NOBODY BEATS US

Congratulations and Best Wishes
on your 90th birthday from
Alan & Gabeltr Hilton

David Tossell has been a sports journalist for three decades and is director of European public affairs for the NFL. Three of his most recent publications, *Nobody Beats Us*, *Grovel!* and *Bertie Mee*, were nominated for British Sports Book Awards.

NOBODY
BEATS US
THE INSIDE STORY OF THE
1970s WALES RUGBY TEAM

DAVID TOSSELL

MAINSTREAM
PUBLISHING

EDINBURGH AND LONDON

This edition, 2010

First published in Great Britain in 2009 by
MAINSTREAM PUBLISHING COMPANY
(EDINBURGH) LTD
7 Albany Street
Edinburgh EH1 3UG

ISBN 9781845967314

This book is a work of non-fiction based on the life, experiences and
recollections of the author. In most instances, names of people, places,
dates, sequences or the detail of events have been changed to protect
the privacy of others. The author has stated to the publishers that,
except in such respects, not affecting the substantial accuracy of
the work, the contents of this book are true

A catalogue record for this book is available
from the British Library

Typeset in Caslon and Hammer

Printed in Great Britain by
CPI Cox and Wyman Reading RG1 8EX

CONTENTS

ACKNOWLEDGEMENTS

All the research material in the world, important as it is to a story like this, is nothing compared with the contribution of those who were central to the action it describes. Therefore, I am greatly indebted to those former Wales internationals of the period with whom I have spoken during the writing of this book: Phil Bennett, Tom David, Mervyn Davies, John Dawes, Gareth Edwards, Charlie Faulkner, Steve Fenwick, Stuart Gallacher, Ray 'Chico' Hopkins, Barry John, Arthur Lewis, Brian Price, Graham Price, Derek Quinnell, Clive Rowlands, Delme Thomas, Clive Williams, J.J. Williams, J.P.R. Williams and Bobby Windsor. I am also grateful for the chance to interview Kevin Bowring, Ieuan Evans and Max Boyce.

Important thanks are due to David Power of the Welsh Charitables RFC, without whose support this project might not have got off the ground. A percentage of royalties from the book is being donated to one of the Welsh Charitables' beneficiaries, the Welsh Rugby International Players' Benevolent Association, whose own J.J. Williams has been a constant source of support and contacts and who generously provided a foreword. Details about both organisations can be found at the end of the book.

I am grateful to others who have contributed in a number of ways, including Alex Luff and Gwyn Dolphin at the Welsh Rugby Union, Stephanie Branston, Amanda Kirk, Haydn Parry, Neil Reynolds, Kath Thomas, Richard Whitehead and Robert Whitlock. Colorsport's

Andy Cowie and the staff at Getty Images and Rex Features offered their usual expert assistance in sourcing photographs, while the British Newspaper Library provided its customary efficiency. I have endeavoured in this book's bibliography to acknowledge the many writers whose work has assisted my research. To everyone at Mainstream, including Bill Campbell, Iain MacGregor, Graeme Blaikie, Emily Bland and others, thanks for your backing of this project from the outset.

Final thanks, as always, to Amy, Sarah and Laura and especially to my wife Sara, who has uncomplainingly shared a year of her life with a bunch of old rugby players and is wondering who the next lodgers in our marriage will be.

FOREWORD

BY J.J. WILLIAMS, WALES AND BRITISH LIONS

The 1970s was a memorable decade for rugby in the British Isles. In some ways it laid the foundation for the modern game as it is today. The 1971 Grand Slam was won in superb style by Wales, and that was followed by the historic victory by the British Lions in New Zealand. Interest in the game, especially by the media, had risen to new heights, and when the '74 Lions became the first team to win a series in South Africa, the BBC had at last given rugby the coverage it deserved. Players like Barry John, Gareth Edwards, J.P.R. Williams, John Dawes, Gerald Davies and Mervyn Davies became household names.

Throughout the decade, Wales was at the forefront of British rugby, and further Grand Slams were won in 1976 and 1978. It was the style of rugby played by Wales that captured the imagination of the public. New stars had emerged, like Phil Bennett, Ray Gravell, Steve Fenwick, me and the indestructible Pontypool Front Row. The key to all of this success was the flair and panache shown by the Welsh players. We also had top-class coaches such as Clive Rowlands and John Dawes, who although completely different in their styles, were leaders of the top order. Clive was the coach who would appeal to players' emotions, while John was more the calm, calculating type. Of course, they had certain individuals at their disposal who were world class and also a wealth of other top players who provided enough strength in depth for Wales to remain at the top for the whole of the decade.

Having a big nucleus of players from clubs like Llanelli and London Welsh was a tremendous help and it was the style of those two famous clubs that Wales adapted during the period. We were also the first country to have organised squad coaching sessions, and the infamous training camps on the beach at Aberavon were watched by thousands of supporters, who all wanted to know what the magic formula was. Of course, there wasn't one: we simply had outstanding individuals who blended together so well. Many of the '70s team had played schoolboy rugby together and that understanding continued throughout the years.

The decade was more or less divided into two parts. The 1971 Grand Slam team had Gareth, Mervyn, JPR and Gerald as the backbone. When the new stars arrived – many of them in the epic victory in Paris in 1975 – it established a new regime, which was to take Wales to an even greater height. The new team won two more Grand Slams and four consecutive Triple Crowns. That record is still in place today and it will take a very special team to match that and to replicate the manner in which it was achieved.

There were some regrets – for example, the fact that Wales never beat New Zealand, even though the 1978 defeat was rather questionable. Maybe Wales just never played the touring All Blacks when we were ready and prepared for them. The autumn games never had the importance granted to them back then that they have now. Also, losing the 1977 Lions series in New Zealand was a major disappointment, especially as the touring party included 18 Welsh players. The other shame is that there was no World Cup at that time. The top teams in the world were New Zealand, France and Wales and winning a Grand Slam meant that you had beaten one of the top sides to do it.

However, there were so many glorious memories throughout the decade. The famous tries and individual skills of the Wales team took the game to a new audience. Even today, some 30 years later, the names of the Welsh players of the 1970s are held in admiration throughout the rugby world.

PREFACE

GOLDEN YEARS: GARETH AND ME

'Nobody ever beats Wales at rugby. They just score more points' – *former New Zealand captain Graham Mourie*

How do you judge greatness in sport? It's an argument that has filled many a pub happy hour or workplace coffee break. Numbers of trophies and titles won; the manner of their acquisition; longevity of success – all are valid means of measurement. Perhaps one of the most reliable is that the achievements and personalities should transcend the particular arena, both geographical and cultural, from which they have originated. Thus even the most casual sports follower of a certain age would tell you that Brazil's magicians of 1970 constitute the greatest national team ever to step onto a football field. Likewise, you don't need to be either German or a grease-stained Formula One fanatic to know that no one has handled himself behind the wheel of a car in recent years as brilliantly as Michael Schumacher. Understanding of the dominance of the West Indian cricket team under Clive Lloyd or the supremacy of Steve Waugh and Ricky Ponting's Australians is not the exclusive purview of those who rush out to buy *Wisden* on the day of its annual publication.

If you'd played word association in the 1970s with members of the British public and opened up with 'rugby', the chances are that 'Wales' would have been blurted back at you. In fact, within the experience of the British fan there was no other team in a major sport whose achievement spanned that entire period in the manner of the Welsh national rugby team. In football, for example, it took a few years before Liverpool usurped Don Revie's Leeds United – symbols of the early '70s – to dominate the second half of the decade and stride unchallenged throughout the next. Welsh ascendancy in European rugby began in the same season that Leeds were winning their first League Championship, 1968–69, and continued unabated until Liverpool were clinching their third title in four years and Revie was counting his Arab millions, having long since quit Leeds and then abandoned the England team.

The bare facts are that from 1969 to 1979 Wales won the Five Nations Championship outright six times, shared it twice, were denied another title by politics and gathered three Grand Slams and six Triple Crowns along the way. Never were they beaten at home in the tournament during that time.

Such detail cannot even hint at the vibrancy of the team. A simple roll call, however, brings to life the dash and daring that held fans in thrall, whether the passionate congregation in the Cardiff Arms Park – even the name had its own captivating rhythm – or the millions watching in their homes. For the television audience of the time, winter Saturday afternoons meant *Grandstand*'s live coverage of the athletic and mental power of Gareth Edwards, the floating genius of Barry John or the cavalier bravery of J.P.R. Williams. Not to mention the twinkling toes of Phil Bennett and Gerald Davies – their sidesteps defying the laws of physiology – or the relentless courage of 'Merv the Swerve' Davies, whose lack of actual swerving on the field did nothing to discourage a catchy nickname.

What divine conspiracy determined that, within a couple of years of each other, such a large number of players would emerge who are still widely regarded as their nation's (maybe the world's) best-ever in their positions: full-back, scrum-half, outside-half, winger, number eight? And what outstanding fortune for those of us around to witness such a union. In colour no less. Even before the widespread introduction of this new-fangled development across the BBC network, rugby was among the first sports to benefit, with Saturday evening highlights among the corporation's early experimental colour transmissions on BBC2. Every try, every tackle now seemed more spectacular, more authentic for the blood-red shirt in which we saw it being performed; every personality a little more three-dimensional.

These, remember, were the days when the only live football on television was the FA Cup final and the occasional international. Five Nations rugby, therefore, held a special place in the calendar, providing an exotic Saturday afternoon break from the parochial, mud-splattered endeavours of rugby league's artisans or the manufactured *World of Sport* alternative of the ITV Seven and professional wrestling. Quite simply, it was the most exciting, passionate and glamorous live televised sport that the public got to see on a regular basis. It was an audio experience as well, the choral elevations of 'Hen Wlad Fy Nhadau' – 'Land of My Fathers' – and 'Cwm Rhondda' offering stark contrast to the hooligan element on the football terraces who forced television directors to keep their fingers permanently on the fader button. It meant that certain Saturday afternoons became an almost religious experience. And in the pulpit was Bill McLaren, all reverence and rolling Rs on the microphone, the poetry of his delivery making Eddie Waring and David Coleman sound like tongue-tied schoolboys approaching voice-cracking puberty.

Excitingly for us television viewers, a rugby union international also offered one of the rare opportunities to see Frank Bough outside of his natural studio habitat. Of course, we didn't know then that he was, thank you very much, getting his kicks away from the confines of BBC Television Centre via a far headier cocktail than horse liniment and prop forwards' sweat. In the early '70s, the opportunity for him to present *Grandstand* from a tunnel underneath the main stand at Cardiff Arms Park, Twickenham or Murrayfield – if he was lucky, with a big green 'G' on the wall behind him – seemed exhilarating indeed and something that Frank would not have sniffed at. Little did we expect news reports of later years that suggested he would have sniffed at pretty much anything.

Quite apart from the rich television experience, there was another reason why the early rugby internationals I saw seemed so mystical. I had never participated in the sport in any form. It simply wasn't something that primary schoolkids from my part of north London did while playing in the park or the streets outside their homes. I had re-enacted thousands of Arsenal matches and World Cup finals with school pals or with my next-door neighbour, who being almost three years older than me usually assumed the mantle of the more favoured team as we spent winters playing out entire FA Cup tournaments. We also passed the summers contesting full Test series in the back garden, with various plants as fielders, or recreating Wimbledon by knocking a tennis ball back and forth over the fence.

Yet even for someone who took every opportunity to replicate major sporting events and role-play its big names, actually attempting to play rugby was never within my early consciousness. I knew no one who even owned a rugby ball. I had been England batsman Geoff Boycott or Arsenal midfielder Jon Sammels any number of times – never Gareth Edwards. It all added to the sport's air of other-worldliness and enhanced the mythical qualities of men such as John, Davies and Williams. Yet when I arrived at my new secondary school in 1972, with Barry John's shock retirement still a talking point, that all changed.

Discovering that my football ability was not enough for a place in the first team I decided that, rather than kicking my heels on the sidelines, I would switch sports. I seized the opportunity to join the newly-formed rugby team and spent the rest of my schooldays playing at scrum-half. It has to be said that in the early days of the team, many, with admirable pragmatism, had made a similar decision to me, which explains the preponderance in our squad of weedy wingers and overweight forwards.

So it was that most of my autumn and winter Saturday mornings for seven years were joyously spent, albeit often in defeat, on frosty or mud-ridden school rugby pitches around north London and Hertfordshire. And on a few of those days each year, the bus journey home – often taken with the soil of conflict still caked beneath my school uniform – held the promise of something special: a live international on the telly. Sometimes even the second half of a second game if kick-off times worked in favour of such extravagance. I was an England fan, I suppose, but you don't need to be much of a rugby historian to know that England in the '70s were crap. David Duckham, for many years my most fondly remembered long-legged blond, could be breathtaking if the ball ever reached him on the wing, while Steve Smith was my preference among the revolving door of scrum-halves. But while I might have rooted for England out of inbred patriotism, my favourite team was Wales; my hero Gareth Edwards.

I drove my teammates mad by spending ages at after-school or lunchtime training sessions in a vain attempt to perfect the behind-the-back reverse pass with which Edwards could extricate himself from the deadest of ends. The fact that our team wore light- and navy-blue hoops – close enough in my mind's eye to Cardiff's light blue and black – only encouraged me further to attempt emulation. I was relieved to discover, though, that Edwards could not spin a pass off his left hand, thus saving me the bother of any attempt at ambidextrousness.

I was not alone in such acts of adulation. Our full-back, while trying hard to cultivate extravagant mutton-chop sideburns out of teenage bum fluff, settled for paying tribute to JPR by playing every game with his socks rolled down and resolving to become a doctor, which he ultimately did. How many of today's sporting icons can claim to have inspired their fans to save lives for a career? And our ritual warm-up before practice became re-enactment, complete with full Cliff Morgan commentary, of 'that try' scored by the Barbarians against the All Blacks in early 1973 and fashioned out of Welsh brilliance.

For a decade, Wales were the standard against which rugby excellence was measured by the average sports follower. Failure against the southern hemisphere giants of New Zealand did little to detract from general public acknowledgement. The rugby universe was smaller back then. There was no World Cup to worry about. Games against the All Blacks were infrequent and better left to the British Lions, whose triumph in 1971 owed much to the 17 Welshmen on tour and whose impact, while great, was still limited by live coverage being restricted to Saturday morning radio commentary. While the closest followers of Welsh rugby felt fully the pain of defeats at the hands of the All Blacks in 1969, 1972 and 1978, to those more casual fans, which meant the majority of the British population, it was the more visible, annually relevant Five Nations which determined the vigour of a rugby country. This is not to say that Wales did not come mighty close to toppling New Zealand in Cardiff in 1972, when Bennett missed a game-saving kick, and six years later, when a blatant piece of play-acting in a lineout won the All Blacks their decisive injury-time penalty.

The response to the latter incident prompted visiting captain Graham Mourie to comment that 'nobody beats Wales at rugby, they just score more points', echoing a sentiment expressed previously by one of his predecessors, Ian Kirkpatrick. While those men might have been intending to take a dig at what they saw as Welsh sour grapes, they actually succeeded in encapsulating the pervading mood of the nation and its rugby team in that glorious era. Whatever the final score, the population of Wales knew that their on-field representatives would have bled for the cause and fought for their countrymen until the final breathless scrum. The spirit of Wales, personified in JPR's bloody face or prop forward Graham Price's tireless 75-yard charge to score in Paris, remained invincible.

To the Welsh people, fortunes on the rugby field have always been an integral element in determining the nation's emotional health. The narrow high streets of valley towns might not be barricaded Kolkata-style by mobs burning effigies of failed captains in times of defeat – the people are too grounded in reality and perspective for that – but victories at Twickenham can create an atmosphere of carnival from Cardiff to Carmarthen.

Across the southern belt of Wales, rugby has always been the working-man's game. In England it has stereotypically been associated with the southern middle classes; in Scotland it was the domain of Borders farmers. It is hard to imagine an English Triple Crown – had such an unlikely occurrence materialised during the years of Welsh rule – creating much of a buzz in the car factories, cotton mills and collieries of the Midlands and the north of England. Yet such triumphs were seized upon hungrily in Wales in the '70s, a period when national pride was a valued commodity, when the industrial landscape was changing and the contraction of the traditional industrial strongholds of mining and steel was causing redeployment of the workforce and, in many cases, lengthening dole queues. Each victory added a splash of colour to the lives of valley communities that, as comedian Max Boyce poignantly noted, could too often be coloured 'Rhondda Grey'.

And just as the exploits of teams led by John Dawes, Mervyn Davies and Phil Bennett underpinned their own countrymen's sense of worth and self, so they helped to create a Welsh national identity for us unworldly schoolkids on the other side of the Severn. The Scots, we knew, had waged numerous wars with the English and saw trips to Wembley as a continuation of such hostilities; the Irish were either cheerful, ruddy-faced types, mocked by comedians on TV variety shows, or, thanks to news pictures from Belfast, political and religious fanatics. The Welsh, we now discovered, were, well, rugby fans. The best known of all of these was Max Boyce, whose frequent appearances on shows such as *Parkinson* exposed us to Welsh culture and lore and introduced the characters of the valleys. The more games his team won, the more he seemed to be on our screens. You have to wonder whether he would have earned such a prominent place in the national consciousness had his boys been as bad as England's. Is it any coincidence that as Welsh rugby endured the dark years of the 1990s, Max disappeared from our screens?

On the field, the rugby played by those featured in this book was a very different game from the bruising, muscular matches contested by today's beefcakes. While many words will be spent extolling the virtues of Edwards and company, some of whom will naturally relate their game to the modern era, the point of this book is not to argue the comparative merits of historical periods. It's entirely possible to celebrate one era without denigrating another. Edwards himself sums it up by saying, 'We did achieve a certain standard and there was a style of game that we were fortunate enough to play in that particular era. Of course, if I was 21 now and somebody asked if I would like to be paid to play a game I loved, I would say yes. I would like to play at the highest level. But if I could wave a magic wand and change everything, then I wouldn't. That's not being detrimental to the game today, but I am content with what we did and have the satisfaction of what we achieved.'

The differences in the modern game compared with the 1970s are so obvious to even the most casual rugby observer that measurement of relative merits is rendered worthless. It all comes down to personal preference. My own inclination is that the honest endeavour and occasional mistakes of the age of amateurism contributed to a more exciting spectacle than the practised, repetitive professionalism of today. Rucks and mauls used to be something of a lottery, encouraging teams to endeavour to keep the ball moving from hand to hand. New rules, combined with improved techniques, fitness and physique – all enhanced by daily training sessions – mean that today's rugby offers only rare opportunities for turnovers and, therefore, fewer forwards are committed to loose scrums. Instead, they loiter among the backs, clogging up the defensive lanes or executing crash balls in attack. It used to be that the only forward you'd see positioned away from the fast-mounting pile of bodies was the open-side flanker preparing to launch himself at the opposing halfbacks. The result is that there is less space in today's muscular, well-rehearsed game for Barry John's brand of light-footed running rugby.

But the truth of all truly great sportsmen is that they would have adapted to prevailing conditions and been just as effective in any era. John would have been a very different player if he had been born four decades later, but if anyone seriously believes that he or Edwards or JPR would not have been outstanding in the 2000s they understand little about the qualities that made those men what they were. Qualities that transcend the passing of the decades. Qualities that can fill a book and take us back to a time when Dragons roared, Cardiff voices soared and, as the All Blacks skipper noted, nobody beat Wales.

1

WITH A LITTLE HELP FROM MY FRIENDS

'The step up was made easier by playing a familiar style and with familiar people' – *Mervyn Davies*

Local shoppers were in the minority on Edinburgh's Princes Street as the clock made its way impatiently towards midday and the thermometer gauge battled to stay above the freezing level that had caused the sleet and slush of recent days. On this first Saturday in February 1969, the chill of the Scottish winter was keeping the locals away from the city's most historic and busiest commercial avenue. Their places, meanwhile, were taken by visitors decked out in red and white, 'up for the match' from the Welsh valleys. As one reporter would comment, 'They were said to number 10,000, but there seemed like a million of them.'

To a teenaged student like John Williams, it was a daunting sight as he stepped out of the elegant surroundingsof the North British Hotel (now the Balmoral) and into the excited bustle of fellow countrymen. Some were shopping for souvenirs, others just seeking out the best place to discuss the upcoming action over a pint and perhaps a chaser of the local hard stuff. On one level the presence of such a vast community from his homeland was a comfort to a young player facing an international debut in that afternoon's Five Nations Championship contest against Scotland. Yet it hit home, with something of a shudder, that he was one of those entrusted with making sure these hordes of happy travellers did not go home disappointed. It was a sobering experience; 'a pang of responsibility', as he recalls it. Murrayfield, with most of its crowd of 80,000 packed onto three vast, steaming banks of terracing, would offer no sanctuary for a faint heart.

The purpose of Williams's morning stroll, also undertaken by several teammates, was to kill a little more of the time that had dragged interminably since the Wales team had taken its flight from Cardiff's Glamorgan Rhoose Airport the previous afternoon after completing preparations in a training session at Bridgend's ground on the Thursday. They had landed to disgruntled mutterings among the locals about having assembled for technical purposes earlier in the week, sidestepping the international recommendation that teams should not convene for a match more than 48 hours in advance.

The trip north had contained extra tension for the second newcomer to the side, Williams's London Welsh colleague Mervyn Davies, for whom the journey represented his first time in an aeroplane. Coach Clive Rowlands decided that the best way to put the new full-back and number eight at ease was to place them in the care of two of their Old Deer Park teammates: club captain John Dawes, among the replacements for this game, and wing-forward John Taylor, who was to share a room with Davies, his back-row partner and future flatmate.

Had this been a home game, Friday evening would have been spent at the cinema or theatre, with team physiotherapist Gerry Lewis responsible for acquiring and distributing tickets and ice creams at the latest James Bond movie or whatever live variety show was in town. Some would have interrupted their slow stroll back to Cardiff's Angel Hotel by stopping for a pint, while Gareth Edwards would seek out Lewis for one final rub-down before lights out. On this occasion, the London Welsh quartet sat playing cribbage until nearly midnight, Dawes's prize for victory being bragging rights rather than a pot of money. The stakes were high enough when teachers and trainee doctors were trying to juggle the demands of international sport with everyday life, without adding gambling debts to the mix.

In later years, when the newcomers had become comparatively nerveless veterans, Williams would turn up in the room he habitually shared with Gerald Davies weighed down by textbooks and determined to revise for his latest medical exam. Mervyn, meanwhile, would spend peaceful evenings free of the apprehension that gripped him on this nervous night in Edinburgh. With his country's first game of a new campaign only hours away, sleep could not be grasped in the same effortless way he used his near 6ft 5in. frame to routinely snare balls at the back of the lineout. Davies knew that doubts existed among Welsh fans and media about his place in the team. Typical was the reaction of Cardiff's *Western Mail*, which felt that Newbridge's Dennis Hughes would have been a safer, wiser selection.

Many had scarcely heard Davies's name until it appeared on the Wales team sheet. He had, after all, played barely three months of senior rugby for London Welsh before earning a call-up for the national team trials. Before that, he had been playing for Old Guildfordians, having completed teacher training in Swansea and accepted a position in Surrey. Even his appearance – tall and slender, with a near-Afro hairstyle sticking out above the protective bandage round his head – put observers more in mind of a Harlem Globetrotters basketball star than an international rugby player.

Earlier trials for the Wales Secondary Schools and the Welsh Colleges XV had not amounted to much and it was only as something of an afterthought that he'd approached London Welsh. 'Old Guildfordians was the nearest team when I was looking for someone to play for,' he explains. 'Although the college rugby I played was absolute rubbish, Guildford was even worse. I could not abide the thought of playing this sort of rugby. I'd had the odd game for Swansea over the New Year when they couldn't raise a team so I took this letter from them to London Welsh and I played for the third team. That was crap as well. The following week I was in the second team and I thought it was quite good and I enjoyed it. During half-term I came back to Swansea and I got a telegram telling me I had been selected for the first team [against Moseley].'

It was a selection that teammate Williams recalls 'amazed' most people at the club, but Davies explains, 'They were not a very big team and someone had got the message that there was this long, lanky streak of rubbish playing for the seconds who could win the ball in the lineout.'

Fears that the international arena would expose him as nothing more than a freakish force at such set-pieces swirled in Davies's mind as he sought elusive sleep. Foremost were the uncertainties that he knew existed in the mind of his scrum-half, Gareth Edwards, who had been thinking, 'I could take a lot of stick from the Scots if this fellow doesn't know his trade.' The fact that the heated room was bringing Davies out in a sweat didn't help, nor did the noise of the workmen labouring through the night on a new shop, ruling out the option of opening a window.

Meanwhile, Williams – having previously appeared on tour for Wales and won the Junior Wimbledon Championship almost three years earlier – had a little more experience of the tightening tension that occupied the hours before a big game. In fact, he has no doubt that his tennis career, including his straight-sets win over top seed David Lloyd in that 1966 final at the All-England Club, gave him a mental toughness that he carried to the rugby field. 'If you can play on your own in front of 2,000 people, then playing in a team game in front of 60,000 is no problem,' he says.

Even so, he was relieved when the 9 a.m. knock on the door from physiotherapist Gerry Lewis signalled that only the routine of the morning separated the team from kick-off. Breakfast for Davies, taken in bed, was a fry-up, which would allow him to get by with just a small portion of fish, perhaps with a few chips, when lunch was served. Team management made sure that every culinary preference was catered for on the day of the game, whether it was Williams's toast and honey or the bunch of grapes insisted upon by second-row forward Brian Thomas.

Once everyone had returned from their morning excursions along Princes Street, bodies were crammed into one bedroom. Some, like flanker Dai Morris, were already dressed smartly, ready for the trip to the stadium; others looked as though they had barely risen from their beds. All were quickly engulfed in new coach Rowlands's cigarette smoke as he delivered the first of what would become famous pre-game team talks. His words, fiercely and passionately delivered, were intended to inspire. Without achieving the fluency he would grow into with each passing game, he made his mark, calling upon the *hywl* – the emotion – that he wanted his team to carry into battle. 'There were no tactics,' Williams remembers. 'It was all about heart. Give your heart for Wales, for your wives and girlfriends, your family.'

Audience participation was encouraged, with players urged to shout responses to individual challenges such as, 'What are we going to do?' The usual response was 'Win!', although Bridgend prop John Lloyd once famously brought the room to uproar by yelling back, 'Eat 'em!' Inevitably, it was the forwards who reacted most visibly to their coach's rhetoric; the backs, conscious of their reputations as the more cerebral set of players, listened impassively. The final part of the ritual was for all 15 players to be reminded of the lineout signals and for Edwards to rehearse his call of 'coming in – now', so that everyone was attuned to his rhythm. Brian Price recalls an occasion before a Test in New Zealand where, as captain, the meeting was held in his room. 'We were practising "ball coming in now" and Clive said, "No, I want it louder and sharper." In the end we were screaming at the top of our voice. It turned out Ted Heath had been in the next room shaving and almost cut his throat in shock.'

At the pre-match lunch table, Lewis handed a game programme to each man, watching as most quickly turned to the page of biographies to check whether information was up to date or to laugh at a teammate's unflattering mugshot. That left around half an hour before departure from the hotel. Some tuned into BBC's *Football Preview* to hear Sam Leitch discussing title contenders Leeds' and Liverpool's games that day against Coventry and Sheffield Wednesday. Mervyn Davies, meanwhile, passed the time by checking his boots and kit. Shorts and socks had been delivered to his room the night before but the shirt would have to wait.

On board the team bus heading through the drizzle to Murrayfield, the Wales players looked out upon the fans making their way somewhat belatedly to the ground on foot. Scarves and rattles in the red of Wales were mixed in among tartaned Scots hurling good-natured abuse at the opposition. Even such a short journey was enough time for song to break out, with Edwards, Taylor and hooker Jeff Young instigating rousing battle tunes.

Out on the pitch with an hour to go before kick-off, Davies's nerves were helped little by the sight of the terracing already three-quarters full. But back in the spacious dressing-room butterflies gave way to a moment of pride for the newcomers as they were handed their first scarlet Wales jerseys. The smell and feel of the thick cotton and the sight of the embroidered Prince of Wales feathers made up for a lack of ceremony that had disappointed Davies, who had been wondering if perhaps a cap would be forthcoming as well. Instead, he discovered that such a precious prize would be dispatched later by post. John Dawes even remembered his first one arriving in a used shoebox without any kind of covering note, although a few years later the custom would be for new caps to be presented at the post-game dinner. Meanwhile, the Scots next door would have looked enviously upon the riches being dolled out to their opponents. Their players were given one jersey that had to last the season.

An occasional Welsh Rugby Union committee man appeared incongruously in the dressing-room, but the players were too preoccupied to notice. Edwards was receiving his final massage, having made sure, as usual, that he was at the head of the queue for Lewis's services. With everyone changed and ready, it was the turn of captain Brian Price to give the final address, as much a ceremonial duty as a strategically relevant undertaking in the new age of squad training sessions. Price had been relieved just to be in the team, let alone leading it, after losing his place the previous year. 'At the end of last season I felt quite out of the reckoning and in September I was thinking of retiring from international rugby,' he'd said after his appointment. 'It was hard work getting fit but I have enjoyed this season.'

Now it was time for the traditional team photograph, a ceremony that impinged upon Mervyn Davies's ritual final smoke before kick-off. Rowlands even had to warn him on one occasion, 'Make sure the cigarette is behind your back when the picture is taken.' Then, at last, came the summons from the match officials. Running out in front of veteran prop forward Denzil Williams, fresh-faced John Williams

– sideburns still narrow and neat – looked like a youth-teamer who had taken a wrong turn under the stands and found himself swept along by the senior players. National anthems were played and sung lustily, even by English-raised Welshman John Taylor, who'd had to learn the words before his international debut two years earlier. Not by Davies, however. His throat had been locked with emotion as he surveyed the scene before him. It was a long way from Old Guildfordians. As he lined up for the kick-off he ran through his game plan one final time: concentrate on winning the ball in the lineout and maul, the role for which he had been selected, and don't stray too far from Taylor.

In front of Davies, the country's selectors – 'The Big Five' – had looked for strength and experience ahead of mobility, partnering Thomas and Price instead of the second-row duo that finished the previous campaign, Max Wiltshire and Delme Thomas. Rowlands explains, 'I got them to bring back players who had played for me when I was captain. I said to Brian Price and Brian Thomas, "Give me one more year, boys." I needed those hard men. I still believe you can have the best backs in the world but if you don't win the ball, what is the point?'

It was a decision that appeared to pay off as the pair, aided and abetted by Davies, held their own in the lineouts and offered solid support to the front row against a Scotland team who had won their first game in France three weeks earlier. In the backs, Barry John offered the occasional flicker of promise in what was a mostly safety-first opening 40 minutes and Williams belied his inexperience with a performance of promising authority. His unyielding defence was supplemented by a dash of adventure that would have produced a try were it not for the mishandling of Newport winger Stuart Watkins.

Four decades later, Williams easily recalls the moment that John banished his first-game nerves. 'The best experience for me in that game was taking the first high ball and hearing Barry say, "John, spin the ball," and then him kicking it sixty yards to within five yards of the Scottish line. I thought, "Right, that's international rugby!" Barry didn't fear anything. We even had a ridiculous situation in New

Zealand [on the 1971 British Lions tour] in Hawkes Bay, where Gerald Davies had scored three tries. Barry just sat on the ball and said, "Come and get me." Nobody moved.'

This, of course, was no occasion for party tricks and it needed centre Keith Jarrett, another who was back in the team after missing the second half of the 1968 season, to dig out two early penalties against the wind to give Wales a 6–0 half-time lead. And Scotland were unable to prevent Wales stretching away for a convincing victory after the teams changed ends. As the visiting halfbacks exerted their influence, Edwards scored the first try after the wheeling of a Scottish scrum forced Ian McCrae into a hurried pass towards fly-half Colin Telfer. When the ball failed to reach its destination, Edwards was in like a shot to pick up and force his way past tacklers for a score typical of the opportunism that was to be such a feature of the next decade.

A move created in Newport produced the next try when, adopting a tactic employed regularly at his club, Price moved to number two in the line and deflected the ball to the blind side for the fair-haired winger Maurice Richards to burst over the line. Some questioned whether Price's tap had gone forward but a wave of Welsh attacks resulted in further points that made any such argument a moot one. On the retreat once more, Telfer had his clearance charged down by John, who collected the ball and dummied his way past full-back Colin Blaikie to score between the posts. Jarrett converted and, with Blaikie's penalty having been the only Scottish reply, a final score of 17–3 was achieved.

The places of John Williams and Mervyn Davies were secured. Williams would be there throughout the next decade of success, while Davies would remain untouched in his position and become a Grand Slam-winning captain before being struck down by illness at the peak of his success. He would no longer be mistaken for a basketball player, while Williams would never for a moment regret the sporting choice he had made several years earlier.

The year has begun with the Western Mail lamenting the lack of Welsh representation in the latest honours lists, saying that two knighthoods was 'scanty recognition'. It promises, however, that with the summer's investiture of Prince Charles as Prince of Wales, 'The world will be made aware of the Principality in a way which has never been possible before.'

No one will ever know how much the loss of John Peter Rhys Williams to British tennis meant during the sport's dark days of the 1970s, when the odd flash of brilliance from Roger Taylor or John Lloyd was barely enough to prompt a whispered 'Rule Britannia' in comparison with the 'Henmania' that would engulf Wimbledon a quarter of a century later. Who could tell whether a Junior Wimbledon title would ever have developed into something meaningful in the senior game? We know, however, how great Welsh rugby's loss would have been had Williams decided to pursue the new opportunities being presented by tennis's open era. Picturing the Wales team of the era without his sideburns, rolled-down socks and reckless disregard for personal safety is like imagining Max Boyce without his giant leek.

The sideburns are grey, although only slightly less fulsome, and the socks are missing completely as JPR – as he became universally known once another John Williams arrived on the scene – chats about his career. He has half an eye on the Wimbledon action unfolding in front of him and is keen to discuss the five-setter Andy Murray, the Scot who has become the latest hero of middle England, has won the previous evening. As a national hero himself, he understands the pressure of expectation, but adds, 'It is all for such a short period of time. Two weeks of Wimbledon, then nobody wants to know after that.'

One of four brothers, he had already decided upon a combination of medicine and rugby rather than full-time tennis by the time of his success on the hallowed grass of SW19. He had spent long enough on the tennis circuit during school holidays to know that the endless grind, much of it filled by card schools, was too monotonous to stimulate him. The amateur sport of rugby, on the other hand, would enable him to follow his parents in becoming a doctor. Besides, the two sports were becoming increasingly difficult to juggle and Williams recalls performing poorly for the Welsh Secondary Schools against Yorkshire after playing tennis for five weeks during the Christmas holidays. And in the British Covered Court Junior Championships, his tennis was hindered irredeemably by the fractured left shoulder he'd acquired playing for the Wales Under–15s.

Something had to give. So, after growing five inches within twelve months and enjoying a year's scholarship at the sporting hotbed of Millfield School in Somerset, he gained entry to medical school at St Mary's Hospital in London, from where he continued to play for Bridgend during his inaugural student year of 1967–68. He admits that his career choice might have changed in the modern age of professionalism. 'We live in a different era and there is all the money around. And would I have even got into medical school now? Possibly not.'[1]

In 1968, the game's most significant rule change in years was about to help Williams become the dashing, daring full-back of legend. The International Rugby Board agreed in March to trial the 'Australian dispensation' of banning kicking directly to touch from beyond the 25-yard line, a tactic that was stifling attacking play. From now on the ball would have to hit the ground before crossing the line. 'That was great for me,' Williams recalls. 'I could never have been the old-fashioned full-back: catch the ball and kick it into touch wherever you are. There had been full-backs who were attacking players – Vivian Jenkins, Ken Scotland and people like that – but not many. I always wanted to run the ball; kicking was always the last resort.'

Contrast that to the description of duties by Gerwyn Williams, a Wales full-back of the 1950s, who explained to author Huw Williams in the book *Dragons and All Blacks*, 'Your role was completely defensive. The skills required of you were catching, kicking to touch and a skill which has now completely disappeared and used to frighten me – falling on the ball in the face of a dribbling rush by forwards.'

---

1   Williams would continue to play tennis when his rugby career allowed and in 1970 lost only 6–4, 6–4 in the Welsh Open to three-time Wimbledon semi-finalist Roger Taylor, who had that year beaten defending champion Rod Laver on Centre Court.

WITH A LITTLE HELP FROM MY FRIENDS

Early in the 1968–69 season, JPR was to join London Welsh, a club where his approach fitted perfectly with the outlook of captain John Dawes. 'Those days were unbelievable,' he continues. 'We had people of all nationalities coming to watch. We didn't have a big pack of forwards so we ran the ball. It was exciting to watch and even more exciting to play and it was the best thing that could have happened to me. I had been brought up watching Bridgend play that kind of rugby in the '60s and I was lucky that every team I played for favoured an expansive game. From kicks at goal we would always run it back and we would always get to the halfway line. Everyone knew if I got the ball we were going to run with it. It was good for the forwards because they just ran back to the halfway line and we would be there.'

Williams's expertise under the high ball had been developed on the windy seafront at Porthcawl, where his father Peter would spend Sunday afternoons hoisting up-and-unders for his boys. 'Even with the new rules, taking the high ball was, and still is, very, very important, although it is much easier now. If you go up to catch the ball people can't touch you. We used to get hit so we had to turn our backs as we caught the ball.'

When Wales visited Argentina in the late summer of 1968 for a pair of unofficial tests, they did so without any of the senior players who had been on that summer's British Lions tour of South Africa. It meant an opportunity to blood youngsters like Williams, who recalls the trip as being 'pretty traumatic'. He adds, 'We were without about ten players and lost the series 1–0 with one drawn. We came back to Wales in absolute disgrace.'

He had at least impressed the locals, who nicknamed him 'Canasta' – meaning 'basket' – for his unfailing catching. He had also caught the eye of Dawes, who 'hadn't even heard of me before that tour', prompting the invitation to play his club rugby at Old Deer Park.

The quality that is most frequently listed among Williams's attributes is the self-belief that was required to play his cavalier style of game. 'I was always confident playing sport, even though I was a late developer physically,' he says. Clive Rowlands adds, 'He had this confidence he gave to everybody in front of him. Taking the high ball, I have never seen anyone better. I can't remember him ever dropping it.'

And, just as Williams cites Barry John as having relaxed him during that debut international, so John acknowledges the contribution of his teammate to his own game. 'He epitomised everything required in a full-back. He was a great tackler, he was solid under the high ball, he made devastating bursts into the line and he possessed great pace, strength and positional sense. Knowing that JPR was behind me gave me the freedom to express myself on the field because if I made a mistake I knew he would be there to cover.'

It had all begun with a pang of guilt, however, with Williams feeling he had 'abandoned' his St Mary's Hospital team on the eve of a game in order to make his debut for London Welsh as a stand-in for the injured Gareth James, an old tennis buddy. Yet it was obvious from that first match that the club had found its new full-back. A couple of months later, a skinny-looking teacher strolled in to claim the number eight position.

Two businessmen, Raymond Glastonbury and Raymond Godfrey, begin High Court proceedings in an attempt to prove that Wales's leading entertainment export of the decade, Tom Jones, agreed to pay them each five per cent of his earnings to act as his managerial team. The singer is now reckoned to be clearing £500,000 per year, and Glastonbury claims, 'We gave him the faith to believe in himself.'

Mervyn Davies remembers the unexpected moment of discovery. 'I was about 10 or 11 and I was rooting through my father's drawers when I came across this Welsh jersey and thought, "What is this? He played for Wales, did he?"'

Far from regaling his son with tales of how he had represented Swansea and Glamorgan and been picked for Wales in the unofficial 'victory internationals' that immediately followed the Second World War, Dai Davies gave his son 'a back-hander' for going through his belongings. 'My father hid his light under a bushel. He never talked about playing for Wales – like he never spoke of his time in a prisoner of war camp.'

There was certainly no passing of the torch of international ambition from father to son. 'I remember thinking, "I wouldn't mind one of those shirts," but it was a sort of fleeting moment,' Davies continues. 'I just played rugby at school because it suited my personality and my stature. I was too tall and gangly for soccer. I had no great ambition because again my school was not a recognised rugby school. I just got a job teaching and was out of Wales for the first time and looking for somewhere to play. It all snowballed so quickly there was no time to have any real ambitions.'

Asking permission to smoke a cigarette in his own Swansea home and then walking around to keep the smoke away from his visitor, Davies – hair now short and grey but retaining a tendency to its former unruliness – explains that, like Williams, he was the beneficiary of changing rules and attitudes in his sport. 'It coincided with the time when the number eight was being looked at more as a tall ball-winning player and I fitted the bill.'

So well, in fact, that when he picked up the morning newspaper in his local newsagent in Guildford shortly after the final Wales trial, he found a small story informing him that he had been picked to face Scotland. The next day he received a letter from the Welsh Rugby Union confirming his selection and giving him five days to send back an acceptance card. He had it back in the post inside a minute. 'There were numerous guys playing in the back row who were well put out by my selection,' he says.

Yet it didn't take long in a Welsh shirt for Davies to prove that his influence extended beyond the back of the lineout. Derek Quinnell, a Wales and British Lions teammate, explains, 'Swerve was a great team member. You would always find him making the tackle on the people in the centre and he had great ability in the lineout. He was such a long, gangly thing and he was light with it as well and could get off the floor. You would find him at the bottom of every maul and ruck. You could kick him all day and he would just get up and get on with it. He was very durable and had the capacity to recover as well. Some days you would look at him and think he will never be fit for Saturday and then he would play as well as ever. He was a dog of a forward and a great asset to any team.'

According to Barry John, 'He had an almost built-in radar, which would tell him where the ball would go next. He was simply brilliant at reading the game.' And Clive Rowlands states, 'He had this gift to win difficult ball and turn it into good ball for the scrum-half.'

Davies continues, 'Actually, I found when I started playing in internationals that it wasn't that onerous a task. I don't want to sound big-headed because the step up from club rugby to international is massive, with the pace of the game and the speed of thought and fitness required, but it didn't seem too much of a problem to me. London Welsh was the right place, right time for me. We were the in-vogue team at that time, along with Llanelli under Carwyn James, and were playing a style of rugby that was about movement of the ball to the wings. The Welsh team played the same.'

From harbouring no great thoughts about international rugby a few months earlier, Davies was hooked on the high of the most elevated level of his sport. 'Over the years club rugby was a means to an end. I enjoyed playing it but there weren't that many games in a season where you felt personally challenged. In 40 club games in a season there might be only 12 games where I would be really challenged from a personal perspective, because I would be playing Hefin Jenkins of Llanelli or someone like Andy Ripley. International rugby is what I lived for because you were playing the best. You weren't going to get opposition just trying to take you out. The lower quality of rugby you played the more of that you got. You were not in fear of being sneakily knocked down. It was man against man and I loved it.' There could, however, still be moments when back street tactics were called upon, as Davies was to discover in his second international.

More than 3,000 protest outside Caernarfon Castle over Prince Charles's forthcoming investiture. 'No English blue blood for Red Dragon of Wales,' reads one banner, while loudspeakers play Dafydd Iwan's song 'Carlo', which satirised Charles's supposed love of the Welsh language. Meanwhile, 21 students begin a four-day hunger strike in protest at the Prince's plans to study at the University College of Wales at Aberystwyth.

The vagaries of the Five Nations scheduling at this time meant Wales had to wait five weeks before hosting Ireland, who by then had won three games in the competition and were chasing their first Triple Crown and Grand Slam since 1949. Present at the game was Prince Charles, undergoing some cultural education before his scheduled investiture as Prince of Wales three months later. The stadium that confronted him could hardly be described as palatial, the rebuilding of the North Stand leaving one side of Cardiff Arms Park's National Stadium as a mere building site and reducing capacity to 29,000. The Welsh Rugby Union was busy raising money for the construction by selling 8,000 seat debentures for £50 and £100.

Concern had been expressed that hordes of excited Irish fans would arrive in Cardiff ticketless in the hope of watching the game from vantage points within the skeleton construction. Police and the WRU both warned that such attempts would be immediately repelled. Meanwhile, reports circulated that five-shilling tickets were fetching up to £15 on the black market.

Within five minutes of kick-off fears grew for royal sensitivities when it became clear that the entertainment unfolding before the Prince was to be a little earthier than his family members were used to. Normally, a few slaps from Eric Morecambe on the cheeks of Ernie Wise and a five-minute performance from the Czechoslovakian State Song and Dance Ensemble – both features of the most recent Royal Variety Performance – were as brutal as it got when the Royal Family enjoyed a day out. Now Charles looked down on ensuing mayhem as Brian Price, the muscular, chisel-jawed Welsh captain, landed a right uppercut on veteran Irish wing-forward Noel Murphy. There were some claims among the Welsh, however, that Murphy was himself auditioning for a place on the stage when he grabbed his face and hit the deck in the manner of a modern-day Premier League footballer.

Mervyn Davies chuckles as he recalls, 'That was an interesting introduction to international rugby in Cardiff. I came across something I had never come across before: we were going to duff a bloke up because he was a nuisance. It was the Murphy Plan and we had rehearsed it at the squad sessions. We had John Hickey playing the part of Murphy, whose forte was killing the ball in rucks and mauls. He could frustrate you and he didn't mind being stamped on as long as the opposition didn't win the ball. Someone who shall be nameless came up with the plan. Gareth Edwards was supposed to pick up from the first scrum, allow Murphy to tackle him and then the entire Welsh pack was going to stamp all over him – hopefully so badly he would have to leave the field.'

Price recalls, 'I think it was the French player Benoit Dauga who had said to us, "You have to make the Irish quiet. If they are on the floor, we go all over them and they don't talk so much." Noel, who was a good friend of mine, was the main inspiration to the side, so much of our discussion with Clive was about stopping him. Somehow it got out and at the Friday press conference at Bridgend I was asked about the Murphy Plan. I said, "I don't know what you are talking about."'

According to Davies, 'It didn't quite work out because we hadn't been awarded a scrum and it was frustration on the part of our captain. When Murphy's head popped up in a maul, he hit him. Murphy took about ten seconds deciding whether to fall down or not.'

Price continues, 'Somebody was grabbing me from behind and there were fingers all over my face. I swung a fist – it could have been at the referee for all I knew – and it happened to be poor old Noel. Their captain, Tom Kiernan, came running up shouting, "It's the Murphy Plan!" I should have been sent off and after that there were fights and blood all over the place.'

Murphy's reaction was felt by some to have been contrived and his punishment no more than he deserved. In the end, it may only have been the Irishman's dramatics that saved Price from becoming the first player dismissed in a Five Nations match[2] – something that would have caused considerable hand-wringing and disgrace in an age before disciplinary measures became routinely administered

---

2   When England's Mike Burton was sent off in Australia in 1975 he was only the third player to be dismissed in international rugby, with none yet sent off in the Five Nations Championship. There would subsequently be nine dismissals in the championship between 1977 and 1995.

in the form of red cards on the day or retrospective suspensions based on video evidence. Price later apologised to his team for his actions and the Welsh press were prepared to forgive, but *The Times* was in no such mood. Rugby correspondent U.A. Titley called it 'a deplorable act of ruffianism' and 'the depth of bad manners'.

Davies adds, 'There was a lot of that kind of thing at that time, but I am glad to say it changed within the space of about six months. The elder statesmen playing international rugby retired and there was a new breed of player who had ambitions beyond their predecessors. We didn't like losing but there was a new thinking in the way we approached the game.'

For Price, however, the incident lingered. 'Tom Kiernan didn't speak to me for about ten years after that,' he says. 'Even six years ago I was working for the BBC in Limerick in Ireland and I met Noel, as I had done many times since. His wife was with him and she wouldn't speak to me.'

While the tension and bad temper continued on the field, Ireland took a 6–3 lead, the crop-headed Kiernan landing penalties either side of a dropped goal by Barry John. With half-time approaching, fists flew again among the forwards and Irish hooker Ken Kennedy was laid out. Kiernan, a vocal force who was never slow to attempt to influence match officials, threatened to take his team from the field unless order was restored. Yet referee Doug McMahon would say later, 'I've had rougher matches to control.'

This was far from being the final time in the period covered by this book that a game between Wales and Ireland featured acts of skulduggery. In fact, it would be a contest between the two Celtic tribes that eventually did produce that first Five Nations dismissal. As Derek Quinnell comments, 'Ireland would always be tough no matter where you played them. There were always guys who would kick the shit out of you, and then they had the talented players as well.'

Such had been the disjointed nature of the action that more than five additional first-half minutes were played, during which Wales took the lead with a piece of incisive thinking that was out of keeping with the offerings up until then. Having won a penalty inside the Irish 25, the whole stadium assumed that Keith Jarrett was preparing to kick. The Irish players had even turned their backs on the action. Instead, Jarrett tapped the ball and passed to the 16st. Denzil Williams, who was virtually untouched as he pounded over in the left corner, the only try of a 36-game international career. Jarrett's conversion made the half-time score 8–6 and Wales pulled away in the second half.

The try seemed to have a tranquillising effect on their mood, undisturbed even by losing Brian Thomas for ten minutes to receive treatment to a head wound that required ten stitches. John released the three-quarters with greater frequency and, although some reports ventured that the Irish had been literally beaten into timidity, what really undid them was the ability of the Welsh to execute the basics of the game simply and at speed.

John, enjoying perhaps the most fruitful day yet in his three-year partnership with Edwards, barely needed to reach full stride to make the outside break that set up Stuart Watkins. Eight minutes later, Edwards gathered up untidy lineout possession and kicked back into the box. He won the race for the ball, hacked it forward and then found Dai Morris, true to his nickname of 'Shadow', on his right shoulder. The wing-forward scored from 20 yards.

Full-back Williams then joined the back line in a move that had begun from deep, selling a dummy and feeding Watkins on the right wing. When he was stopped short of the line, Taylor picked up the loose ball and dived over. There was some Irish consolation when Taylor's fumble allowed Mike Gibson to kick downfield and score under the posts, but Jarrett's penalty accounted for the final points of an emphatic 24–11 victory that left Wales as firm favourites to win the championship.

2

MY WAY

'Clive [Rowlands] made us all feel very proud of what we represented; all the people we represented and what the game meant to those people. He had an uncanny knack of reminding us of that' – *Gareth Edwards*

Local legend has it that Cwmtwrch, which in English translates to 'Village of the Wild Boar', was so named because it was the site upon which King Arthur killed the leader of a pack of beasts that was terrorising the region. Arthur, so the tale goes, achieved his feat with nothing more than a giant stone and a strong arm. It is exactly the kind of against-all-odds heroism that makes this little corner of the Swansea valley the perfect home for Clive Rowlands, a man who was never afraid to conjure up the myths, heroes and history of the region when it was time to inspire his players.

His home is barely a Gareth Edwards spin pass away from the village rugby pitch and as he recalls his six years as coach of Wales it is easy to feel the passion that filled his meeting rooms, especially when his voice rises and reverberates and his most emphatic points are punctuated with silence and a fixed stare that almost dares a contradiction. It would take a brave man to offer one.

'I remember Scotland had appointed Bill Dickinson as a special adviser to their captain,' he recounts. 'He had been reported as saying to his team before an England game, "If you have a bed of roses and you put one thistle among them, within a year the roses are dead and the thistles have taken over." So I said, "Boys, let's get one thing straight. It will take a year for the thistle to take over the rose. [Pause for dramatic effect] Put a dragon in there for two seconds and there is not even a bloody garden left!" When you can pick up little things like that you can see the effect on the players. That was my gift really. I was a motivator. I used to read articles and cut them out and put them on the wall. I used to love milking it.'

Even though he had captained his country in all 14 of his international appearances, the nationalist fervour that the former scrum-half brought to his role as coach and for which he would become famous was something of a surprise to those who knew him of old. Brian Price explains, 'He was the sort of captain you hardly noticed, which you could never say about Clive now. He had an unobtrusive way of captaining the side and then we didn't see much of him after the game. But when he became coach, my god alive, you couldn't get away from him. He changed personalities and was demonstrative in everything he did. He would be there at training, legs astride and shouting. We thought, "Christ, is this the same bloke?"'

But Rowlands knew he needed to offer more than fire and brimstone if he was to justify the elevation the Welsh Rugby Union had bestowed upon him. It explained the anxiety that had accompanied him into the Murrayfield stands as he took his seat for his first game in charge. He had been wracked with doubts: a mixture of uncertainty over the effectiveness of the preparation he'd overseen and fears that he would fail to reward the WRU's faith.

'I had a lot of letters saying, "The coaching system depends on you, Clive,"' he recalls. *Western Mail* writer J.G.B. Thomas had captured that feeling by describing the Scotland game as 'one of the most important in Welsh rugby'. Rowlands continues, 'A lot of influential people didn't like coaching and felt it was wrong for Wales to have a coach. They came out with silly statements, saying we would stop the guys developing the skills they had. Well that was bad coaching, not good coaching.'

The irony of Rowlands's first game as Wales team coach having been in Scotland on the day his team played their first full international under the new kicking rules was not lost on many observers. It had been on the same ground in his second international match where he had hastened the death of kicking to touch from outside the 25. On that day in 1963 he had stubbornly done little other than boot the ball over the sideline at every opportunity. By the end of the game, an astonishing 111 lineouts had been awarded. Wales won 6–0, Rowlands kicking all the points, and outrage had exploded across the world of rugby. He was held culpable for such an ugly scar on the face of the game and was even informed by a huffy Barbarians committee member that he would never be invited to play for them.

Fly-half David Watkins recalls receiving the ball only four times all day, yet over the years Rowlands has remained unrepentant, recalling that his first two passes were followed by a loss of territory and pointing out that he played strictly within the laws of the game. 'I have seen film of the game and there are long periods when you don't see me kicking the ball. You see other people kicking it, but I got the blame for each one of them. I am not saying I didn't kick a lot but if I kicked to touch 111 times then Scotland must have thrown it in 111 times, which wasn't the case.'

Often in sport, teams become a manifestation of the on-field style of their mentor. Yet, just as the cynical element of the great Leeds team of this period belied the thoughtful, imaginative playing style of manager Don Revie, so the reverse applied to Rowlands. A hard-nosed realist as a player, his Welsh team would reveal a streak that often bordered on the romantic, particularly once John Dawes, a renowned aesthete, was its captain. 'As a player, I can't ever remember Clive running with the ball,' says Price. 'As a coach, there was none of that. Once we were in a certain position he would say that we were going to use the ball. And he always emphasised the talent people had. Gareth Edwards was not a terrific passer at first, so he would say, "Gareth, you are strong, you can go through him."'

Rowlands was the first coach to reap the full benefits of the new kicking rule, which placed restrictions on full-backs and fly-halves with limited handling ability while giving rein to the attacking élan of the likes of J.P.R. Williams and Barry John. 'When the new law came in, people said, "What is he going to do now?"' he remembers.

'Well, we counter-attacked and the key to its success was that people knew what to do. I always had JPR go for the near touchline and we had the wingers running back and John Taylor and Dai Morris there in support. Before you knew it, there was an attack on and moves like the dummy scissors would come into it. It didn't work every time, but if it didn't then JPR was a safe kicker, even if not the longest.'

The son of a miner, Rowlands had been a club player for Llanelli, Pontypool and Swansea. His international debut in 1963 had been against England as one of six new caps, including David Watkins, Denzil Williams and Brian Thomas. Nicknamed 'Top Cat' after the cartoon character of the time, he retired at the age of 30 because of ongoing lumbar pain and was immediately elected to the WRU committee, which was followed by an invitation to coach the Welsh squad on its trip to Argentina in the late summer of 1968. 'When you were captain in my day you were always coach,' he adds. 'I was a PE teacher, so I was trained to be a coach. It was nothing new; it was man management.' Following the tour, he was offered a three-year appointment to continue guiding the team. 'In my opinion any shorter period would have been unfair,' he said.

If Rowlands had been worried about critics making snap judgements on his coaching ability, those fears had been eased by victories over Scotland and Ireland. The *Western Mail* had even called the Irish game 'a triumph of organised coaching'. But now came a trip to Paris, always a testing contest, even if this particular France team had lost seven straight matches at both ends of the world since their Grand Slam of 1968. Captain Christian Carrère had been jettisoned and the team was rebuilding without the retired Camberabero brothers, Guy and Lilian, at halfback. They were soon facing the prospect of an eighth defeat as Wales built an 8–0 lead on the wide open spaces of the Stade de Colombes, where the passionate, unpredictable fans traditionally did their best to compensate for the distance to the playing field created by the athletics track. Edwards had subdued them with a run at the line from 20 yards, completing it by forcing his way through tacklers like an impatient Metro commuter in rush hour. With typical vision, he then kicked into the corner for Maurice Richards to run on and score a try that Jarrett converted.

Pierre Villepreux, the elegant full-back with the narrow features, landed a penalty as France began to move the ball with urgency and fluency. Suddenly a Welsh lead that could have been more emphatic but for Jarrett's failure with seven kicks in unhelpful conditions was looking more tenuous. When Wales kicked off the second half, France countered with a swift passing movement. Villepreux kicked high and diagonally to the left corner and saw the bounce beat Stuart Watkins and Williams, allowing winger Andre Campaes to touch down. Villepreux's conversion levelled the scores, a stalemate that remained to the end of the game. The most notable footnote was the debut of Llanelli's Phil Bennett as a late substitute after Gerald Davies injured his elbow.

The draw was enough to mean that victory in the final game against England in Cardiff would secure the championship outright, along with the Triple Crown. That would be a more than satisfactory outcome for Rowlands in his first season as coach and would help to justify the very existence of his role.

> Newly announced defence cutbacks mean that 2,600 military personnel will be withdrawn from Wales over the next four years. The closures of selected training bases and administration centres will also cost 1,100 civilians their jobs and have a significant detrimental impact on local economies. Meanwhile, 1,650 workers are laid off by the British Steel Corporation at the Spencer Steelworks in Llanwern.

The position of national team coach was still a new addition to the century-long history of rugby in Wales, a chronicle that started in the mid-19th century when doctors, teachers and clergymen brought back to the valleys a love for the game they had acquired at their English universities. Over time, the sport spread beyond the domain of the educated professionals into the lives of ordinary working men. While English professional football was growing out of factories paying players to represent their workplaces, rugby in south Wales became the means by which communities could flex their muscles against the neighbours. By the end of the century, more than 70 clubs were in existence.

The efforts to properly bring those clubs together under one organisation are generally believed to have stemmed from a meeting at the Castle Hotel in Neath in March 1881, when the foundation was laid for the Welsh Football Union, later to become the Welsh Rugby Union.[3] The national team played its first game in 1881, a thumping loss to England at Blackheath that would have been 82–0 using modern scoring, but recorded a victory in Ireland when it played its second game almost a year later. By the early 1900s, matches were being contested on an annual basis between the four home countries and Welsh rugby was entering what is commonly referred to as its 'First Golden Age'. In the meantime, an event that would have far-reaching effects on the sport in Wales had taken place in August 1895, when a group of northern clubs broke away from the Rugby Football Union to form the Northern Football Union – the starting point for professional rugby league.

The steady exodus of Welsh rugby talent to the working towns of northern England had yet to get fully under way as Wales marched triumphantly through the first decade of the new century. Between 1900 and 1911, they won the Triple Crown six times and the Grand Slam on three occasions, the last of those representing the first such achievement after games against France became part of an expanded Five Nations Championship instead of mere friendlies. In among those successes was a famous 3–0 win over the first touring New Zealand team at Cardiff in 1905, when the referee's disputed ruling that the All Blacks' Bob Deans had been held up while attempting to score a game-saving try helped fuel a century of rivalry.

Even with the relatively primitive communications of the era, tales of star Wales players such as diminutive scrum-half Dickie Owen and skipper Gwyn Nicholls, the 'Prince of Three-Quarters', passed via newspaper reports or word of mouth from town to town, creating

---

3 Dispute about the roots of the governing body exists among historians, some of whom cite a meeting of clubs a year earlier at the Tenby Hotel in Swansea as the point of origin. The WRU celebrated its centenary during the 1980–81 season.

inspirational figures for a generation of players whose own ambitions in the game would, in too many cases, be ruined by the First World War. In fact, it would not be until after the second great conflict of the century that Wales would produce worthy successors to those baggy-trousered heroes, when John Gwilliam led his country from his position at the heart of the back row to Grand Slam triumphs in 1950 and 1952. Bleddyn Williams, a powerful, strong-running centre and a gifted passer of the ball, took over the captaincy to achieve another memorable win against New Zealand in 1953.

In the last game of that 1953–54 season, Wales played their final international at Swansea's St Helens ground, elevating Cardiff Arms Park, which had previously shared Wales games, to the status of exclusive home of the national team. The stage was thereby established for decades of theatre, most of it broadcast live, that would grip the nation more than any of the soap operas about to fill living rooms as the new age of prosperity and consumerism brought televisions into the majority of homes.

Originally a piece of swampland behind the Cardiff Arms Hotel on the bank of the River Taff, the Cardiff Football Ground had first been developed as a stadium in 1912. Following the repair of Second World War bomb damage and the opening of a new South Stand in 1956, it reached a capacity of 60,000, staging the Empire Games – as the Commonwealth Games were then known – two years later. On rugby days, the stadium housed the greatest male voice choir in the country, yet it had only intermittent cause for outbreaks of verse over the next decade or so. Even though Wales, led by the spirited talents of outside-half Cliff Morgan, won the Five Nations title outright with three wins in 1956, the Triple Crown remained out of reach for thirteen years until the three home rivals were finally overcome in 1965.

By that time, a mood of reflection had descended upon Welsh rugby following the national team's ill-fated visit to South Africa in the spring of 1964. Arriving as joint winners of the Five Nations, they were soundly beaten 24–3 after being level at half-time. Rowlands, captain and scrum-half, called it 'a lesson in the art of taking advantage of each and every opportunity'.

Speed of reaction was not something for which the amateur rugby administrators of the era were known, so it probably seemed like a rather racy response when the WRU's general committee guided clubs later that summer to conduct a full examination into the state of their game. They were directed to appoint team coaches, while the question of whether the country should appoint an individual to oversee such developments raised its head.

To many, coaching felt intrinsically ill-fitting within a strictly amateur game. At both club and international levels, it had been left to the captain to guide whatever tactics and preparation existed. It sounds primitive, of course, yet it should be remembered that even in the professional world of the Football League, managers had only begun coaching their teams in the previous two or three decades. Until clubs saw the results achieved by innovators such as Herbert Chapman, the former Huddersfield and Arsenal boss of the 1920s and '30s, the manager-secretary – as he was usually known – had been little more than an administrator.

Cliff Jones, a former Wales fly-half who became a national selector, was named head of the working party appointed to examine the sport. Jones was a known coaching advocate and of the three sub-committees created, covering fitness, laws and tactics, it was the last – chaired by Jones himself – that met most frequently. Brian Price, one of the players co-opted, recalls, 'We met every month and were looking at ways in which we could improve coaching throughout Wales, trying to set up schemes for people who wanted to get involved. We felt we should have a person who set out a programme, so the result was the appointment of Ray Williams.'

In June 1967, Williams, who had played for Northampton and London Welsh, took a pay cut to accept the job of national coaching organiser at a princely wage of less than £2,000 a year, thanks to the grant approved by Minister for Sport Denis Howell to fund two-thirds of the salary. Kept out of the Wales team by Cliff Morgan, Williams had trained as a PE teacher at Loughborough and coached England's West Midlands region. He had staged courses to help teachers train as rugby coaches and had been one of the key forces in the creation of English rugby's coaching manual in 1951–52. The

WRU was said to have been so impressed by that publication that their adoption of many of its points played a key part in their success in the mid-1950s.

With Williams installed in his position, notable developments ensued. Rowlands explains, 'Ray got courses going and was turning out coaches. The game was alive with people who wanted to help. Even the little village teams suddenly had a coach and instead of six people turning up for training there would be twenty. Through that development of really good coaches you got great players.'

Stuart Gallacher, these days chief executive of the professional Scarlets, had been a novice Llanelli player at Stradey Park and vividly recalls the revelatory nature of the introduction of Carwyn James as team coach. 'Having started there at 19, I became captain in 1967 at the age of 21 and I was lucky that it coincided with the arrival as Carwyn. Rugby took on a different perspective from that day on. We started to prepare and train and play what I called proper rugby. It was a revelation and it eventually began to reflect in the Welsh set-up.'

The three seasons between the loss in South Africa and the appointment of Williams had seen a decline in the fortunes of the Wales team. From winning the Triple Crown in 1965, they lost at home to Australia for the first time when beaten 14–11 in December 1966 – a game notable for the international debuts of Barry John, Gerald Davies and Delme Thomas. 'We were anything but a dream team,' John recalls. 'Deep down the players sensed we could be on the verge of something special, that we could be an exciting team if we gelled, but the results suggested otherwise.'

The 1967 Five Nations campaign was rescued from complete disaster when a solitary win was achieved in the final game against England in Cardiff. Making his debut at full-back was Newport's Keith Jarrett, usually a centre, whose dark hair, strong jaw and coolness with the ball at his feet belied his 18 years. With a straight-ahead style, he kicked five conversions and two penalties and ran down the sideline for a try, equalling the Wales record of nineteen points in a game.

As well as being charged with establishing a structure and guidelines for the technical development of players around the country, Williams would soon be proposing that those in and around the Wales team should train together on a regular basis, introducing the squad system that blazed a trail in European rugby and succeeded in upsetting the neighbours. 'Whatever next?' barked the retired army types at Twickenham, who had already been left choking on their gin and tonics when the WRU announced the appointment of its first national team coach in David Nash, a former Ebbw Vale, Wales and British Lions number eight, for the 1968 season. Nash had been on the short list for the organiser's role and was felt by some to have been offered this new position as a consolation prize. Gerald Davies recalls sensing that the more senior players were sceptical about Nash's appointment – as they would have been about any man in the position – while 'younger team members, including myself, welcomed his arrival on the scene'.

Meanwhile, the All Blacks' tour of Britain in late 1967 offered further proof of the benefits of coaching. Players from the four clubs forming the West Wales team practised together under the direction of James, the future British Lions coach, and were rewarded by putting up an honourable display in losing only 21–14 to Brian Lochore's team. The tourists then needed a late try to salvage a draw against East Wales, who had trained as a unit under former Wales flanker David Hayward.

Nash's season in charge of Welsh fortunes can hardly be said to have heralded a new era. For a start, he found himself having to go cap in hand to his employers to be allowed to travel to the Five Nations games in Dublin and London. It was only the support of the players that led to the WRU putting their hands more deeply into their pockets. Results, however, did little to make a further case for Nash. Even with Barry John now established as the team's outside-half following the departure of Watkins to play professionally for Salford, Wales had only a home win against Scotland to show for the 1968 campaign.

Nash quickly discovered that he was not required to accompany the under-strength Wales team on the late-summer trip to Argentina, where WRU president Glyn Morgan was to be manager and selector Harry Bowcott, bereft of coaching experience, his assistant. Chairman of selectors Alun Thomas made a stand for the cause of coaching by resigning his position in protest and when the clubs made similar sentiments known at the WRU annual meeting, Rowlands was hurriedly asked to join the tour party. 'A lot of people didn't want me because I wouldn't listen,' he laughs. 'Other people said, "That is why we are having him."'

Back in Wales, the direct influence of Ray Williams on the team was to increase thanks to his relationship with Rowlands and his constant presence as an adviser, along with Cliff Jones, at squad sessions. Mervyn Davies refers to Williams as a 'mastermind', adding, 'When Ray opened his mouth we listened'. With others on hand to help with the technical and organisational elements, one of the major responsibilities that Rowlands believed fell to him was to make his players take pride in the red shirt they wore. It is the aspect of his coaching approach that is most widely acknowledged, although sometimes from differing perspectives.

Gerald Davies recorded, 'His major contribution, initially, was to sow those seeds which would blossom into a strong sense of colourful destiny; an appreciation, respect, and acknowledgement of who we were and what we all represented. He insisted that we should play in such a way that all of Wales could feel proud of us. He needed some reining in now and then but you should have been there when Clive was in his prime and in full flow.'

Price says, 'Maybe Clive didn't think he was the top notch as a player so he kept himself quiet, but being coach brought out the best in him. Clive is an actor. I have seen him teaching and he was an actor there as well.'

Edwards called Rowlands 'just the sort of motivator I needed' and spoke of his blood pounding by the time he took the field. 'Clive was great for Welsh rugby at a time when coaching was relatively new,' he says. 'He had great knowledge of the game, a very strong personality and a wicked sense of humour. There was a lot of emotion and rhetoric and you couldn't help but respond. I remember one team talk where a couple of selectors were almost running on the spot. He was great at motivating.'

Meanwhile, John Dawes recalls the human touch that accompanied the coach's oratory, saying, 'Even though he had this motivating technique he always had a degree of humility about him. He never put himself above you.'

Yet, despite the memories of his supporters, not everyone responded so readily to the Rowlands approach. Former British Lions flanker Tom David argues, 'The only thing I ever felt when Clive did his Henry V bit was embarrassment. It might have worked for others but not for me. Clive was not really a coach; he was just a ranter and raver. He was very emotional and was 100 per cent Wales, but from a technical point of view we did very little.'

Rowlands describes team meetings as 'the key to the day'. He continues, 'When I said 11 o'clock, I meant five minutes to. Nobody would consider being late, but occasionally I would designate one player to come late. It was usually John Bevan because I knew he could take it. He would come in sweating and I would bollock him. He only looked like he was sweating because he had thrown water on himself. It was daft, but we all left that room feeling together.

'I walked out of the room one day and said, "We are not going to win today because you are not with me, so I am off. All the best to you." Later on I thought, "Oh fuck, I shouldn't have said that to the boys. I don't want to lose this game." I went over to the changing room a little bit early and they were all in already. I was not saying much, talking to one or two. There was Dai Morris seated next to Delme Thomas as usual, with his head down and his hands over his ears. I said, "Boys, let's have another go. We can't lose today. Look at the concentration on Dai." Dai said, "Shut up, will you? I am listening to the two o'clock race." Everyone burst out laughing so I just said, "Righto boys, we are now back together because we have laughed together," and they went out and won.'

Memories of Rowlands's pre-match addresses tend to obstruct discussion of his tactical acumen, but former Wales second-row Gallacher suggests that there was more to him than urging his team to 'win for Auntie Gwladys'. He says, 'People forget that he was a very canny coach too. He knew the game inside out and surprisingly, having been a scrum-half, he knew forward play very well.'

Long-standing administrator Keith Rowlands, no relation, highlighted his ex-teammate's outstanding rugby knowledge when he noted, 'He had a catholic approach to the game, which included a feel for the player, the match, the venue, the opponents, the referee and, if he could forecast it, the weather.'

But, without meaning to understate the ability of Rowlands, Mervyn Davies offers a view that is typical of many. 'Clive was very successful mainly because he had good players. I think anybody could have coached that side. In saying that, what he did was bring us all together and put a discipline and structure into the way we played.'

> Land-owner and caravan site operator Goronwy Evans sees an opportunity to cash in on interest in the new Prince of Wales by selling 500,000 one-foot square plots in Snowdonia at £4 each. The dormant grazing land, in which he shares ownership with the Queen, is selling well, he says, to Canadians and Americans.

The structure and leadership of the national team continued to be one of the hot topics in the build-up to the potential Triple Crown decider against England, with Ray Williams offering, 'There are those who question the desirability of a national squad. I would venture to suggest that after Welsh performances this season no one any longer can question its effectiveness.'

For the first time in the international season, changes would be needed in the Wales team, due to injuries to Price and Gerald Davies. The five men charged with such decisions were Cliff Jones, who had been in his role as selector for ten years; Rees Stephens, a former national captain who won thirty-two Welsh caps over a decade after the Second World War; London Welsh stalwart Harry Bowcott, who picked up the first of his eight caps in 1928; Jack Young, a fiery WRU representative – and uncle of hooker Jeff Young; and Vernon Parfitt from Newport, a member of the WRU coaching committee.

'I certainly believed in the selection committee,' Rowlands asserts. 'It was fairer for players because if someone was the sole selector and didn't like a player then he didn't get a look-in. The selectors in my time were so experienced they were a big help to me as captain and coach. I knew they would go with me on certain selections and on others they would argue. You picked your battles.'

On this occasion, the committee opted for Delme Thomas to fill the second-row vacancy and John Dawes in the centre in place of Davies. The choice as captain was Edwards, who the previous year, at the age of 20, had become the youngest Welshman to lead his country. Along with Denzil Williams, Brian Thomas and Stuart Watkins, Dawes brought to four the number of survivors from the last Triple Crown triumph. Rowlands, skipper on that day in 1965 when Wales beat Ireland in Cardiff, delivered one of his most impassioned team talks. Then pack leader Thomas issued instructions that England scrum-half Trevor Wintle should 'look like he's been sunbathing in the Bahamas with a string vest on' by the end of the game.

But what had been expected to be a war of attrition turned into an exhibition, especially once Wales had the strong wind at their backs. Most of all, it was a day of triumph for Cardiff's Maurice Richards, whose four tries equalled a feat not performed for his country since 1908. Capped for the first time the previous season, Richards had hinted at his potential by scoring in two previous games in this campaign, but 12 April 1969 was forever to be the day with which his brief international rugby union career would be associated. It was the 24-year-old left-wing more than any other who benefited from the domination Wales exerted up front.

Bob Hiller's penalty had England ahead until Edwards fed John in front of the posts and a further spin pass put Richards over in the corner. It was still only 3–3 at half-time, but Thomas's success in the line gave Wales the possession from which Jarrett kicked two penalties early in the second half. It was then Jarrett's poor pass that inadvertently led to a brilliant solo try by John. Picking up the loose ball on the bounce, John worked his way in from close to the left touchline with a series of sidesteps and swerves, beating four men before flopping over the line. According to the scorer, it was this game more than any other that convinced him he could be a viable force in the international game. 'I had had enough of doing what other people said; deciding to be the puppet-master, not a puppet.'

After Wales won a ruck inside the England 25, John became creator once more when his quick up-and-under set up a passing movement that ended in a second try for Richards. A Hiller penalty was followed by the only left-footed dropped goal of John's international career, and after full-back Williams was held up following one of his forays into the three-quarter line, he snaffled the ball back for the opportunistic Richards to grab and dive over. Appropriately, Richards's day in the sunshine ended with a flourish. In a planned move, he came inside to take the ball 40 yards out and charged through and away from England defenders, a smile, minus his front teeth, bared in a mix of grin and grimace as tacklers grabbed at him in vain.

His had been the most emphatic single contribution to the final score of 30–9, yet the overwhelming excitement surrounding John's try was an indication of the media's growing infatuation with the young fly-half. John himself admits, 'Maurice never received the credit he deserved.' And Phil Bennett, watching from the substitutes' bench, commented, 'Maurice showed he would have been one of the greats had he not gone off to play rugby league.'

That move was still a few months in the future. First of all, Richards and the champions of European rugby were about to embark on a trip to the other side of the world, where events would help to shape a new, harder attitude within the Wales team.

3

SOMETHING IN THE AIR

'Surely a sprinter with your dazzling skills would find
life more comfortable on the wing?' – *Clive Rowlands
to Gerald Davies*

The flight from Wellington, on the foot of New Zealand's
North Island, up to Auckland, the country's biggest city, lasted
barely an hour, yet it was long enough to change Gerald Davies's
international career. The Wales touring team was en route to a
second meeting with the All Blacks, overwhelming winners of their
first contest a couple of weeks earlier. A pair of victories in the
meantime against Otago and Wellington had raised spirits, but had
also left coach Clive Rowlands with important personnel issues
to resolve in the few days before the match at Eden Park. Of the
three wings included in the 23-man squad, Stuart Watkins and
his uncapped Newport teammate Alan Skirving were unavailable
because of injury. The answer, Rowlands believed, was to play John
Dawes and Keith Jarrett in their favoured positions in the centre
and ask Davies to make a switch.

Taking a seat next to a man whose 11 Wales caps had all been
won at centre, Rowlands used all the communications skills he'd
learned as a teacher to deliver what he sensed would be a difficult
lesson. The gist of his conversation – conveyed, according to Davies,
in 'a conspiratorial whisper' – was this: 'The change in the kicking
law means that wingers will have a far more prominent role in the

future. You don't want to get involved with the heavy mob in midfield. I can assure you that you'll get sufficient possession.'

Davies was less than effusive about what he saw as a demotion and feared being isolated on the touchline, but Rowlands recalls, 'The game was starting to change and the centre's job was to knock down the little guy. Gerald was not interested at first, but I said, "When the ball reaches you, Ger, what are they going to do about it?" He was good defensively as well. Maybe not in the centre, but brilliant defensively on the wing, where you thought it out.'

The deal was clinched, although Davies recalled later, 'He might just as well have wielded a knuckle duster as talk as he did with honey on his tongue. There was hardly any point in carrying on with my protests.' Davies did, however, retain the impression that this was merely a short-term solution to a problem that would be resolved at the completion of the tour.

Growing up in Llansaint, a small village overlooking Carmarthen Bay, Davies had received much of his rugby education through listening to his father, a miner, discussing the big games with his pals every weekend. As a teenager who had represented Wales Schools at outside-half and centre, he appeared for Llanelli during school vacations and was sufficiently assured in his understanding of the game to sit out what would have been the biggest match of his life. Asked to play out of position on the wing against the 1963 All Blacks, he declined.

Having moved from Llanelli to Cardiff during his period as a trainee teacher at Loughborough University, he had become an international regular by the time Clive Rowlands buckled his seat belt next to him. He had scored only twice for Wales, but in his next 35 internationals, all on the right wing, he would amass 18 more tries. Barry John would come to refer to him as 'the Nureyev of the flank', explaining, 'He was blindingly quick, possessing the most remarkable balance, which enabled him to use that sidestep which so often wrong-footed defenders.'

According to Rowlands, 'He epitomised everything that was good about a rugby footballer. That balance, that ability to change pace, that sidestep that you knew was coming and you could do nothing about. He was something special.' When, in 1970, Davies applied to join London Welsh, Dawes said it was 'like Pelé or George Best asking to be taken on'.

Davies insists that the act of setting up a score for a teammate continued to bring him as much pleasure as crossing the line himself, putting it down to a need to demonstrate that he retained the powers of invention he'd possessed as a centre. 'There are a great number of games when the wing does not see much of the ball. A winger does not mind this too much as long as he is looked upon as a creative player in his own right.'

And often overlooked were those defensive abilities; a willingness to throw his body into the path of oncoming trouble. Of which there was plenty on the trip to New Zealand.

The Registrar General releases figures showing that people born in Wales have a two-year shorter life expectancy than those from England. A higher risk of bronchitis and stomach cancer and greater rates of infant mortality are highlighted as the main reasons for the statistic.

Wales had taken their European title proudly to the southern hemisphere, where the media spoke of 'New Zealand awaiting the coming matches with some apprehension, if not dread' after the local television screening of the season finale victory over England.

But, in truth, their trip was doomed to failure before the players selected for the seven-game tour arrived at the departure gate in London. The party, managed by Llanelli club secretary Handel Rogers, travelled for thirty-six hours via Teheran, New Delhi, Singapore and Sydney to New Zealand, before being squeezed into a turboprop Fokker Friendship for a final two-hour jaunt to the town of New Plymouth. Despite arriving at 4 a.m., and with the first game of the tour less than four days away, the locals were determined to mark the arrival of the first full Wales team to visit their country with a parade and festival. Only once the Welsh players had wearily delivered a chorus of 'Sospan Fach', led by choirmaster John Taylor, were they allowed to retire to their beds. Even an earth tremor in the early hours could not disturb their sleep. Not surprisingly, they were only half awake during training and throughout the drawn game against Taranaki. Far more energetic was the battle of rowing boats that the players waged among themselves when given some time off at a local lake.

Having picked the fringe players in the first match, for fear of some not getting a game later in the tour, Wales went into the first Test in Christchurch with several key men having seen no prior action on tour. *The Times* decried the authorities' scheduling:

> To commit them to an international only eight days after their journey across the world and after only one preliminary canter is an act of sadism, the perpetration of which condemns the International Rugby Board as an institution unsympathetic to the players.

As Clive Rowlands recalls, 'I don't care who you are, if you go to New Zealand and play the first Test like we did you have no bloody chance.'

It was immediately clear that on a heavy pitch, upon which two curtain-raiser games had just been played, the All Blacks pack, which included six farmers, was too strong for the visitors. In addition, local referee Pat Murphy's interpretation of the rules allowed more blocking and compression in the lineouts than Wales were used to in Europe, meaning Brian Price and Brian Thomas rarely had a clean opportunity to win the ball. Conversely, Murphy was quick to penalise the Welsh for not releasing the ball in the tackle, often without offering any opportunity for them to do so. 'The refereeing made a heck of a difference,' says Rowlands. 'The fairest one we had was a man called John Pring, who we had in the first match. I remember talking to Carwyn James about him before the [1971] Lions tour and telling him there was only one ref they should have. He did all four Tests on that tour.'

The result of Murphy's officiating was a bad-tempered game in which Welsh frustration increased. With eight minutes remaining, Jeff Young grabbed the jersey of Colin 'Pinetree' Meads, a legendary figure in New Zealand rugby. The big second-row – who had left his brutal mark on Clive Rowlands and David Watkins in previous internationals and had been sent off for a kick in Scotland two years earlier – swung a punch that broke the Welsh hooker's jaw. Refereeing and All Blacks tactics aside, however, Wales could have no complaints about their 19–0 margin of defeat. 'We got absolutely slaughtered,' J.P.R. Williams admits. 'The first game was a nightmare. It was like a wall of black coming towards me.'

Opining on the Meads assault and the outcome of the match, the editorial column in the *Western Mail* as good as suggested that Wales should leave the All Blacks to their own game and give up hope of ever beating them:

> To New Zealand, Test match rugby has become warfare without weapons, not a mere game. The home countries cannot again field sides to match the hardness of an essentially agricultural community, for our softer way of life does not breed the big hard men necessary to cope with Meads and company.

Slight and slender, Barry John looked like a choirboy pitted against a mob of angry bikers and, with little ball to work with, Wales posed only an occasional threat to the home team's try-line. Defensively, Wales were constantly tested by the positional kicking of fly-half Earle Kirton and their forwards spent most of the match retreating against the marauding group of Meads, Ken Gray, Brian Lochore, Ian Kirkpatrick and Bruce McLeod. Notably, three of the four New Zealand tries came from pack members, the exception being the first, scored by winger Malcolm Dick.

Jarrett, who had been on target from the halfway line during training, scuffed and sliced a series of penalties – five in all, from a range of distances. The slippery surface also hampered Stuart Watkins's attempt to deal with a loose ball, allowing prop forward Jazz Muller to feed his hooker, McLeod, for the second try. The New Zealand front-row men were involved again two minutes later to offer Lochore an easy run to the line and New Zealand held a 13–0 half-time lead after Richards was manhandled to the ground a couple of yards short.

With Sid Going buzzing around the base of the scrum in typically belligerent fashion and McCormick composed at full-back, New Zealand eventually increased their lead with six minutes remaining when Gray flopped over following a break from centre by Grahame Thorne. McCormick's late penalty completed the beating, leaving Rowlands to lament, 'When we made mistakes we didn't lose six yards as we did at home, we lost eighty.'

Two weeks after the first Test, a reorganised Wales team gave a more spirited performance in the second, but ultimately suffered an even bigger margin of defeat, this time 33–12. As well as the enforced changes in the back division, there had been moves in the pack, where Brian Thomas switched to prop, allowing Delme Thomas to partner Brian Price in the second row, while Dennis Hughes replaced the injured Taylor in the back row. The true superiority of the All Blacks in this game lies somewhere between the final scoreline and the fact that they only outscored Wales in tries by three to two.

Yet Wales made too many mistakes and gave away too many penalties to feel truly hard done by. The 24 points scored by McCormick, then a world record, was an indication of their carelessness – as well being evidence of more questionable officiating, crystallised by Mervyn Davies's claim to have seen referee Murphy jumping with delight at a successful New Zealand kick. Barry John commented, 'I am seething. No fewer than 12 All Blacks players came to me after the game apologising for the refereeing. I am seriously thinking of giving up rugby as a protest.'

Wales were again unable to match the relentless home forwards, even though they held the lead after 20 minutes. By the time New Zealand had established complete dominance in the second half, they were able to start tossing the ball around and even Going was spinning it out rather than sticking to the incisive running close to the scrum that had troubled Wales earlier in the match.

Jarrett had another forgettable day, making two of seven kicks, and when he squirted an easy penalty wide in the sixth minute the pattern was set. He and McCormick traded penalties before Wales scored the first try of the game with their best sequence of attacking play in the series. First, Gerald Davies gave a clear sign of the danger he could pose from wide positions, bursting outside his opposite number and feeding inside to Jarrett, who kicked ahead and was ruled to have knocked on as he and Davies went for the touchdown. Moments later, and from the same right-hand corner, Wales launched a move that showcased what would become familiar strengths. Thomas palmed cleanly to Edwards, who quickly fed John, and then Dawes timed a neat pass to Williams bursting into the line from full-back. He found Maurice Richards, who paused exaggeratedly as if planning to cut inside before accelerating beyond two black shirts to score in the left corner. 'The try itself was sensational,' Dawes recalled. 'But so was the effect on the crowd. An eerie silence prevailed over Eden Park. It was born of complete puzzlement about what actually happened.'

Within eight minutes, though, New Zealand were ahead 11–6 after Going fed debutant winger George Skudder to score on the blind side and McCormick landed the conversion and a penalty. Further kicks either side of half-time saw McCormick extend the lead – reduced by Jarrett – and a long period of pressure finally produced a try for the powerful centre Ian MacRae. McCormick thumped over a dropped goal from just inside the left touchline, struck another penalty from a similar position, and completed his tally for the game by converting after Ian Kirkpatrick scored from the back of Wales's own lineout. A little more respectability was added to the score in injury time, when John chipped ahead and Richards, Williams and Dawes took turns to keep the ball alive long enough for Jarrett to complete the move.

There was no chance for Wales to slope off home just yet. One week later, they found themselves playing Australia in Sydney, a contest many felt should have been used as a warm-up prior to facing the more powerful All Blacks. The game at least allowed the tourists to conclude the serious business of their trip with a victory, playing a tight, forward-based game to counter the speed of their hosts and emerge as 19–16 winners.

After twenty-three minutes they found themselves trailing 11–0, but any thoughts of getting on the plane and escaping this southern hemisphere nightmare were put to one side as Jarrett kicked a penalty and Edwards made a blindside thrust and passed to his right for Dai Morris to score. Still trailing 11–6 at the change of ends, it took only three minutes of the second half for Gerald Davies, with the wind at his back, to gallop forty-five yards for his first try as an international winger after Williams had made another of his timely entrances into the line. Davies's recollection of his first two internationals in the number 14 jersey is that 'both games went very well'.

Jarrett's conversion from under the posts and a 50-yard penalty gave Wales the lead and that advantage was stretched to 19–11 when Davies set up Taylor for a converted try. But Wales again conceded a string of penalties that halted their momentum and allowed Australia to exert pressure. Full-back Arthur McGill was awarded a try, despite Richards arguing so forcefully that he had help up his opponent that a penalty was awarded against him to restart the game. The failed conversion meant that the visitors' margin of victory was preserved.

After a brief stop to enjoy some welcome hospitality on the beaches of Fiji – against whom Dennis Hughes scored three times and Taylor twice in a 31–11 win – it was a re-educated and chastened group of players who returned home and turned their thoughts to a stretch of sand in Wales.

4

JUST CALL MY NAME, I'LL BE THERE

'We would pile into one Mini and would all claim it on our expenses. You had just played a game on the Saturday and you were injured, bruised and knackered. You had a few beers afterwards knowing full well you had to be up at 4 a.m., drive down, train, drive back and be at work Monday morning' – *Mervyn Davies on squad training sessions*

These days, Afan Lido, on the Aberavon seafront at Port Talbot, is a 21st-century facility. Part of a leisure centre chain, its squarely functional structure hosts a swimming pool, gymnasium, bowling lanes and floodlit all-weather pitch, offering amenities for a range of occasions, from business seminars to kids' birthday parties. To the nation's rugby players of the 1970s, however, this modest attraction on the south-west Wales coast represents primitive dormitories, lukewarm soup and cold winter Sundays, usually spent across the road on the wide two-mile stretch of sand. It was where the 30 men in the Wales training squad would don their red tracksuits and go through their paces with thousands of fans leaning over the promenade railings for a glimpse of their heroes.

When the team convened to prepare for the 1970 Five Nations Championship, those spectators saw a group fired with a new intensity, a deeper determination. Humiliation in New Zealand had seen to that. 'We got a right stuffing and realised there was more to this international rugby,' Mervyn Davies explains. 'The younger tourists felt rather nonplussed when some of our older players appeared to throw in the towel and settle for an easy ride through our final three matches. That was the moment I and few others made a conscious decision that we were not going to get beaten like that in the future and we started training more seriously and looking at diet.'

Phil Bennett, a fringe player on the tour, describes it as 'one of the defining moments of the era'. He says, 'They thrashed us. I think the old players who were coming to the end of their career perhaps didn't really fancy a war against the All Blacks down there. But the young players learned lessons from New Zealand's attitude and the way they wanted to win so ruthlessly.'

It had been the youngsters, such as Davies, who were the notable successes of the trip. He had earned particular praise for neutralising the threat of the All Blacks peeling from the back of the lineout, one of their favourite tactics. Back in Britain, he acknowledged that the new Welsh generation needed to improve their readiness for international rugby. 'I'm not saying we wouldn't have a drink any more because we did,' he says. 'But we wanted to take a more professional approach, even though it was down to trial and error more than having a dietician or a fitness guru.'

According to Davies, the starting point was a mental one; simply making a greater commitment to the sport. 'The amount of time you spent on the training field was limited because you had a job. The theory was you trained twice a week with your club side and played once a week, but quite often if you made, say, five training sessions out of eight in a four-week period you were doing well. It wasn't enough.'

An opportunity to invest a few more hours was provided by the Welsh squad training sessions, which had been introduced prior to the 1969 Five Nations season. There, the desire of individual players to demonstrate a new, more focused approach was perfectly in keeping with the demands imposed by coach Clive Rowlands and national organiser Ray Williams. Afan Lido on a Sunday during international season was not the place to be if you were lacking dedication to the cause. For a start, the fact that the two grass pitches were frequently rendered unfit by the winter weather meant that training was more often than not carried out on the energy-sapping beach. Davies recalls, 'The wind would really blow and sand would get everywhere. There are no horizons on the beach; on a rugby pitch there is a white line telling you where to stop. You took a deep breath and carried on through the wind and rain. One time Clive said, "Run along there," – it was with the wind fortunately – "and when I blow the whistle turn round." He let us go so far that we couldn't hear the whistle. He had to get in his car and come and get us.'

Rowlands explains that the location played a big part in the success of the squad sessions, believing that just another rugby field would not have produced the same results. 'The boys who came down from Pontypool or Ebbw Vale perhaps never saw the sea. It was important to give them something different. I used to let everyone know when we were training and the more who came to watch us the better. Nobody wanted to drop a ball in front of all those kids.'

Gareth Edwards describes the Aberavon sessions as 'unique', adding, 'They developed into a must-see event. I would not be exaggerating to say there were thousands there. All along the front, people had come to watch us train. It put the pressure on you and, although I don't want to be too dramatic in my choice of words, it gave you a sense of belonging and gave you a sense of what this game meant to the people.'

Simply getting to training was a challenge for many, especially those based in London. But geography was no excuse for non-attendance. Winger J.J. Williams would not make the national squad for another couple of seasons, but his memory of his first session illustrates the intensity emanating from those in charge. 'We met at Afan Lido and it was snowing. We talked about what we were going to do and about 45 minutes after we started, in came the boys from Ebbw Vale, like Denzil Williams and Arthur Lewis. There were about four of them. "The valley is closed with all the snow," they explained. "Then why couldn't you have stayed here last night?" Ray shouted back. "Get down here and give me 40 press-ups and 40 sit-ups." They were still in their suits. I thought, "Fucking hell. No one is messing around here."

'Clive and Ray set very high standards for the players. It was strong leadership and we all bought into it. We changed in the dormitory among the bunk beds and we had something like half a sandwich and some soup for lunch. The wind would be blowing off the beach and there would be a couple of thousand people watching.'

Some of the London Welsh players would ensure their prompt arrival by staying at the home of J.P.R. Williams's parents in Bridgend. 'We would play on the Saturday, have one pint and then all get into a car,' he recalls. 'We would take it in turns to drive. We stayed at my parents' and would go down to the local working-men's club and have a few beers. The following morning, my mother would make us a big breakfast and then it was off to Aberavon. We would stop at Kingston Bagpuize in Oxfordshire on the way back for some game pie. It was fun and we would all be back at work on Monday. That was the norm and we didn't think anything of it.'

In the days before the completion of the M4, the discovery of short-cuts through Berkshire and Wiltshire became almost as important as learning moves on the field. John Dawes says, 'We looked forward to it. There was great banter on the journey down and back and it enhanced team spirit.'

Cliff Jones, chairman of selectors, explained in a 1971 interview how important squad training had become to the national team. 'In Wales, players are involved in too many first-class matches, with the result they have insufficient time to practise. Of course, there is always the danger in an amateur game that the squad system at national level will take up too much time, but demands are kept to a minimum by selectors.'

However, those demands did mean that there were instances when the Welsh players would have to spend the night in Afan Lido's primitive accommodation. Derek Quinnell recalls, 'We would meet on the Saturday evening and all sleep in this big dormitory. It was sometimes difficult to sleep with 30 guys there, but it was important for team building. There was a bit of an SAS survival feel about everything.' Delme Thomas adds, 'It might seem terrible looking back, but it paid dividends.' Besides, while the younger players obediently adhered to the 11 p.m. curfew, the older ones would slip out for a late-night curry.

Once out on the sand, J.P.R. Williams describes the training sessions as 'fantastically competitive'. He says, 'It was an absolutely bizarre thing to be playing a game on Saturday and then having a training session that was like warfare. People like Derek Quinnell and Tommy David, Lions players who were in the second team so to speak, were hitting the shit out of the players in the first team. There was no real malice but most players will tell you that the training sessions were harder than any international. There were no poseurs. It was hard going playing on sand and nobody held back – well, possibly the halfbacks.' Recalling a condition that became known as the 'Cardiff hamstring', he laughs, 'They spent a lot of time on the physio's bench.'

Quinnell continues, 'We had a lot of talented players and to get into the squad was very difficult, so they were tough sessions. The backs used to run and Clive enjoyed pounding the forwards against each other.'

Tom David, who was to become a teammate of Quinnell's at Llanelli and would spend more time on the fringe of the Wales first XV than as a full member, admits, 'Squad training was lively; harder than games. There is no doubt that as a wing-forward I was desperate to get in the game and be selected. You would have a short penalty move or something like that and, well, I was a bit of a lunatic half the time and when I had the ball I used to go out to hurt people – because I wanted to prove a point. It was a difficult balance but that was the rivalry in Welsh rugby at the time. That was why in the '70s we were so successful.'

Davies recalls, 'You could be standing next to a guy in the lineout who, if he had half a chance, would step on your foot, break your hand or knock out your teeth. I felt early on there was a certain amount of jealousy with some people, wondering who the hell I was. You had to prove yourself to the other players, particularly because London Welsh were looked upon as the pretty boys of club rugby. It steeled you and gave you an extra incentive.'

Second-row Stuart Gallacher, who would win his only cap in 1970 after several appearances in official trials, recalls the sessions as 'eye openers'. He says, 'Clive Rowlands was very canny and knew there was great hunger in a lot of us. I was up against guys like Brian Thomas, Brian Price and Delme Thomas to try to break into the team, so it was hammer and tongs. We did scrummaging sessions that were a cut above what you did at your club.'

Centre Steve Fenwick, another whose introduction to the squad was not too far away, says, 'I have never seen so much fighting. Everyone wanted to get in the team and the only chance was to prove yourself against your opposite number. I remember the Pontypool Front Row giving John Richardson of Aberavon a hammering because he was pressing for their position. The three of them wanted to stay in so they hatched a plan to kick the shit out of him in a practice game. It came down to a toe-to-toe, one team against the other.'

Another Aberavon prop, Clive Williams, who was also trying to dislodge one of the Pontypool boys, adds, 'I am sure John would have been trying something as well. Training there was full-on and a bit of fighting would be a regular part of it. It was always best to be in the red jersey, and if you weren't then you made sure you were a nuisance.'

Fisticuffs aside, the Sunday sessions are acknowledged by all to have had a great unifying effect on the team, as JPR confirms. 'It was really about getting to know each other. We had a lot of London Welsh, Cardiff and Llanelli players and it was question of learning how to play with each other.'

Dawes, who assisted coach Clive Rowlands in the execution of the sessions, explains, 'The little flaws were brushed up and we eliminated those silly errors so we could play a more constructive game. We did it without losing any natural ability. We would never ask Barry John or Phil Bennett to do a crash-tackling role. So this was organisation rather than coaching. What we did was get used to each other and recognise what each other could do. There was plenty of ball work. Gareth Edwards wouldn't want to come out of the changing room unless we had a soccer ball to start every session.'

Rowlands recalls, 'In the warm-ups there was always a ball involved. It was the same when Dawesy was coach. We would work on individual skills, Gareth's kicking or whatever it was, and then the backs and forwards would split up. Backs would practise their moves and, whether you used it or not, the point was that they would be able to do a scissors without calling it. If you practise something enough it comes instinctively. The players thought for themselves and the best scissors move was the one that came off the cuff.'

Dawes and others remember the time spent together away from the field being every bit as important as the training. 'We seemed to gel naturally: the teacher, the doctor, the coal miner, the steelworker and the Cambridge graduate. There was no regime that said you must mix, but it just happened.'

Edwards confirms, 'Clive would work us hard but we would have a great time. It was all new and there were a lot of characters in the team. There would always be the sound of people laughing.'

Delme Thomas adds, 'We were amateurs, from different jobs, and when we got together there was a great comradeship. We played for the love of the game and I would hate to be playing now, even though they earn big money. Their livelihood is on the line in every game. They can't enjoy it as much as we did. We had a great bunch of boys.'

For the forwards in particular, squad training was an opportunity to enhance their status and feel a more integral part of the team, with their skills appreciated by all. In the old days they had been dismissed by some as 'donkeys' whose role was to traipse around the field trying to keep up with the backs. It was assumed that they thought little about the wider game and were content simply to enjoy a dust-up against their opponent in the scrum. As David Hayward, the late Cardiff and Wales flanker, observed of the front row, 'It didn't really matter to them what the score read in the *Football Echo*, if they had taken two against the head they had won.'

Mervyn Davies recalls, 'Clive worked harder with the forwards. What you were trying to achieve was to make space for the next man, therefore the speed of the ball along the line was intended to give them half a yard on the opponent. It was kind of like chess and it was all about keeping the opposition close to the ruck or maul, not letting them spread.'

Rowlands frequently made the first-team forwards test themselves against ten opponents, watching with satisfaction as the sand turned into a swamp. But even though he 'wanted to develop the unit to be the best ball-winning machine in the world' it was not all about brute force and scrummaging technique. 'Speed of action and speed of thought' were just as important. One day, he even decided to give Barry John a taste of life in the pack. John had jokingly asked hooker Jeff Young, 'What do you blokes in the front row think about when you are in a scrum with your noses on the ground?' So at the next session the fly-half was called forward by the coach to take his place as a prop forward. 'Listen, Barry,' Rowlands explained. 'If you drop the ball or knock on these eight ugly gits have to go through a scrum. You don't know what it is like. So have a go and find out.'

Banter between John and the forwards was nothing new. When Rowlands asked Young one Sunday to run across the road to check if the tide was in, he shot back, 'Why not send Barry, because if it's in he'll be able to turn it himself.'

Rowlands carefully observed such interaction between his players, making sure he knew their personalities as well as their playing styles. 'He treated each and every one of us as an individual, knowing everyone's idiosyncrasies,' John noted. 'In doing so it created a team. If that is not management, what is?'

What most players agree was absent from the squad sessions was detailed discussion about opponents and rigid implementation of strategy, although Rowlands explains, 'The longer I went on as coach, the more you started getting into that side of it. In the beginning I couldn't care less about the other side. I remember losing one game and getting a lovely letter from a Welshman, the Reverend something. He wrote, "I read in the paper you didn't put too much consideration to the opposition. Pity."'

More attention was paid to making sure that the Welsh players understood their roles and could execute them to the highest possible standard. Few dispute that it was the right approach, given the individual ability sprinkled liberally throughout the team. J.P.R. Williams recalls having 'very good coaches who were not as dogmatic as I think they are today. They let you make decisions,' while Tom

David states, 'There weren't too many planned moves because you had such great players who were blessed with natural talent. Nobody had to tell Gerald Davies when to sidestep.'

Mervyn Davies remembers Rowlands leaving the backs to create their own strategy. 'Wales in those days weren't the greatest side in the world, but we were successful because we quite often relied on individuals to do something special – Gareth or Gerald or JPR. If we had been a bit more cohesive we would have been an even better side, but Clive did instil that discipline. We couldn't just throw the ball willy-nilly; we had to go through the phases and follow a game plan, but often that game plan was out of the window when Barry and Gareth got the ball. They were such individuals that you just had to react to what they did. It is an almost direct antithesis of what happens today. People of their stature took the onus upon themselves and said, "Bugger that. There is a gap and I am going through." They knew full well the coach wouldn't drop them because they hadn't done what they were told.'

Edwards explains that Rowlands was adept at maximising his time with the players. 'People today would laugh at it – it was Sundays and then the Thursday afternoon run-out. Tactics were kept to a minimum because Clive didn't have time to get too complicated. He had confidence in the players and some of his early tactics were as simple as, "Gar, if it's good ball, use it. If it's bad ball, kick it." He acknowledged that we could determine that. He would work hard with the forwards in the time we had in order to make sure I got the possession I required to give Barry or Phil the service they needed so we could give our backs every opportunity to score. That was our approach early on.'

Dawes recalls his own role at the sessions. 'If Clive was with the forwards, he would tell us as backs to go off and "go through things". That was the expression he used. I can't remember that I took the lead; we just went away and did it. I wouldn't worry about the things the players couldn't do. I was trying to avoid situations where they would be exposed by a weakness. It seemed to work. The fact I was a trained teacher, like Clive, was definitely influential. You didn't shout and bawl; you quietly got on with it. We always rehearsed or practised what we could do, and looked at it as the opponents having to stop us.'

Offering further enlightenment on the nature of the coach–captain relationship, Dawes adds, 'All the talking was done by Clive and even as captain I said very little. But we weren't told what to do by him. We knew what we were going to do and he let us get on with it. It was the perfect match. As captain, I would only suggest things to players, not tell them – although such was the class of someone like Barry John that you only had to suggest something once. Clive never interfered. He had his personal relationships with the players and they were different to mine.'

Although never captain, it was John, in the pivotal position of fly-half, who made most of the crucial decisions in the heat of battle. And Dawes, the most successful of his skippers, was happy to let him express his talent. 'I had complete freedom to run games instinctively as I saw fit,' is John's memory. 'Sid never grabbed the headlines as much as the rest of us but he deserves a large chunk of the credit for what we achieved because he was so positive in everything he said. He was more likely to tell me to go for it and for a running fly-half that was like letting a greyhound off the leash.'

According to Fenwick, Dawes would continue the same approach when he was appointed coach. He explains, 'There were some planned moves and he had input, but I remember him saying, "You are the people on the field and I can't make decisions for you. I will be really pissed off if you don't try something. I'll never criticise you for trying something that doesn't come off but I will for not trying." It gave people licence to alter tactics during the game. If things weren't going well in one department we could change. Everyone was encouraged to chip in with their own thoughts. We were given responsibility and John encouraged you to express your talent. When Alan Davies was coach [in the 1990s] players would look up to the stand for instructions.'

J.P.R. Williams does recall, however, that his famous excursions into the three-quarter line had to be rehearsed. 'The lineout was so much more unpredictable in those days that you had to practise your timing. You had to take the ball flat out because if you took it slowing down there was no point. We practised a lot of that so that the backs knew where and when it would happen. It wasn't all off the cuff.'

One tactic that needed no preparation was taking advantage of their own language. John would suggest to Edwards in their native tongue where to throw the ball, recalling that 'the opposition didn't have a clue what was going on'. Mervyn Davies continues, 'I would often speak Welsh with Barry or Gareth. It meant that we knew exactly what we were doing and there was no need for signals. It gave us an edge, especially in pressure situations and at the base of the scrum.'

Delme Thomas was another who shouted lineout instructions in Welsh, although it helped to remember who among the team did not speak the language. Bobby Windsor, who became the Welsh hooker in 1974, recalls the hilarity among his teammates when Edwards bellowed a command prior to Windsor throwing into the line and was greeted with, 'What the hell did you say?' by his English-speaking colleague.

Meanwhile, discussion of the individuals against whom Wales would be lining up was kept to a minimum. JPR explains, 'You were left to do a lot of the thinking for yourself and I studied the game a lot. With David Duckham, I knew which way he was going to sidestep. And big guys by and large have to slow down to step, whereas people like Gerald Davies and Shane Williams don't. You could see the big guys slow down to sidestep, so you can do the opposite. If they go off their left foot, which was what Duckham used to do, I would go off my right so that I hit him. We didn't have all this video analysis they have now.'

J.J. Williams confirms, 'We didn't talk much about the opposition. We would look at our game, though, and look at the errors. I remember one Scotland game, when we had beaten them quite comfortably but Andy Irvine had scored a try. I'd kicked the ball downfield and it went too high. It went through a few phases and Trevor Evans put up another kick and then Irvine started an attack down in one corner and it ended with a try up in the other corner. I was told it was my fault! That is what you are talking about, the minutest detail. If I hadn't done that kick then Trevor wouldn't have been in trouble. We attempted to eradicate every mistake.'

Such attention to detail was a far cry from the days prior to squad get-togethers. Looking back on his days as Wales skipper, Rowlands says, 'We had a Friday afternoon training session and then everyone went home and came back on Saturday morning. You had to get your organisation in very quickly on the Friday.' Edwards even described the national team set-up during the 1960s as a 'Steptoe outfit'. Yet the new regime, augmented by the lessons of New Zealand, meant that Wales were going to enjoy most of the last laughs as a new decade arrived.

5

GIVE ME JUST A LITTLE MORE TIME

'You hear reserve players say, "We are sitting there and we want Wales to win." Do you, shit!' – *Ray 'Chico' Hopkins*

It was always going to be interesting to gauge the approach of the Welsh selectors to the 1969–70 season. Would they see success in Europe as a base from which to apply only small, subtle upgrades, or would the experience in New Zealand prompt more wholesale changes? In the end, the personal choices of several players made their strategy more straightforward, turning the campaign into one of transition.

The services of three key players among the backs would be denied to the selection committee, upon which coach Clive Rowlands had taken the place of Vernon Parfitt. Instead of settling into his new position on the wing, Gerald Davies opted to take a year's sabbatical from international rugby to focus on his studies at Cambridge University. Meanwhile, two British Lions three-quarters had taken rugby league's money, winger Maurice Richards signing for Salford for a reported £7,500 and Keith Jarrett joining Barrow.

Both were significant losses, Richards having scored seven tries for his country in the previous season and Jarrett, despite his miserable run in New Zealand, being the incumbent goalkicker. Incredibly, given the success he was to enjoy in 1971, Barry John would not yet be considered for that role. Clive Rowlands says, 'We'd had Keith Jarrett so we had not had to think about it. Barry wasn't even kicking much for Cardiff at that time. He could drop goals brilliantly but we'd done without him as a kicker.' Instead, J.P.R. Williams and Gareth Edwards would handle the bulk of the duties, with support in one game from Laurie Daniel, the Newport winger. Williams, despite his innate confidence, is honest enough to recognise that he was not an international-standard kicker and admits that he hated the pressure that went with the role.

The loss of so many important players would lead to the selectors trying ten men in the three-quarter positions during the five games of 1969–70, including four different combinations in the centre. Several men played out of position, while Phil Bennett appeared in three separate shirts in as many games. With such a lack of cohesion it was little wonder that only one try was scored by a Welsh three-quarter all season.

In the pack, Brian Price had retired after 32 caps and Brian Thomas chose to bow out of the highest level of the sport after 21 appearances for his country. Having captained the team as a stand-in, Edwards was now given the leadership in his own right. Meanwhile, a place in the second row was found for London Welsh's Geoff Evans, a lecturer in biochemistry who had started his career at centre and hooker.

Another change was enforced for the first game of the season against South Africa when flanker John Taylor, appalled at the examples of apartheid he had seen in that country while touring with the 1968 British Lions, made himself unavailable on moral grounds. There were plenty of people who shared Taylor's view that the Springboks' tour of Britain should not be going ahead. The walls of global disapproval were beginning to close in on South Africa, leaving them isolated from the rest of the sporting world. FIFA had suspended them from world football as early as 1961, with the International Olympic Committee following suit three years later. In 1968, the Marylebone Cricket Club famously cancelled its proposed visit after the South African government announced that all-rounder Basil D'Oliveira, a 'coloured' cricketer from Cape Town, would not be welcome as part of the England team. The South Africans would shortly embark on their final series of Test cricket for more than two decades, thrashing Australia at home early in 1970. When the proposed tour of England later that summer and the 1971–72 series in Australia were both subsequently cancelled, it increased the pressure on rugby to play its part in excluding the regime of John Vorster from the international sports community.

In Britain in the autumn of 1969, the recent wounds of the 'D'Oliveira Affair' meant that passions were running high when the Springboks began their march around the country. From the very first game, a defeat against Oxford University at Twickenham, the presence of anti-tour protestors clearly unsettled the South African players. The Oxford game had been moved belatedly from the university's Iffley Road ground after police said they could not guarantee the safety of the public or venue against likely demonstrators. It was hard to shut out such distractions, especially when the chants and jeers turned into ugly, violent scenes, as they did in the game against West Wales at Swansea, where protestors broke on the field. Stewards were accused of being heavy-handed, while 11 police were among the injured and 63 people were subsequently charged with offences relating to the day. Home Secretary James Callaghan, the MP for Cardiff South-East, responded by calling an emergency meeting of all chief constables in areas still to host a tour match.

By the time they played Wales in January 1970, the fragile tourists were still seeking an international victory, having lost to Scotland and England and drawn the previous week against Ireland. They had also suffered a couple of defeats in the Principality, against Newport and Gwent. They had at least become accustomed to the site of barbed wire on walls and railings and a vast presence of mounted police.

On the field, Dennis Hughes, the experienced Newbridge number eight who had won a second cap in New Zealand, was chosen at flanker – as he would be for all six of his Wales appearances. Newport's Barry Llewellyn, who had missed out on a Test in New Zealand through injury, was given a debut in the front row, while the wingers selected were Phil Bennett, usually an outside-half, and Ian Hall, the Aberavon centre who had threatened to pull out of the combined Neath-Aberavon team to face the tourists when selected out wide. Billy Raybould, a 1968 British Lions selection, now enjoying his first season with Newport, was recalled alongside John Dawes in the centre.

Heavy rain and thick mud wrecked Welsh hopes of executing the running game they believed would expose their opponents. The Arms Park surface, like so many of those brown, boggy football pitches that regularly featured on *Match of the Day*, left much to be desired. Until the ongoing construction was completed at the complex, providing Cardiff RFC with a new ground outside the National Stadium, the club was playing all its first-team and reserve games on the pitch and the tractors had been working overtime in trying to get fertiliser into the soil. Wales persisted in their attempts to overcome nature, even though it took until late in the second half for the crowd to witness a successful passing move. The first half ended with only an exchange of penalties between Henry de Villiers and Edwards on the board.

South Africa kept Wales on their heels with accurate kicking into the box and took the lead early in the second half through left-wing Syd Nomis. But while the home team stared defeat in the face, the visitors approached injury time with thoughts of Ireland's last-gasp escape in Dublin seven days earlier etched deep in their fragile psyche.

If Welsh fans came to expect anything above all else in the decade just beginning it was the reliability of Edwards to produce a piece of brilliance when needed most. On this occasion he was in the right place after Nomis was caught by the combined efforts of Hall and Dawes near the left touchline. Llewellyn ripped the ball clear and passed to Edwards, who displayed all his strength as he charged his way over the line. His conversion missed – he was still human – but the excited Wales fans greeted the final score of 6–6 in the manner of victory. It was, after all, the first time they'd avoided defeat in six games against South Africa.

Welsh coal merchants announce they will make the public pay the entire ten per cent cost increase agreed by the Prices and Incomes Board. Jack Harris, secretary of the Coal Merchants Federation of Wales, explains that such increases are always passed to the consumers, although observers fear it will hurt the industry by reducing the competitiveness of coal against other fuels.

Comparative results against the tourists appeared to put Wales behind Scotland and England in the pecking order as the new Five Nations season kicked off. The schedule of fixtures had designated those two teams as Wales's first two opponents and by half-time against Scotland in Cardiff it appeared as though the recent form guide would hold up.

Playing with the wind, the Scots took a 9–0 lead, the scoring having started when Ian Robertson evaded a tackle and dropped a goal. That appeared to inject self-belief into their backs, who stretched a Welsh unit that had again been chopped and changed. The hard running of Daniel, supported by his kicking ability, had been preferred to the lighter footwork of Bennett on the right wing, but such was the determination to keep the Llanelli man in the team that a place had been created for him in the centre.

The Wales forwards, unchanged except for props Llewellyn and Denzil Williams switching sides, were struggling and a long-range penalty from Wilson Lauder stretched the Scots' lead. After J.P.R. Williams failed to make touch, Robertson sold a dummy and cut inside for a try that Barry John believes is one of the best scored against him by an opposing outside-half. Edwards once again led the recovery by forcing the Scots onto the retreat, but Daniel clunked the bar when presented with an easy opportunity. Wales did score before half-time, though, after Edwards ran from a penalty and Mervyn Davies set up a ruck. Morris, Edwards and John formed the conveyor belt that got the ball to Daniel and he finished the move, before adding the conversion.

Now it was all Wales, with Edwards and his loose forwards like slavering wolves. With 13 minutes of the second half played, Edwards gambled again from a penalty and this time Llewellyn emerged from the ruck as the try scorer after good work by Denzil Williams. Having helped to set up a try in his first game and scored in his second, Llewellyn was making quite an impact and is still rated by Rowlands as 'one of the best prop forwards I have ever seen. He could run like a three-quarter and his hands were amazing.'

A third try arrived when Robertson's kick was blocked by John, who was almost climbing up his leg at the time, and touched down by Dawes. It was a worthy reward for Dawes, whose support play and intelligent passing made him the pick of the Wales backs. Edwards converted and was on target again after Dai Morris picked up and dived over as Wales drove ahead at a five-yard scrum. Final score: 18–9.

It was the back division that continued to give the Welsh selectors reason for concern as the game against England approached. Barry John had not been at his best in the past two games, but it was Bennett, for now, and Daniels, for ever, who were discarded. Back came Raybould and the inconsistent Stuart Watkins. Criticism of Welsh selection in the media concentrated on them entering the game without a specialist place-kicker. England had no such concerns. In full-back Bob Hiller, whose dark-haired good looks appear now like a cross between Leslie Crowther and Liam Gallagher, they had one of the most consistent kickers in world rugby, and one of the last to achieve such status with his straight-ahead style. After ten minutes he was called up to convert a try that stemmed from winger John Novak dislodging the ball from the grasp of J.P.R. Williams as he attempted to call for a mark, the move ending with David Duckham being sent away for the score. Wales replied after John kicked deep into the corner and Mervyn Davies fell over as he caught the ball at the back of the line, defying English efforts to stop him grounding the ball.

Novak and fly-half Roger Shackleton missed dropped goals, but the pair were involved at the start and finish of a move that brought a second try. Shackleton juggled the ball, recently ruled legal under the revised knock-on law, and the powerful Novak marked his debut by scoring on the overlap. Hiller converted and added a penalty ten minutes later for a 13–3 lead. There was an unfortunate diversion when French referee Robert Calmet suffered what turned out to be a cracked shin bone after being squashed in a ruck and was replaced at half-time by English official Johnny Johnson. Home scrum-half

Nigel Starmer-Smith quickly appeared to suffer some other kind of distraction when he crouched in hesitation after Edwards's kick to the corner, allowing John to steal in for a try. It hardly signalled a significant shift in momentum, however, and after a break sparked by Starmer-Smith it needed a fine smother tackle by Williams and Dawes to stop John Spencer two yards out when a pass to Novak might have made the game safe. Williams would say later that it was the moment when 'England blew the game'.

It was also the moment that led to a piece of rugby history, with Edwards left holding an injured ankle after teammate Hughes had fallen on it while tackling Starmer-Smith. At 13–6 down with twenty minutes remaining, the home side in the ascendancy and one of Wales's key players off injured, many of the visiting fans who had made the pilgrimage to the headquarters of rugby were despairing of rescuing the game. They had reckoned without Chico Hopkins.

The National Union of Teachers confirms plans for a series of eight-day strikes throughout 43 schools in Wales, part of a nationwide campaign affecting 450 schools. Most will be temporarily closed but Cardiff Education Authority plans to keep schools open by using non-striking teachers to perform additional duties.

The timing of the interview for the book has been carefully planned. 'Let's make it at three o'clock,' Ray 'Chico' Hopkins has suggested. 'That way I can watch *The Antiques Roadshow* first. I collect antiques like Gareth Edwards collects money!'

By the time of the match that carved his boyhood nickname into Welsh rugby lore, 23-year-old Hopkins had spent plenty of time either watching Edwards from the Wales bench or filling in for him in provincial tour matches. A cheerful character with an impressive collection of punch lines and light-hearted put-downs, he explains how his performances for Maesteg had brought him to the attention of the national selectors the previous season and earned him a place in a national trial in Llanelli.

'I was picked for the Possibles and Allan Lewis, who had played for the Lions, was in the Probables. I thought, "Great, we have got all the head bangers in our back row." I wasn't frightened of playing against Mervyn because he was a gentleman and John Taylor and Dai Morris were good players but not ones to give you a dig. Then Allan Lewis got blocked in by snow and they moved me to the Probables. I thought, "Shit." But the Probables pack dominated. I got the ball from everywhere, scored three tries, went through to the final trial and got picked to go on the 1969 tour to New Zealand.'

Although understanding that his role was to understudy Edwards, he denies that it was a source of frustration. 'Gareth had good days and he had bad days, but I never ever felt inferior to him. The man in my day who I would say was the difference was Barry John. Overall, Gareth probably had the edge on me because he was a 440 yards man, but he was a different player behind a beaten pack and he never played in many games when the pack was beaten. Some of the Cardiff players told me they preferred it when he wasn't playing because they were better as a team then. But if the pack was on top he could exploit it more than me. I couldn't have scored that try against Scotland [in 1972].

'I got on with him all right, as long as he knew he was the top dog. But when I was out in New Zealand in 1969 and putting him under pressure, they couldn't decide who they were going to play at halfback and everybody forgets that. I sound a right big-headed bastard here but I played six times in his place at the top level, for the Lions and on the Welsh tour, and we didn't lose a game because we were such a good side. He didn't play in the provincial games in '69 and Clive Rowlands always says to me he should have picked me in the Test matches because Gareth had a niggling hamstring. I won the man of the match against Wellington before the final Test and everyone thought I was bound to play, but Gareth got in again.'

Hopkins happily admits to the reality of life on the Welsh bench, where he usually found himself alongside reserve fly-half Phil Bennett. 'You want something to go wrong so you get picked. Phil Bennett said to me against Scotland, "You'll be in the next side because Gareth is playing crap." Then he made that break and scored a great try and someone turned to me and said, "You can forget the next fucking five internationals. You've had it now."'

After returning from New Zealand, Hopkins had suffered a knee injury and was only just easing his way back when the Twickenham game came around. 'I had hardly played for months and was about a stone overweight,' he says. Recounting what turned out to be his only Wales cap, he continues, 'I said to Phil, "I have got a feeling I am going on today." He said, "That bastard won't come off." All of a sudden, Gareth is down. We sat in the stand in those days and I went down the stairs like bloody greased lightning. It was like I was in a trance. You were thankful to be part of a great side, but me and Phil were always under pressure because Gareth and Barry were always pushed to the front so much by the Cardiff papers. We were shitting ourselves that if we went on and made the slightest mistake the first thing they would say was that we missed the other guys. I had played a lot with Barry in provincial games so I was playing with someone I knew, but that is all overrated anyway. If you are a fair player you can fit in. You play on your instinct and good players can adapt to each other.'

Within minutes of his arrival, Hopkins, full of energy and instinct, had helped to bring Wales back into the game. Jeff Young, back at hooker for the first time since his broken jaw, won the heel from a five-yard scrum and Hopkins slid to the blind side and delivered a well-timed pass to J.P.R. Williams, who charged past Hiller and scored a try that reduced England's lead to 13–9. A sign of the changing times was that it was only the third try for Wales from the full-back position, yet Williams would go on to score six over the next seven years.

Hopkins, typically, has a down-to-earth recollection of the moment. 'If the ball had come out in the middle of the scrum I would have passed to Barry John under the posts, but it came out on the blind side and it was a bit awkward to turn. JPR was there and it looked like it was a move but we never planned anything. If he hadn't come up on the outside right then I'd have ended up in the fucking stand.'

Wales still trailed as injury time approached and, having driven towards the English line, they prepared to receive a lineout beneath their fans straining to see from the South Terrace. Breath was held as England threw to the back of the line, a dangerous ploy deep in defence. When the ball dropped on the Welsh side, time seemed to pause as history prepared to deliver its latest offspring. Hopkins was the first to react, snatching up the ball, throwing a quick glance to his left and diving into the gap before him and over the line. 'The ball bounced over Dai Morris's head and into my hands,' says Hopkins. 'You can't legislate for that, can you? It was just meant to be my day.' There was still the conversion to be executed, far from a formality, yet Williams stabbed the ball goalward and watched it reach its destination for a 14–13 lead.

Far from losing concentration in the euphoria of the moment, Wales regained possession in the final seconds. Hopkins again takes up the story. 'I put the ball in the scrum in the last minute and in those days they would penalise you if it was crooked. I thought, "Please, God, please don't let Bob Hiller kick a goal from the 25." Anyway, it comes out but it was on the far side again so I picked it up and kicked from my own 25. The ball landed on their 25-yard line and rolled up the touchline. I was under no control of it really. I bet you're thinking, "If he could play like he can talk he'd have been a fucking world beater."'

From the set-piece, John dropped a goal on the run. 'If I scored we would be 17–13 ahead,' he said. 'If I did not, England would have a 25-yard drop-out and would probably concede possession back to us anyway.' Even for a team with an increasing reputation for pulling games out of the fire, it had been a remarkable turn of events. Tough characters like Denzil Williams and Jeff Young had tears in their eyes in the dressing-room, such was the emotion of the victory.

And that was the Welsh international career of Chico Hopkins, all 20 minutes of it. It was enough to see him named Player of the Year by the *Welsh Brewers' Rugby Annual for Wales* and it is still celebrated more than some players who appeared in upwards of 20 matches. 'I know Gareth was shitting himself,' says Hopkins of the aftermath of Twickenham. 'But he was in the team in Ireland and he and Barry were disastrous and they lost us the Triple Crown. Gareth was still there against France and I thought, "Well, I am never going to get in the side now." It would have to be a broken leg or something.'

There would be further international recognition, though, when Hopkins was selected as the second scrum-half on the British Lions tour of New Zealand in 1971, replacing the injured Edwards in the first half of a famous victory in the first Test. He even beat the All Blacks again after switching clubs to Llanelli. 'Carwyn James always wanted me to go there,' he explains. 'I'd had great satisfaction playing for Maesteg but we were going for the championship and people weren't turning up for training, plus about six of them were about to retire. I thought, "If they can't train now to win the championship I am going to get murdered if I stay here."'

Soon after the All Blacks game, he made an even more dramatic move, to play rugby league for Swinton. 'I went when I was in my prime and in as good a position as ever with Wales,' he admits. 'I'd had good reports on the Lions tour and now I was with Phil Bennett in Llanelli, which would have been an advantage. But my father died when I was playing for Llanelli against Cross Keys. Dropped dead on the touchline. We were very close and he always wanted me to go to rugby league eventually. And I had met a girl up north who became my wife. Money didn't come into it. I had a good job as a sales rep and public relations officer, a good family life and wasn't struggling in any way.'

But he concedes, 'I didn't really make it. I went to a poor side and it is the positions, you can't get used to the angles. I used to be frustrated and it made me think I couldn't have been as good as I thought I was!'

Hopkins is not a man with regrets, however. The form and fitness of Gareth Edwards meant that, even if he had stayed in Wales, those 20 glorious minutes would have remained his only full international appearance for his country. According to Barry John, the only disappointment Hopkins feels is over Edwards's own response to his performance at Twickenham. John stated a few years ago, 'I know that to this day Chico feels let down and aggrieved with Gareth because he feels the great man did not properly congratulate him on his wonderful performance.'

It's an issue that Hopkins now skirts around, saying, 'There are no sour grapes because I had a great time. The game has been a godsend for me. I would have been a bastard reclusive without it because I was a bit shy. And now people remember me because the name Chico sticks with them. There were better players than me around and people think "Who?" when you mention them. What more can a player want than to be remembered after more than 30 years?'

Art imitates sport as Welsh singer Mary Hopkin loses out to Ireland's Dana in the Eurovision Song Contest. Pontadarwe-born Hopkin, a winner of *Opportunity Knocks*, spent six weeks at number one in autumn 1968 with 'Those Were the Days', but 'Knock, Knock, Who's There?' is beaten into second place by 'All Kinds of Everything'.

It might be an exaggeration by Chico Hopkins to say that John and Edwards cost Wales the Triple Crown when they visited Dublin, but there is no doubt that the 14–0 defeat to Ireland was hardly the duo's finest hour. Edwards admitted, 'That bleak day in Dublin was the day when Barry and I grew up.' He even confessed to fearing for the first time that he was going to be dropped, especially when selector Jack Young said to him at the post-match dinner, 'Make the most of this evening, Gareth.'

Playing their Welsh-record 16th game in tandem, Edwards and John struggled against a home side that appeared free of inhibitions and in the mood to make their considerable weight advantage pay off. When Wales did have possession, their own mistakes prevented them progressing. J.P.R. Williams was even accused of leaving too many gaps at the back after launching his trademark sorties against the kicking of Barry McGann.

With Cambridge University winger Keith Hughes having replaced Ian Hall, Wales were indebted to a strong tackle in the corner by Raybould on Irish number eight Ken Goodall to maintain parity at half-time. But then Ireland dominated and, after the scoring was set in motion by McGann's fifty-seventh-minute dropped goal, two errors by John produced tries. First, his pass went behind his three-quarters to allow Ireland winger Alan Duggan an unopposed run. Then, three minutes after a Tom Kiernan penalty had made it 9–0,

John chipped into the arms of the spindly Goodall, who ran from inside his own half, gathered his own kick and completed what *The Belfast Telegraph* described as 'one of the finest solo tries ever seen at Lansdowne Road'. The burst of 14 points had taken only 12 minutes and skipper Kiernan, celebrating a record 47th cap for his country, ended the game being carried on the shoulders of the home fans.

Interestingly, the real hero of the hour, Ken Goodall, was to enjoy no more Irish triumphs. He announced after the game that he was joining rugby league team Workington for financial reasons. Even though he was only 22, such was the esteem in which he was held among his peers that Mervyn Davies would say, 'I will never know if I was the best number eight in the world because Ken wasn't around to challenge me.'

For Wales, the repercussions of Dublin were far-ranging. The Welsh press, keen to apportion blame, tossed around a theory that a fall-out between Edwards and J.P.R. Williams had been at the root of the unforeseen disaster. The cause of their argument was supposed to have been anything from goalkicking to girlfriends. 'The story was totally wrong,' Williams insists. 'We simply got hammered. Sport is about there always being a chance for one team to beat another.' Edwards did, however, write about a misunderstanding between him and JPR about who was going to kick a penalty.

According to Mervyn Davies, who heard allegations that the team had been out on the beer until late the night before, 'The excuses were legion. One of our players had thrown a punch at a teammate in the changing-room and unsettled us – rubbish! Our real enemy that day was complacency.'

Clive Rowlands can now cite that game as one of the pivotal moments in the development of his team. 'The games that made these players better were ones we lost. I will never forget the game in Ireland. Normally if you have five good players and one of them is off form, the other four will get you through. If all of them are off you have a problem. I told them after the game, "Don't enjoy this, but don't forget it either." We came down from our hotel rooms for the dinner that night and the players walked in singing "Calon Lan". I thought, "Good boys."'

For the last game against France, Edwards was relieved of the captaincy, as he would be again after being re-appointed to the post in 1974. In fact, one of the great arguments over his career – and one to which we shall return – was the extent to which he was, or wasn't, suited to leading the Welsh team. On this occasion U.A. Titley wrote in *The Times*:

> It is under pressure that a captain's influence counts for most, but Edwards was not up to it, and no captain should allow any member of his team to argue with him in public. It is not surprising therefore that John Dawes has taken over for this match.

Edwards, it was noted by observers, had appeared slower than usual to release the ball throughout the season. Add that to John's own misfortunes in Dublin and it was ironic that it was in the three-quarters where wholesale changes were made for the France match. New caps were awarded to Jim Shanklin and Roy Mathias, both usually centres at London Welsh and Llanelli respectively but now picked on the wings. The withdrawal of Stuart Watkins through injury marked the end of a twenty-six-cap Wales career that had produced nine tries and the selectors clearly wanted to replace his physical presence. In fact, Mathias was such a powerful player that after he went to St Helens to play rugby league two years later he eventually ended up as a back-row forward. There was a suggestion by some reporters that JPR should play in the centre to allow Cardiff full-back Robin Williams to be drafted in as place-kicker, but it was a third newcomer to the side, the granite figure of Ebbw Vale's Arthur Lewis, who was named alongside Dawes, the only member of the three-quarters to retain his place throughout the season.

At the age of 28, Lewis, who had spent several years at Ebbw Vale after moving from his home-town club, Crumlin, admits, 'I thought playing for Wales had passed me by. Personally, I thought I was playing better rugby earlier in my career. I knew that not many players got picked for Wales from Ebbw Vale and I had been offered the chance to go to Newport, but I wasn't interested. I was at a great club, which was run very professionally.'

Lewis had helped his cause with a strong performance in a B international in France. 'I was marking Joe Maso and on the plane going over Bleddyn Williams had said, "You're up against one of the best but he doesn't have a lot of bottle. Stir him up a bit." I handed him off early on and his nose splattered a bit and after that I had a good game. They stuck with Billy Raybould against Ireland but he didn't play too well so I was in.'

Two days before a game that could still give Wales an opportunity to win the championship, there was another change when John withdrew injured and Bennett was at last given the chance to represent his country in his position of choice. Given a more consistent service than Edwards had delivered in previous games, he kicked accurately and thoughtfully, while the defensive work of the three-quarters and the captaincy of Dawes also earned good reviews.

France, already winners over Ireland and Scotland, were generally considered the more talented side, but their speedy runners, such as Jean-Marie Bonal, who had recorded 10.6 seconds for the 100 metres, made little use of their opportunities. That their possession was not more plentiful was due to a purposeful performance by the Welsh pack, where Taylor was back at flanker and John Lloyd returned in place of the injured Denzil Williams. A back injury to Evans allowed Scottish-born Stuart Gallacher, dominant in the lineouts, to make the most of his only cap at lock before his conversion to the professional game.

Bonal won the race for a bouncing ball to open the scoring, but two penalties by J.P.R. Williams meant Wales led 6–3 after a first half in which they had been territorially disadvantaged. From the second-half kick-off, French fly-half Paries was put under pressure by a pass from his partner Puget and made a panicky attempt to get the ball to full-back Villepreux. It ended up in the arms of Gallacher inside the 25 and he passed for Morris to score under the posts, with Williams converting. 'The day went in a blur, although I had played in big games before, for the Barbarians against South Africa at Twickenham,' recalls Gallacher. 'But I will never forget the moment their outside-half threw a crazy pass into my hands. I took off and kept running and no one tackled me. Ten yards from the line I saw a blue shirt in front of me and then I heard a voice inside me. It was Dai so I popped the ball to him.'

The Welsh defence ensured that winger Jacques Cantoni's try was only a consolation effort and preserved the 11–6 advantage. France duly beat England to ensure they shared the title, but Wales would be able to reflect on a campaign in which they had partly erased the blot of the New Zealand tour and proved they had depth at halfback and in the pack, and could now look forward to the return of a key player to improve the three-quarters. They had also appointed a captain who was about to embark on the season of his life.

6

ALWAYS ON MY MIND

'People wanted to see our type of game. You don't talk about the Brazil soccer team just because they win, you talk about what you see and the way they play. People enjoyed our game, even in England, where the media always liked us' – *John Dawes*

Not even the rattling seats and creaking suspension could divert the concentration of the teenaged boy deep in thought as the north-bound bus made its winding, tedious way into the Ebbw valley from Cardiff. The jolts from the uneven road surface seemed to synchronise with the images of tackles and tumbles that played in his head, adding an additional textural layer to the memories of his red-shirted heroes in battle.

It was these homeward journeys undertaken by John Dawes after attending international matches in the capital during the 1950s that helped to develop one of the most influential minds in the history of Welsh rugby. 'I went to all the big games in Cardiff and of course it was by public transport,' he remembers. 'I would enjoy watching the superstars of the day and, without television, you had to go to the game to see them play. It made much more of a personal impact, being there to see them perform. I always had a desire to play in a certain way and I wanted to do certain things. We used to have a lot of ten-man rugby in those days, which was effective and hard to break down, but it didn't stop me thinking about how I wanted to play the game my way.'

Born in the Chapel of Ease section of Abercarn, a mining village, Sidney John Dawes (hence the nickname 'Sid') inherited his physical ability from his father, Reg, a well-known player for several local rugby clubs. From his teachers at Lewis School in Pengam, an institution determined to graduate to the fixture list of the country's leading grammar schools, he gained a thorough grounding in the fundamentals of the game. From that sprang the keen analytical mind that was not content merely to celebrate the victories or mourn the losses of the Wales teams he witnessed at Cardiff Arms Park. He wanted to expand his understanding of the key moments and tactical decisions that had shaped the outcome of the games; to appreciate the geometry and physics of the action's ebb and flow.

It was a trait that continued upon his arrival at Aberystwyth as a chemistry student. On a practical level, he would try to figure out ways of beating teams of burly farmers or miners with a group of students yet to reach physical maturity. But such an intellectual approach to the game was not merely to formulate the most efficient method of achieving victory. 'I have never believed in winning at all costs,' says the man who saw from an early age that rugby had the potential to achieve heights of execution and thinking that transcended the mere result. J.P.R. Williams adds, 'In 1971 we didn't have a lot of ball, but under John we played some majestic rugby. Being the romantic that I am in all sports, I like class rather than grind.'

Dawes had started his rugby life in the forwards, switching to scrum-half and finally being introduced to the three-quarter line while playing for his local club, Newbridge, during school holidays. At Aberystwyth, he settled into the centre and in his final year earned a call-up for the Welsh international trials. He was also appointed university captain, giving him the opportunity to put his theories about the game into practice. His blueprint, which he would carry into senior club and international rugby, was to get the ball into the open spaces as quickly as possible and to unleash a fleet-footed set of back-row forwards who could arrive promptly at the breakdowns and recycle possession.

After continuing to play for Newbridge while earning a PE diploma at Loughborough, he took a teaching job in London. Even though he could hardly have been said to have been brought up as a Welsh nationalist – he didn't even speak the language – it was London Welsh where he turned up to play in the autumn of 1963.

Full-scale victories over Welsh clubs had been a rarity in the six years the Exiles had been at Old Deer Park since moving from Herne Hill. Dawes was disappointed to discover he had joined what amounted to little more than a social club. First-team players treated training as something to be avoided at all costs, while the side was characterised by over-sized, immobile forwards. In his second season, however, not only was Dawes named vice-captain but, following the WRU suggestion that clubs should appoint coaches, that job fell to him as well.

'There was talent there but it was not harnessed,' he explains. 'They used to turn up on Saturday, play the game, have a few pints and go home. I was appointed coach because of my background as PE man but in those days it was the captain who was in charge and he was not particularly interested in training. So I didn't have the results I would expect, but I persevered and after two years I was made captain as well. Then I could insist on the coaching and people used to say that, with me, if you didn't train you didn't play. If you couldn't be bothered then another person would get the nod, so we gradually were able to bring the level up.'

A good nucleus of the team was now training twice a week and accepting their coach's directive for improved fitness levels. Sunday morning discussions in the pub with three or four senior players became another regular feature. Dawes recalls, 'We had a large teaching intake and out of 160 players in our seven teams, between 100 and 120 were involved in teaching. I put in a degree of organisation and the enjoyment factor was paramount. We had the Welshness, the singing and the camaraderie – all the ingredients of a good weekend out. And it worked.'

As the 1970s arrived, Dawes was achieving his wish of combining a powerful yet athletic front five – anchored by tall second rows such as Geoff Evans and Mike Roberts – with a mobile back row, which not only featured the ball-winning ability of Mervyn Davies but had marauders like John Taylor. The running game that been born out of necessity in earlier years because of a poor pack was now an option that could be unleashed from a position of strength. In that respect his club side offered a foretaste of the Wales team he would coach in the middle of the decade, with its all-conquering forwards. The 1970–71 season would see London Welsh beaten in only four games, earning them the *Sunday Telegraph* pennants as unofficial champions of both Wales and England.

While constructing his club side, Dawes had been in and out of the national team. Selected in 1964, he helped set up a crucial try on his debut against Ireland but had to be content with watching Clive Rowlands and David Watkins monopolise the game from the halfback positions. He retained his place throughout the next season's Triple Crown campaign, but it was France – who denied Wales a Grand Slam in Paris – who made a bigger impression on him than Rowlands's safety-first kicking. Dawes watched in awe as they raced into a 19–0 first-half lead, combining flawless execution of the game's basic skills with a willingness to improvise and innovate.

Picked only once over the next two seasons, he was chosen as captain for the first time against Ireland in 1968 before seeing the job go back to Gareth Edwards in the next match, after which he was discarded again. He was asked to captain the weakened touring team in Argentina and invited to participate in the squad training sessions that began the following season, but still was unable to win back his place until the final Five Nations game of 1969. 'There were better players around of my type,' he says without regret. 'I didn't expect to be selected. I would never dream of being in the team ahead of Gerald Davies.'

It was Dawes's greatest strength as a player that often stood in the way of his elevation to the national side, whose selectors could be influenced by media members with a preference for more eye-catching individuals. 'There was nothing flashy about him,' says JPR. 'He was a great passer of the ball and a great thinker.' National team partner Arthur Lewis adds, 'He was a steady player. His defence was good and he never made mistakes. We were renowned for giving the right pass to people.'

Here, Dawes's natural modesty again comes to the fore. 'It was down to my own limitations,' he says when discussing his reputation as an unselfish player. 'There were people who were faster and more skilful than me. I knew what I could do and what they could do. Our forte at London Welsh was using the ball, catching and passing. I leaned towards players who could do something special and my job was to get the ball to them. That simple philosophy was what I enjoyed.'

Dawes was the perfect centre for a Welsh team able to boast devastating wingers in Gerald Davies and John Bevan, a new arrival to the side in 1971. What was needed was someone to get them the ball with timing and accuracy, and who could accommodate the thrusts of Williams into the line. 'He had this great ability to bring out the best in the players around him,' says Clive Rowlands. 'He was a good defender as well and never missed his man. His ability to make the right decision at the right time was amazing.'

Barry John even said that the absence of Dawes from a critical game could induce 'a mood of panic' among teammates, even though the crowd might not realise its significance. 'I believe Sid has never received enough credit for his own playing ability for he was a master of passing superbly under pressure.'

According to a Cardiff Public Health Laboratory report, the River Taff, from whose banks the new National Stadium rises, is more contaminated by 'super germs' than any other British waterway. The worst area is between Aberfan and Clifynydd, where sewage is pumped in at several points, and experts say that even new treatments to reduce toxic levels are unlikely ever to make it safe for swimming.

The completed National Stadium at Cardiff Arms Park was ceremonially opened in October 1970, with a new capacity of 52,000 and a gleaming North Stand that included 13,000 seats in its top tier and terracing for 11,000 below. In the grounds outside the main arena stood a new compact stadium that would house Cardiff, with the Glamorgan cricket team now relocated across the river at Sophia Gardens. A commemorative game was won 26–11 by Wales against an RFU President's XV – Gareth Edwards scoring the arena's first try – but there could be no better way to anoint the new home of Welsh rugby than by presenting the faithful with some meaningful victories.

Dawes approached the Five Nations season comfortable in his position as team captain. He felt that the way in which he had ordered fly-half Phil Bennett to keep his attacking instincts in check in the previous season's finale against France had proved to the selectors that he could, when the need arose, display a hard streak to balance his renowned sense of adventure.

Another source of pleasure to Dawes was that after the previous season's revolving-door policy on the wings there appeared the prospect of some stability, with the return of an old favourite, Gerald Davies, and the emergence of a belligerent new talent, John Bevan, a second-year student at Cardiff College of Education. The confrontational style of running adopted by Bevan, who seemingly would have been affronted had anyone suggested he try to go round, rather than through, a defender, was in stark contrast to Davies's delicate, fast-paced skills. A solid 6ft and 13st., long sideburns and cropped hair added to Bevan's destructive image, giving him the look of a football terrace hard man. Renowned Irish prop Ray McLoughlin would comment that he had never known strength like Bevan's after being forced to take him on in a training drill during the British Lions tour of New Zealand. Born in 1950 in the Rhondda Valley mining town of Tylorstown, which had produced a Welsh sporting hero in former world flyweight boxing champion Jimmy Wilde, Bevan's toughness was such that he had played for Wales at Under-15 level as a number eight and was only allowed to play in the backs for the Under-19 side after digging his heels in and refusing a place in the forwards. Eight games for Cardiff during the current season had already produced ten tries.

Picked for the opening match against England at Cardiff, Bevan and Davies were among five changes from the team that had played Wales's last game. 'With the selection policy of the time, you never knew if you would be picked,' recalls Arthur Lewis, who was retained in the centre. 'There was only one Gwent representative among the selectors and I knew I was not a favourite of Harry Bowcott, who was trying to push the London Welsh players. Clive Rowlands told me years later that Harry never voted for me once. We had a trial at Neath that New Year's Day so I only had a couple of sherries the night before and I ended up scoring three tries.'

Ebbw Vale teammate Denzil Williams was back in the front row as pack leader, while Stuart Gallacher's departure to rugby league let in a player whose size had cost him a dream of a career with the round ball. Born in Colwyn Bay, Mike Roberts had caught the eye of Everton scout Harry Cook as a promising centre-half, only to be told after a trial at the club that carrying 15st. on a 6ft 3in. frame made him too big for them to take their interest further. Instead, he turned to rugby, playing in the second row for Dublin and Oxford Universities before joining London Welsh when he took a teaching post in Hertfordshire. Having ballooned to almost 19st. by the time he visited the United States in 1969, he worked hard to lose two stones and was rewarded with a national trial and a place in the Wales B team. His elevation to the full team under the captaincy of Dawes owed much to the influence of his club mentor. 'Under John, one couldn't help but improve,' he said. 'Previously I had looked on backs and forwards as being separate, but under Dawes we were a team, all fifteen players taking part as one unit.'

Even though Wales now had only two forwards under 14st. – flankers Dai Morris and John Taylor – they were still outweighed by almost seven pounds per man against England. Yet, according to Roberts, the passion and pride they put forth on a cold and wet day made light of such a disadvantage. 'Denzil led us well; one could feel the unity of the forwards in the set scrums. It gave us the heart to succeed.'

Roberts played his part in helping Wales dominate in the lineout, while Williams and Barry Llewellyn provided a solid front in the set scrums. Williams went as far as saying, 'I think that was the best scrummaging we have ever produced.' Meanwhile, the Welsh forwards appeared faster around the field, consistently outmanning England at the breakdowns.

Such a platform allowed for a precise and composed performance by Gareth Edwards, while Barry John revelled in the dominance of his team and Dawes helped set up a couple of tries in his superbly understated style. England had gone into the game with seven new caps and their lack of familiarity contributed to wingers David Duckham and Jeremy Jannion barely seeing the ball. Jannion dropped his one scoring opportunity and a 22–6 scoreline was a fair reflection of the afternoon's action. The acerbic J.B.G. Thomas suggested in his report that the visitors would have done better by simply picking the Gloucester pack for the game.

The first score came in the eighth minute after Delme Thomas won a lineout and John dropped a goal with an action so smooth it looked like a slow-motion replay. There was a mishap two minutes later when Taylor tapped back close to the Welsh line and England number eight Charlie Hannaford fell on the ball for a try. It was uncharacteristic of Wales's tidy work in the line and, within two minutes, had been wiped out. Wales won the ball from a maul and, having shaped to drop, John instead fed J.P.R. Williams coming into the line before Dawes's pass paved a clear way to the line for Gerald Davies. Under the team's new cunning plan for attempts at goal, Taylor used the natural curve of his left-footed kicking to convert from near the right touchline.

The maul that led to that try had been set up when Lewis took the ball on a crash move, code-named 'Arthur'. He explains, 'I introduced a bit of that myself. I had been captain at my club and helping out with the coaching, so I had the chance to introduce a lot of the moves we did at Ebbw Vale. I was 6 feet and 13 stone, so I was one of the biggest centres about and was one of the first crash-ball players. The logic behind it was trying to take out the opposition back row and free up our own back row to create more space for our guys. You had flankers then who were never off the back of the outside-half and this was designed to tie them up.'

As England's pack struggled to get a foothold, scrum-half Jacko Page, who already appeared older than his years and compensated for thinning hair with impressive sideburns, was ageing by the minute. Typical of his team's problems was the way they moved their second-phase possession far too slowly after running a 30th-minute penalty, allowing wing-forward Tony Neary to be tackled. When the ball came back to John, he easily eluded Page, chipped round John Spencer and then passed inside for Bevan to score. A third try quickly followed. England's new full-back, Peter Rossborough, looked as brittle as the giant matchstick he resembled with his skinny limbs and mop of dark hair as he fluffed an up-and-under by Edwards right under the posts. Lewis was on hand to flick the ball to his right, Dawes moved it on and Gerald Davies outran the opposition. Taylor converted for 16–3, and it was not even half-time yet.

J.P.R. Williams, who later discovered he had played most of the game with a depressed cheekbone fracture, was still entrusted with some of the longer kicks, connecting with a 40-yard penalty. After Rossborough replied, John struck a dropped goal late in an uneventful second half. The closest Wales came to crossing the line had been when Bevan was stopped by the energetic covering of Duckham.

Fire brigades in Wales will be unable to deal with emergency calls unless an ongoing pay dispute is settled soon. A ban on overtime means firemen in rural areas may stop the practice of being on call at home outside shift hours. Meanwhile, Transport and General Workers Union [TGWU] leader Jack Jones joins Ebbw Vale MP Michael Foot to lead a protest in Cardiff against the government's proposed Industrial Relations Act, which aims to place tighter limitations on strike action. Similar 'Kill the Bill' protests will be staged around Wales over the coming months.

Clive Rowlands recalls his feeling that this 1971 season could be the source of something special. 'In 1969, the only game we didn't win was the draw in France,' he explains. 'In 1970, we only lost out in Ireland. I said to them, "Boys, if you want that Grand Slam you know what it takes." I have never seen such a confident side in my life. They weren't cocky because they thought very highly of the people they played against and the players they kept out of the side.'

John Dawes, however, insists that the players were careful not to gaze too far ahead. 'We didn't dream of Triple Crowns or Grand

Slams. I know it is a cliché, but we only looked as far as the next game. Part of it was this inherent feeling with the selection panel that you might not be there for the next game. Nothing was ever said, but you felt it and wondered if you had done enough.'

Arriving at Murrayfield for the second match of the campaign, Wales had a shock before kick-off when Gareth Edwards discovered he had left his gumshield at the team hotel. Fans making their way to the ground witnessed the comical sight of Rowlands riding pillion on a police motorcycle as he sped back to collect the missing item. If that was a dramatic start to the afternoon, it was nothing to what lay in store in one of the most exciting internationals of any era.

Scotland proved adept at spoiling the quality of the Welsh possession, turning scrums they expected to lose and happily conceding penalties to disrupt the visitors' momentum. The success of such tactics was attributed to Jordanhill's Bill Dickinson, a man with a reputation for the ferocity of the packs he produced at his club. He had been named as 'adviser to the captain' for the game – a step on the road towards a Scottish national team coach. Yet Wales could have scored a couple of times before Scotland put points on the board, with John Bevan kicking too far ahead after full-back Ian Smith dropped the ball and John's dropped goal attempt was charged down by Frank Laidlaw.

It was left to Scotland skipper Peter Brown to squeeze over a penalty from 35 yards after J.P.R. Williams was punished for not releasing the ball. Brown was one of the unlikeliest-looking players of the era: lopsided, coat-hanger shoulders and feet splayed so far apart that he resembled a crab shuffling sideways around the field. Yet he was a highly effective number eight and – apart from one fatal error – on this day he showed an uncanny knack for scuffing his side-footed kicks over the crossbar. He curled another low one between the posts to restore the Scots' lead after John had equalised from close to the left touchline.

In injury time at the end of the first half, Wales scored the day's first try. Delme Thomas won the ball at a Scotland lineout and it went through the backs to Williams, who swept through a hole in the defence, dummied outside and fed Taylor as he cut back in towards the posts. Taylor galloped across the line as Scottish lock Alastair McHarg took a Norman Hunter-style swipe at his legs. John converted for an 8–6 lead. Four minutes into the second half, Wales scored another five points after Edwards sprinted to the blindside from the 25, ignoring the trio of Scots lining up to tackle him and slicing through for the try.

But this was far from being one of those games where Wales stretched away in the second half. When Thomas tapped back Bevan's throw, the bounce of the ball favoured the big prop Sandy Carmichael, who fell through Edwards's attempted tackle for a converted try. Brown's penalty from in front of the posts put the home team in the lead at 12–11, but back came Wales and, on 64 minutes, Bevan was halted on the 25. Taylor kicked the loose ball into the path of John and the light-footed genius picked up and slid between two tackles to cross the line, taking a heavy hit from each side as he did so. While the scorer was being attended to by Gerry Lewis, Dawes stepped up to attempt an easy-looking conversion, at which point John returned groggily to the fray and hit the post with his kick. The score remained 14–12 to Wales and John would remark, 'I can recall some periods of play in that game, but the rest are a total blank. I should not really have stayed on the pitch.'

Two minutes later, another Brown penalty and another Scotland lead. 'It's a scruffy looking one,' said Bill McLaren in the commentary booth as the ball limped over the bar and Murrayfield exploded into excited cheers. Recalling Brown's kicking technique, Edwards admits, 'It used to break our hearts. It looked as if it would never get off the ground.'

With seven minutes to play, surely the home team could make the game safe. Bevan's kick had been charged down by winger Billy Steele and J.P.R. Williams had been tackled. Centre Chris Rea grabbed the ball and bolted for the line, defying the efforts of Dawes to pull him back by his shirt. Brown only had to make the conversion from below the posts for a six-point lead. But, like John before him, he banged the ball against the upright and, at 18–14 down, Wales were still alive. According to Rea, 'As the Welsh shoulders stiffened with resolve, so did the Scots shoulders sag at the prospect of the final onslaught.'

Anxious that his players did not lose their composure in the frantic final search for points, Dawes told them he had spoken to the referee and discovered that, including injury time, there were still ten minutes to play. In fact, no such conversation had taken place and in reality less than half that time was available to Wales. The last minute of it was approaching when Scotland threw the ball in from the right wing, five yards from their own try-line. As was still the custom, it was the winger, Steele, who delivered and it was the arm of Thomas that rose to win clean possession for Wales. Edwards to John to Dawes; centre Ian Hall on a dummy run inside; Williams into the line to take the ball from his captain. Then he passed to Davies, who beat Smith on the outside to score. He'd been blocked, though, from getting around under the posts, leaving Taylor to kick from only seven yards in from the right touchline. Edwards remembers lamenting to Thomas that they were going to lose the game after playing so well and scoring four tries. 'I didn't think John Taylor was ever going to kick it,' he said.

One point behind and the game resting on his left boot, Taylor was actually relieved that the kick was so hard. An easy one would have meant more pressure. As the Murrayfield crowd and a nation of captivated television viewers held their breath, Taylor connected cleanly, which was not always a certainty in the days of imperfect pitches and no kicking tees. He was turning away even before the ball dissected the posts, clenching his fists as he ran back. His successful kick, and the subsequent events of the season, ensured that the game continues to be considered one of the greatest internationals ever played. 'If he did that kick ten times he would probably miss nine of them,' contends Mervyn Davies. 'Although we were the best side in the championship we needed a bit of luck if we were going to win the Grand Slam.'

By the time Edwards had used up vital seconds with a missed drop at goal and the final whistle had blown, the emotional scenes in the dressing-room were like Twickenham a year earlier. This time it was Rowlands whose face was streaked with tears.

7

ALL RIGHT NOW

'With the pressure we were under against the French, even Barry [John] tackled for the first time in his life' – *J.P.R. Williams*

One of the most impressive aspects of the winning Welsh try at Murrayfield is that it all seemed so effortless, like an everyday training routine. That, perhaps, says more than anything about the resolve, nerve and the ability of the Wales team in 1971 and owes a great deal to the way that Clive Rowlands drilled his players in the basics of the game. He sums up his approach thus: 'I believed that the more often John Dawes passed to Arthur Lewis the better the pass got.'

What most pleased Dawes, the captain, was that the basics of their game held up even when confronted by defeat and that every member of his side continued to approach his role with the power of the collective in his mind. There were no desperate individual efforts to rescue the situation. A simple match-winning move actually needed a whole number of things to work flawlessly for it to result in that try. Even Barry John acknowledges that it could all have gone wrong when the ball reached him. 'I was shouting out loud to myself, "Catch it and give it," as Gareth fed the pass to me. Only by concentrating hard like that could I overcome my concussion and focus on what I needed to do.'

Ian Hall, in the centre for Wales for the first time in place of the injured Arthur Lewis, had to execute his decoy run in order to fully draw the defence; then J.P.R. Williams's entry into the line and his final pass both needed to be expertly timed to give Gerald Davies the maximum opportunity to make his speed tell. Dawes's explanation is, 'John did not come into the line unless it was a good ball, but given that first essential he was prepared to come in from almost any situation on the field. JPR would not start his run until the ball was in the fly-half's hands. Then he would go as fast as he could so that he was overtaking the line and going through on the burst when the ball reached him.'

But, before any of that, it had required Delme Thomas to win the lineout, just as he had to launch the first Wales try of the game. Just as he had so many times in his career.

A soccer player in his home village of Bancyfelin until going to senior school just before his 12th birthday, Thomas went on to play so well for Llanelli that his first international appearance was as a 23 year old for the British Lions in New Zealand in 1966, before he had even represented Wales. 'If you weren't in the international set-up you didn't know who was who. I was bundled into the deep end, not knowing most of the Welsh side, let alone the English, Scottish and Irish boys.' He ended that tour playing as a tight-head prop, a position in which the Lions used him again in South Africa two years later. But in the shirt of Wales he set about establishing a reputation as one of the finest second rows and lineout men in world rugby, even if the selectors still occasionally chose to look elsewhere, as they had early in 1969.

Sleeves rolled up high to reveal blacksmith's biceps, Thomas, at 6ft 3in. and around 16st., had the appearance of a cartoon strong man. 'I wasn't the biggest,' he says. 'So I did a lot of weight training and squats and put some spring in my legs. I was a great believer in that – not weightlifting but doing training with weights just to build myself up. I could feel that it was an advantage.'

His partner in the Llanelli second row in the latter half of the '60s, Stuart Gallacher, says, 'Delme was lifting weights when no other forward was. He was before his time as far as conditioning was concerned and was the Charles Atlas of the day. He still does a bit at the back of his garden. He was a natural athlete with a huge spring in his step, yet he was a quiet and reserved man. I sat next to him for five years in the dressing-room and I did all the talking. He had a huge passion for the game and his contribution to that try [in Scotland] was typical Delme. No fuss.'

Most successful teams also acknowledge the odd slice of luck along the way. And so Thomas confesses that it took some good fortune for that decisive throw to be delivered to his area after he had positioned himself as the front jumper in the lineout. 'As I moved up, I heard Peter Brown shout to the scrum-half to change the lineout signal for the wing throwing in, but they couldn't have heard him because the ball was thrown in short and I was able to tap down to Gareth.'

The final piece of the match-winning puzzle was the kicking ability of the very individual figure of John Taylor, a man far removed from the background and profile of most of his teammates. For a start he'd been born in Watford, to a Welsh mother and English father, and had a Home Counties accent that prompted Barry John to call him 'Lord Kew'. He had only somewhat reluctantly started playing rugby when he attended the local grammar school, admitting, 'I wanted at the time to go to a school that played soccer.' In an age when size and weight was increasingly required, even of wing-forwards, he was considered something of a shrimp at less than 6ft and 13st. 7 lb. And a year earlier he had made his famous stand against taking the field with the South Africans, an act that had won him public support from the Welsh miners.

Then there was his appearance: unruly, bushy hair and goatee beard, earning him the nickname 'Bas' after the television puppet character Basil Brush. The French called him 'Le Hippy', while it was easy to imagine him slipping binoculars over his shoulder and yomping across the countryside with Bill Oddie in search of real ale and rare bird life.

Originally a centre, Taylor had moved to the back row after finding his way barred at Loughborough University by Gerald Davies and England international Colin McFadyean. Joining London Welsh in 1966 after taking a teaching job in Putney, it was a series of good performances on the club's Christmas tour of Wales that earned him an early selection for the national team, which in turn led to a place in the 1968 Lions party.

He may have been considered small, but few failed to acknowledge that his mobility and handling ability made him ideal for an attacking brand of rugby in which flankers were expected to do more than knock halfbacks on their backsides for 80 minutes. It was typical of him to be in the right place to score the first Wales try at Murrayfield, although the images of his dramatic kick in that game have become so deeply ingrained over the years that it is easy to overlook the consistent contributions that made him an automatic selection for several years. Alongside Neath's Dai Morris, another thoughtful and athletic player, he formed a formidable wing-forward pairing with which to bookend Mervyn Davies.

Morris, in fact, might have joined his colleagues on the 1971 Lions tour but for the selectors' concerns over his infamous dislike of being away from home. 'He was painfully shy and never really got over it,' says Chico Hopkins. 'Whenever he was on tour he just wanted to come back.'

A colliery welder, Morris would play four-hundred club games for Neath without missing one through injury before a damaged knee sidelined him in 1974. 'I am a fitness fanatic,' he explained. 'It is the duty of every player to get fit and stay fit. I train with Neath whenever there is a session but my work at the colliery also helps to keep me fit and hard.'

His unselfish style of play on the field reflected a modest, quiet personality and, according to Clive Rowlands, made other players better. 'Being that honest type of player with great skill, players played well around him and he fitted brilliantly with Taylor and Mervyn. I always used to tell Dai, "Wherever Gareth is, try to be close to him and look after him." He was only about 12 stone something but he was built like a rock. In a 15-man game you need people like that.'

Famously, Morris was publicly revered by entertainer Max Boyce, who explains, 'Dai played for my local club and I watched him coming through from youth rugby. He was a man of great humility and he epitomised all that was good in rugby football. He gave everything at all times and asked for nothing. He was arguably not the greatest player Wales has ever produced, but certainly the most respected.'

Recalling the back-row threesome that served Wales for a total of 18 games, Mervyn Davies says, 'You can't talk individually about flankers and number eights; you have to look at the back row as a unit because their work is intertwined. The fact that Dai, JT and me played so many games shows it was working. I was still changing my style of game from being a corner-flagging type of number eight who wouldn't get involved in anything, apart from maybe tackling the centre out wide. London Welsh was changing me into someone whose first action was to go forward. When you played with JT and Dai they were so fast that they were just gone in a flash and left me for dead so I would pick up the pieces they missed. They would force the backs to come inside and if they did I would be waiting. That made me a more defensive number eight than an attacking one. They were scoring the tries and I saw my role as a defensive one. The coaches didn't really say anything, but we talked about it among ourselves a bit.'

> Welsh actor Hywel Bennett tells audiences to treat as light-hearted his new film, *Percy*, in which he plays the recipient of the first penis transplant. His money from the film has enabled him and his wife, TV presenter Cathy McGowan, to buy a £30,000 home on the Thames near Richmond, handy for watching London Welsh. He also explains, 'I've got a genuine Welsh dresser as a reminder of my upbringing on a Welsh farm.'

Wales had five weeks to come down from the emotional high of Murrayfield and to re-focus on the game that could bring them a second Triple Crown in three years, the visit of Ireland to Cardiff. Fears that they might have become rusty in that time or would be looking ahead to a possible Grand Slam encounter in Paris were offset by the team's growing air of invincibility at home, where the intimidating atmosphere generated by the fans packed into the newly completed stadium could strip bare even the most resilient of opponents.

In contrast to the new North Stand, in which the crowd appeared to be perched directly above the touchline, the terraced areas behind the posts were separated from the pitch by the semicircular curve of the Wembley-style track, creating the feel of an amphitheatre. 'They say that a stadium is nothing but a stadium,' says Gareth Edwards. 'Well, I looked into the eyes of opponents many times and, believe me, the Arms Park had an effect.'

Clive Rowlands, who consistently urged the home crowd to save their most vociferous support for when Welsh backs were to the wall rather than when the tries were flowing, sent his players out to the Cardiff club pitch for their now customary pre-game routine 45 minutes before kick-off. He explains, 'My warm-up always started in position for kick-off. They would catch, maul and pass to the wing. After a couple of minutes, no one was walking to the stadium any more. They all stopped to watch and there was a huge cheer when we touched the ball down. The best practice you could ever have was to touch the ball over the try-line and nobody ever went over the line in my training session without touching down.'

The warm-up proved to be a prelude to an efficient victory. The 23–9 scoreline stemmed from Wales eventually winning the battle up front and the simultaneous brilliance of Edwards and John. 'They were two mates and both basically had everything,' states Rowlands. 'As a pair they were quite outstanding. The best pair of halfbacks there has ever been.'

Not for the first time, Wales started slowly but did well enough, in concert with the Irish backs' limitations, to limit the visitors' lead to a pair of wind-assisted penalties by Mike Gibson. The game turned in the final six minutes of the first half, starting with a poor clearance by Ireland scrum-half Roger Young. John Bevan carried the ball into a tackle, Morris released the backs and Gerald Davies finished the move by eluding three men to score by the flag. Soon afterwards, John cut towards the blind side with a neat break and caused full-back Barry O'Driscoll more headaches with another skilful kick. O'Driscoll was overwhelmed and Bevan emerged from the melee to hurl the ball back to John, whose dropped goal was his eighth for his country, a Welsh record. He added his first-ever international penalty just before the interval for a 9–6 lead, and the onslaught continued with a 14-point spree in 18 minutes in the second half.

Barry Llewellyn peeled from a lineout to set up a ruck and Edwards dived over from a yard after beating Young to the ball when it squirted free on the blind side. Edwards was then the provider, luring the cover towards him as he broke to the short side from a scrum and freeing Gerald Davies for his fifth try in three games. Rowlands's promise that he would see enough of the ball on the wing to make an impact was certainly being upheld. After John's penalty from close to 50 yards, Edwards took the ball on the run as it bounced behind a lineout and, using his strength and speed, crossed for his second try of the day. The way he slammed the ball into the turf was, he said, an instinctive action, releasing the anger that had been building at the media criticism he felt had been following him around for the previous year. John added the conversion.

So, just as they had six years earlier, Wales would travel to France for the final game of the Five Nations with the Grand Slam within their grasp. Once the party for the forthcoming British Lions tour of New Zealand had been announced, with Dawes as its captain, the full attention of the Welsh media and public was focused on Paris. There was to be no shortage of support for the visitors, with 10,000 travelling fans – including many without tickets – ready to head for the French capital, where they would help the attendance reach 60,000, a record for the Stade de Colombes. Banks in Cardiff reported that supplies of French francs were running low as the mass transportation of the Arms Park to Paris got under way.

Comments from the Welsh camp in the days before the game appeared designed to create a balance between preventing anyone getting too carried away and projecting an air of confidence to their opponents. Dawes said, 'We can play just as well outside Wales as in it. We are in good heart.' Chairman of selectors Cliff Jones warned, 'Paris in the spring with the warm sun favours the French players. The French selectors have now arrived at their best side of the season.'

France went into the game unbeaten, although two draws meant their ambitions were limited to achieving a share of the championship. Having won the toss, Dawes selected to play against the wind. A sunny day and a dry pitch offered the kind of conditions in which the French backs thrived and it quickly became obvious that the game would be as much a test of Welsh character and resilience as skill. In the lineout, Dauga, Biemouret and the Spanghero brothers – second-row Claude and number eight Walter – established the upper hand and the French pack also showed their ability with the ball in hand.

John and Pierre Villepreux were each unsuccessful with early penalty attempts – the latter, ambitiously, from close to 70 yards – and fly-half Berot was wide with a drop at goal. If the old French problem of finishing off their moves had not reared its ugly head, the Grand Slam could have been beyond Wales. Instead, the visitors' defence held firm. Even John stepped forward, and when he and Taylor combined to halt the 6ft 5in. Dauga the fly-half ended up off the field for several minutes with a broken nose. 'As he toppled off balance, the Frenchman fell on top of me and his elbow smashed into my nose with a horrific thud,' John reported. '[My nose] was so bent I could see most of the world on one side, but hardly anything on the other.' Not realising what the French doctor on the sideline was asking, John inadvertently gave his consent to having his misshapen snout straightened there and then, causing pain that was 'totally and utterly unbearable'. Bravely, and with cotton wool protruding comically from both nostrils, John returned to the front line.

J.P.R. Williams admits to surprise at John's heroics. 'What was great about Barry was we all knew he was never going to tackle,' he laughs. 'If the opposition had the ball I would move forward behind Barry to tackle. Tackling was below him. But with the pressure we were under with the French even Barry tackled for the first time in his life.'

A far more familiar sight than John laying his body on the line was the bone-jarring tackle with which Williams halted the right-winger Bougarel. After three years of having Williams as their last line of defence, the Welsh team were well accustomed to such acts and had often been on the receiving end. 'I was a pretty bonkers player and practised tackling a lot,' he explains. 'I was actually banned from training on Mondays on the 1971 Lions tour because I was injuring my own colleagues too much. I taught my son, who had not played for three years, how to tackle and he came back from South Africa with St Andrews University having been man of the match in every game because of his tackling. If you tackle correctly you don't get hurt and it is absolutely true that the person who goes into a tackle harder gets injured less. It is in the so-called "fun" games where people get injured more often.'

Moments such as his tackle on Bougarel offered a reminder that JPR's attacking play, for all its dynamism and athletic quality, was merely a bonus to the essential defensive work of a man occupying his position. As Dawes put it, 'Against a really good side a full-back has to be a full-back. He will be exposed if he is nothing but a runner.'

With John Bevan holding up Lux under the posts, Welsh resistance lasted until three minutes before half-time, when Barrau, a constant threat, foraged to the blind side. Villepreux and Bertranne continued the move and Dauga crashed over the line, with the successful conversion affording a 5–0 lead. With time expiring in the half, a sequence of play arrived that was the undoubted turning point in the game. Villepreux and Bougarel constructed another attack on the right, but this time the winger, perhaps still feeling the shudder of Williams's previous tackle, tried to flip the ball back to his full-back, who had continued his run to the outside. 'The reason I went for the interception,' Williams recalls, 'is because I had taken him out hard previously so I knew he was not going to take me on. I never usually went for the interception but I knew John Taylor was there to take Bougarel.'

Williams grabbed the ball and raced down the left sideline. When he looked around he found prop forward Denzil Williams up in support on the inside, while Edwards was charging up the touchline. Cutting inside to create more room, he passed to his scrum-half who steamed into the corner. What had threatened to be at least an eight-point deficit at half-time had been reduced to two.

When the action re-started Dawes and Bevan both came close to giving Wales the lead before John's boot achieved that feat with a penalty after France handled in a ruck. On 65 minutes, Jeff Young won a strike against the head to set up a moment of Barry John brilliance. Receiving the ball from Edwards, he set off to his left on a diagonal run. 'As their defence stood back I noticed my opposing fly-half, Berot, standing slightly out of position. I stepped nine inches in the other direction and started a sweeping run.' His subtle changes of trajectory and movement of hands were almost imperceptible, but enough to keep the French backs guessing. Almost before anyone realised it, he was in for a try.

It was turning into what John would call 'the game of my Welsh career', even though he said, 'I'm not sure I should have been playing as I still felt terrible, really giddy and weak, after taking that bang against the Scots.' In the past two games, he and halfback partner Edwards had combined to score twenty-six of their team's thirty-two points.

For the final quarter of the game, Wales could do little more than defend for all their worth as France attacked from all directions and distances. They held out to win 9–5 and the Grand Slam celebrations could begin, during the course of which Dai Morris reportedly lost his false teeth down a toilet and J.P.R. Williams ended up running the bar in the Churchill pub in the Palace de Général de Gaulle.

John Dawes recalls the players' initial satisfaction emanating from victory in a special match rather than the larger achievement it represented. 'It was the best Wales game I played in. Both sides played well on the same day and we came off the field absolutely shattered and elated because we had played in something special. The fact we had won the Grand Slam came later.'

Arthur Lewis confirms, 'It was the toughest game I ever played in. It was non-stop. We were too knackered to celebrate at first.'

Workers in Wales take more time off sick than their British counterparts, according to a British Medical Association report. In the past year Welsh workers lost 30 days every year through illness, ahead of the north of England's average of 25. The report states that respiratory diseases are more prevalent in south Wales then anywhere else in the UK and in mining areas they represent 24 per cent of all doctors' cases.

The Welsh Grand Slam team of 1971 has rightly gone down in history as one of the greatest and most exciting in its country's history – enhanced by the continued achievements of many of its members over the ensuing years. At the time, however, much of the reportage of their feats reflected the continued fascination with the question of how much was down to the relatively recent introduction of coaching to the Welsh team.

In the *Western Mail*, J.G.B. Thomas said of the win against France, 'Such was the display that it must earn them the title of the best-organised national XV in the history of Welsh rugby.' It appeared that victory still required qualification, as though it had received some kind of unfair assistance.

For the second time inside two years, that newspaper's Triple Crown supplement had included a piece by Ray Williams analysing the effectiveness of coaching and the squad system. His main theme had been the knowledge that a coach could acquire about his players through working closely with them on a regular basis. 'At international level the coach has to be something of a psychologist,' he said. 'It is said in education that if you want to teach John Latin, you not only have to know Latin, you have to know John. This is just as true in rugby football.'

Naturally, the players, while acknowledging the importance of squad sessions, stop short of laying their success completely at the doors of the coaches and organisers. Gareth Edwards, for example, was never convinced that coaching improved his game technically, but felt it created a collectiveness of thought within the team. 'It certainly built into the Welsh players a deeper understanding of what we were trying to achieve, gave us confidence in our methods, made the smaller techniques more relevant and so gave us a capacity for absorbing pressure. It was almost as if panic stations were unnecessary because we knew what we had to be doing to play winning rugby.'

In discussing coaching in the early 1970s with many Welsh players, however, one can't help but detect an occasional weariness that their achievements are not allowed to stand independent scrutiny. The opinion of J.J. Williams that 'the key was that we had individually brilliant players right across the decade' is one held by the majority.

Clive Rowlands believes the manner in which the players gelled as a team is the key element. 'Each one was a good mate to each other, whether they were from east or west Wales. It's just a shame we didn't have a World Cup at that time because I think we would have won it, as we would have in '76 and '78.'

A debate less frequently aired is whether the arrival on the scene of so many great talents, with more to come over the next four years, was a genetic fluke or the result of something deeper in the grassroots system within Wales. While Max Boyce wrote whimsically of 'The Outside-Half Factory', an underground production line hidden from the eyes of rugby league scouts, Bill Samuel, a teacher who came to prominence as Edwards's mentor, suggested that the role of the schools' physical education programmes had been overlooked. 'The schoolmasters' contribution towards that era was never acknowledged or appreciated,' he argued.

The boom in organised sport all over Britain after the Second World War quickly led to moves to provide schools with better PE instruction, and major colleges such as Loughborough were at the forefront of turning out a new teaching force. Glamorgan was one of the first authorities in which PE became a compulsory subject, with two lessons per week included within the curriculum. While English sports masters concentrated on trying to turn out the next Tom Finney and Stanley Matthews, Samuel described the situation in Wales as 'a dynamic infusion of expertise which resulted in renewed vigour and success in a subject [rugby] which had lain fallow for many years'.

In his book *Rugby: Body and Soul*, he described the involvement of schoolmasters in the development of Welsh rugby as 'immeasurable', citing their 'loyalty, devotion and enthusiasm for the game'. He concluded, 'This collective and irresistible force in our schools paved the way for the euphoric '70s.'

Dawes concurs with that view. 'A large contribution was made by the grammar schoolmasters in charge of rugby,' he says. 'They usually had a big influence and took a personal interest in it. It would be a foolish man who said he was not influenced by some master. He would be known throughout the grammar schools of Wales for his contribution to the team. From the schools, these boys would go into the clubs. We had a healthy continuity about where we got our rugby brains from.'

8

WITHOUT YOU

'It was a great pity that Barry retired at 27. I sometimes wonder what would have happened had he stayed on just as I was maturing as a player. I can't answer it; I just wonder' – *Gareth Edwards*

There were only a few hours to go before the members of the triumphant 1971 British Lions touring party would feel home ground under their feet for the first time in three months. A brief stop for refuelling in New York preceded the final leg of the journey from New Zealand. Then home, where fascination had been creeping towards fanaticism with each passing radio or newspaper report of another Lions victory.

The seemingly invincible All Blacks had been beaten 2–1, with one Test drawn, and now the British public were keen to make up for their inability to watch the team on live television by turning out to see these new sporting heroes in the flesh whenever possible. For example, demand to see Wales in action at Twickenham in the first game of the next Five Nations season would be such that the RFU would refund £75,000 to unsuccessful ticket applicants – which, at £1.50 for a lower stand ticket and 50 pence for a place on the terracing, represented a lot of disappointed people.

At the moment that many of those same fans were setting their alarms in order to greet the Lions' early-morning arrival at Heathrow, Barry John was killing time before the final take-off of the tour by browsing the *New York Times*. When he saw his own face staring back from the front page, he asked himself, 'Has the world gone mad?' He was looking at evidence of the phenomenon that visitors from his homeland had been warning him about during the latter stages of the tour. 'King John' was public property. Life would never be as it had been before he'd climbed on board the BOAC 707 at Heathrow a few weeks earlier. In the valleys, of course, he'd been used to recognition for a long time. Now it was spreading into all corners of the world and would reach unbearable levels of intrusion and embarrassment. When he was greeted at home by curtsies he would realise it had all gone too far.

From the moment he landed back at Heathrow, Barry John's days as a rugby player were numbered. The 1971–72 season would be his last. 'I had simply had enough of being stuck inside a goldfish bowl. Seeing my name in newspaper headlines every single day; being pulled from pillar to post by being continually requested to attend functions, dinners, parties, receptions and award ceremonies. I had become far too detached from ordinary people and I did not like it; retiring was my only escape.'

A rugby career that would reach a premature end just as it reached its peak had suffered its share of early disappointments. Born in the latter months of the Second World War and raised in the western coal-mining town of Cefneithin, ten miles from Carmarthen, Barry John had played in a Wales Under-15 trial as a scrum-half but had not been invited back for the final audition. So upset was he that he considered giving up the game. Instead, fatefully, he switched positions to fly-half. Even so, he was never picked to represent his country at any level until his full international debut.

The son of a miner, John had 'promised my father I would never go underground' and would diligently sit down to his homework. His education continued at Trinity College, Carmarthen, while his rugby progressed at Llanelli to the point where he was challenging David Watkins for his country's number 10 shirt. He took it for the first time in the game against Australia in December 1966, a match in which he 'passed the ball when I should have kicked and vice versa'. After that came a meeting that is revered among rugby followers in the way that Beatles fans talk about the village fete where Paul McCartney was introduced to John Lennon.

Selected to represent the Probables in the Welsh trial at Swansea, John was contacted by the man named to partner him at scrum-half, Cardiff's Gareth Edwards. Yet to play for Wales and determined to leave nothing to chance, Edwards suggested they meet to throw a ball around. By the time a smart track-suited figure in polished boots arrived at the students' residential block at Trinity early one Sunday, John had forgotten all about his date and was still sleeping off the effects of the previous night's party. 'In my fragile state, the last thing I needed was to go out in the pelting rain to the college field one and a half miles down the road.' Even his kit was in the wash, forcing him to knock on the doors of various friends to borrow a tracksuit and plimsolls.

As they squelched onto a deserted field, Edwards suggested creating imaginary game situations and urged John to shout where he wanted the ball delivered. After 15 minutes, John was numb with cold and when Edwards asked him where to pass the ball next, he snapped back, 'Oh you throw it and I'll catch it. Let's go home.'

'You're as confident and big-headed as I am,' Edwards told his new partner as he drove him back to the shelter of his digs.

As it transpired, John left the Welsh trial after virtually the first pass he received when a stray boot cut open his knee. Billy Hullin was preferred to Edwards for the next Wales game and, after one more match, Watkins was brought back in place of John. It was not until November 1967 that the duo first played together for Wales. That loss to New Zealand, Edwards's third international appearance, signalled the start of an alchemic relationship that burned without the aid of anything other than the unique ingredients each contributed. There were no great discussions, certainly no more private practice sessions. 'What happened between us on the pitch just happened,' says John. 'A natural gelling of two talents.'

John had become the permanent owner of the Welsh fly-half berth after Watkins opted to sign for Salford. His acquisition of the position, along with his move to Cardiff, brought the legend of 'King John' closer to realisation. Of course, none of the additional attention he gained through teaming up with Edwards in the Welsh capital would have meant anything had his play not blossomed as it did. He was picked for the British Lions tour of South Africa in 1968 and was first choice outside-half before breaking his collarbone in the first Test. By 1971, there were few who disputed that he was the world's finest in his position. And there are many who argue that there has been no one better before or since.

His mastery when kicking a dead ball was a relatively late phenomenon in his career, but his ability to drop goals with a mixture of arrogance and nonchalance was as renowned as the infuriating accuracy with which he had opponents back-pedalling with his positional kicking. Such control of that aspect of his game should not be underestimated in the days of heavy leather balls that retained the water and could feel like lead weights by the end of 80 minutes in the rain. Yet had that been all there was to his rugby, he would have been remembered merely as a devastatingly efficient exponent of that particular art.

What elevated him to greatness and captured the imagination of those watching him was what happened when the ball was in his hand and the muse of attacking rugby was in his heart. While Phil Bennett's brilliance would in future years be more blatant – exaggerated sidesteps that left opponents grasping at thin air – John's was a more subtle expertise. With an almost imperceptible feint of the hips or move of the hand, perhaps a mere glance in the wrong direction, swathes of open ground would materialise King Canute-like before him. Opponents frequently never even got near enough to make a groping attempt at a tackle. If there was any weakness in his play it was that, because he rarely ran in a straight line, his passing could sometimes leave something to be desired. It was the smallest of quibbles.

J.P.R. Williams, who found himself backing up many of John's breaks, says, 'He was the best outside-half I have ever seen. You see players now who carry the ball in two hands, and that is what he did. He just ghosted through and people couldn't tackle him.'

Arthur Lewis points out, though, that those playing outside John in the three-quarter line had to be at their sharpest. 'He was unpredictable,' he laughs. 'If we called a move he might do something else, so you had to be on your toes. But he was such a cool player and had such an intelligent head. He was a master thinker in those situations.'

Lions teammate Chris Rea said, 'He filled the role of the superstar. The differences between him and we ordinary performers are many, but no player can rise above the rest unless he has total confidence in his own abilities. Unlike most players, he was not the least bit nervous before a game, and he remained totally unmoved by pre-match build-ups.'

Edwards, who knew John's play and personality better than anyone, says, 'He was a fantastic individual and wonderful to play with. He was so full of confidence and nothing deterred him, even when you were under pressure. I knew I could get the ball to him if I was heavily marked. He could look up and read the game like a chess master and he was a fantastic tactician. A lot of people thought he wasn't as quick as all that but he was not slow, that is for sure.'

According to Ireland's Mike Gibson, that cocktail of brilliance and assuredness could leave opponents light-headed. 'Very few fly-halves can have daunted so many opponents as completely as Barry. His attitude was not to worry about what the opposition were going to do. He was only concerned with what he was going to do and he believed that anything was possible. He had this composure about him.'

It was refreshing, and educational, for Gibson, picked as reserve fly-half and used in the centre in all four Tests, to have John as a Lions teammate in New Zealand. 'The fly-half is the person who reflects the attitude and the potential of any team of which he is a member, and no one did that with more individuality and with a greater sense of character than Barry John. His ambitions had very few limitations and the challenge and stimulus this provided for his fellow Lions went hand in hand with a psychologically crushing effect on the opposition. Barry was a player who saw opportunities coming. I certainly found that by playing alongside him my vision became broader.'

A total of thirteen Welshmen had been named in the original Lions party, including Chico Hopkins, named as number two scrum-half after only twenty minutes in a Wales jersey, and Llanelli's versatile Derek Quinnell, chosen despite his lack of full international recognition. Subsequently, lock Geoff Evans added to the number when flown out as a replacement. Flanker Dai Morris and the front-row men were the only members of the Grand Slam team not selected, although prop Barry Llewellyn's absence was at his own request.

Alongside Scottish tour manager Doug Smith, Llanelli's Carwyn James was the choice to coach the team. A deep thinker about the game, James combined tactical astuteness with a human touch that gave him a profound understanding of the needs of his men. Always with a cigarette on the go, he was a man of some humour and an accomplished communicator. Passionate about his homeland, he had stood unsuccessfully as the Plaid Cymru candidate for Llanelli in the 1970 General Election and throughout the tour he would give early-morning telephone interviews in Welsh for BBC Wales. Eventually he would become a broadcaster and journalist.

The recent success of Wales had made John Dawes the obvious choice as captain, although cynics voiced an opinion that the large contingent from his country would either cause a 'them and us' feeling within the party or leave the Lions at the mercy of the notorious Welsh reputation for being bad tourists. Dawes and James felt it was their role to dismantle any misconceptions and prejudices that existed within and around the party. Dawes recalls, 'There were attempts by the New Zealand media to say there were too many Welshmen. We didn't believe that. It was a deliberate tactic to unsettle us and drive a wedge between us but it died out after a few games. My first priority as Lions captain was that I wanted everyone to contribute. If I felt they had, then I had done my job.'

That James and Dawes not only eliminated any hint of national jealousy, but actually harnessed the understanding of the Welsh players to aid coherence throughout the squad, can be seen by one quick glance at the record of a team that has few rivals for the title of the best to leave British shores. As well as becoming the first Lions outfit to win a series in New Zealand, they marched magnificently around the country, winning every provincial game. They turned in some breathtaking performances – whether it was running in 47 points against the powerful Wellington team; surviving the savagery of a Canterbury side that ended the tours of both first-choice props a week before the first Test; or posting phenomenal individual feats such as David Duckham's six tries against the combined West Coast/ Buller unit or the four tries in a game achieved by John Bevan, twice, and Gerald Davies.

It would take a whole book to detail the planning and execution of the Lions' success: the manner in which their forwards adapted sufficiently to southern hemisphere methods to hold their own, and the flourish with which the backs overwhelmed their counterparts. Suffice to say here that the Welsh were at the heart of the tour and dominated the final statistics. John finished as top scorer with 191 points, including 30 in the Tests, while Bevan's squad-leading tally of 18 tries could have been even higher had the latter half of his tour not been hindered by niggling injury and loss of form. Gerald Davies's ten tries were bettered only by Bevan and Duckham, while seven Welshmen played in all four Tests and Delme Thomas missed only one. As important as the facts and figures were elements that helped ensure a happy atmosphere within the group, such as John Taylor as choirmaster, J.P.R. Williams's Gilbert and Sullivan performances and Chico Hopkins's unlikely comedy double act with England skipper Bob Hiller.

For many of these Welshmen, success was vindication after the disaster of the visit to New Zealand two years earlier. Mervyn Davies says, 'In 1969 we got well beaten by a superior side. Many of us felt that if we wanted to be as good as them we had to work hard at it, so 1971 was our chance to prove that what we said was going to be true; that the new generation had come through and could be successful.'

Clive Rowlands believes that 'the crunch for the '71 Lions was that the majority of the players had been there before', noting, 'Some had gone in 1966 and the bulk of the Welsh side had gone in 1969. That really prepared them.'

And the ominous note sounded for the other home nations was that the Welsh players who experienced their first Lions tour that summer returned home not simply basking in the glow of victory but convinced that they'd advanced as players in such an intensive rugby environment. Davies continues, 'It was the only time in your life you knew what it was like to be a professional sportsman. You were properly fit for the first time, training well and doing the right things.'

Quinnell adds, 'You improved because you were a full-time player. We had games every Saturday–midweek–Saturday, travel on Sunday, a heavy training session Monday, travel again on Thursday. With a couple of injuries, you might play four or five games on the trot. That is as tough as it gets. Every team you played wanted to make the most of their chance against the Lions. As a young player you learned a lot.'

Interestingly, Williams, who had already turned his back on professional tennis partly because of the mundane daily existence on the circuit, discovered enough about being a full-time rugby player to know that he does not envy the modern-day professional. 'What I would find difficult now would be spending all day every day training and thinking about rugby. Even on Lions tours we were allowed to relax and have a few beers. Carwyn was a wine connoisseur and he insisted on everyone having a glass with their evening meal. There was no New Zealand wine then, it was all French – Châteauneuf du Pape, which was expensive stuff.'

For Barry John, metaphorically at least, it was champagne all the way. John Reason, covering the tour for the *Daily Telegraph*, said, 'This modest young man was rapidly becoming the rugby writers' dream since he rarely, if ever, failed to supply something of interest on tour. With the passing of each day, the title of King John became more secure and everyone paid homage.'

Mervyn Davies remembers him as being 'the only Lion who got away with murder at training'. On more than one occasion, teammates would learn that he had been excused training because of a sore back and would then spy him playing soccer on an adjoining field. Such was the acknowledgement of his importance to the team that nothing was begrudged, nor was the decision to spare him from what the tour management correctly predicted would be an over-physical game against Canterbury.

It was John's kicking a week later – a penalty, dropped goal and a series of morale-sapping touch-finders – that saw the Lions prevail 9–3 in the first Test on a wet pitch at Dunedin. Delme Thomas, Mervyn Davies and John Taylor featured in the Lions pack, while Ireland's Mike Gibson was the only non-Welshman in a back division that saw Chico Hopkins replace Gareth Edwards after only 15 minutes because of a hamstring injury he'd originally suffered when slipping on a pothole in training. After withstanding waves of All Blacks pressure, manager Smith commented, 'I cannot praise too highly the work of Carwyn James as coach and John Dawes as captain and the way in which the party has worked for this day.'

Dawes recalls that James frequently left him in charge of the backs, mirroring the way in which he worked with Clive Rowlands. 'Carwyn always said that selection was the most important thing. If you select the right players and add a little bit of organisation you have a good team. Carwyn hardly came with the backs in New Zealand because he had selected them and knew what they could do. He stayed with the forwards because he wanted to learn a bit more about forward play.'

The second Test was lost 22–12 at Christchurch, where John had trouble kicking the ball out of a deep layer of mud. However, the spirited way in which the Lions dominated the final few minutes sent them from the field feeling secure in their potential superiority over their opponents. The move of the game was a piece of Welsh wizardry, with J.P.R. Williams galloping out of a deep position and feeding Dawes before Gibson's final pass launched Gerald Davies on a forty-yard sprint past two defenders for the first of his two tries.

Wellington saw the historic 13–3 victory that meant the Lions could not lose the series. The all-Welsh back row of Davies, Taylor and Quinnell, in his first international, nullified the threat of scrum-half Sid Going, whose thrusting play had been one of the keys to the All Blacks' previous win. In particular, Taylor gave what is considered the finest performance of his career. John scored a try, a dropped goal and two conversions, but his contribution extended beyond that. He recalls that a little piece of pre-game psychology helped bring the best out of Edwards, who had been low on confidence after struggling with his hamstring and his opposite number. With Chico Hopkins also fighting for fitness, John was told to convey to his friend the message that Ian McCrae of Scotland was on alert to fly out. Edwards responded by orchestrating a 13–0 lead inside the first quarter of the game by making breaks that set up tries for Gerald Davies and John, who said, 'In the first 20 minute he produced the best rugby I have seen from him. Any self-doubts were cast aside as Gareth realised he was a player who could produce the goods where and when it mattered most.'

The fourth Test at Auckland is remembered not just for the 14–14 scoreline that ensured the first series victory in New Zealand by a British Lions team, but also for the dropped goal from almost halfway with which Williams gave his team a 14–11 lead. The delight with which he turned to raise his arms towards the stands was to signal to his teammates that he had delivered on his promise to score from a drop during the tour. Over the final 20 minutes it was his defensive qualities, along with a dominant pack and the kicking of the halfbacks, that ensured that a draw was all the All Blacks could manage.

South Wales miners vote to support national strike action, backed by other unions' decisions not to handle any coal shipments. More than 1,000 Welsh children stay at home because of dwindling coal stocks in schools. Meanwhile, 18 men at Blaenserchan Colliery in Pontypool are fired after their 17-hour sit-in to protest at pay cuts.

As the 1971–72 Five Nations games approached, there was hope that the success of Wales and the Lions, coupled with the increase in the value of a try to four points, would lead to more positive play in international rugby. The ability of J.P.R. Williams to attack from deep was highlighted by Vivian Jenkins in *Rugby World* as something that should be an integral component of any team. 'Unless a side can find a type of player who can do these things it is bound to start at a disadvantage,' he wrote.

Clive Rowlands, the lucky coach who was able to harness the cavalier approach of Williams to the class of men like Edwards and John, was now chairman of the five-man Welsh selection panel, whose first task was to find a replacement for Dawes at centre and as captain. The latter role went to Bridgend prop John Lloyd, a 28-year-old schoolmaster, with John as vice-captain. Lloyd had led the Probables to victories in two trial games, but doubts were expressed about how effectively a captain could manage the game from the front row, where much of his time would be spent with his head buried close to the ground. Llanelli's Roy Bergiers, who owed his untraditional surname to his Belgian father, was picked in the centre. Yet another teacher, his finesse and pace, with a preference to go for the outside space rather than crash through the middle, was expected to blend well with the direct approach of Arthur Lewis. Meanwhile, Geoff Evans, overlooked for the Grand Slam campaign after originally losing his place to a back injury, returned to the second row after performing well on the Lions tour.

Fitness was a concern in the build-up to the opening game against England, with Bergiers and Edwards cleared to play only after training in Cardiff prior to the squad's departure for London. Edwards thanked the staff at Manchester City for the healthy state of his hamstring, saying, 'I have been having treatment twice daily with City and without their help I could not have recovered.'

The measure of the two teams was that Wales did far more with less possession than their opponents. England hooker John Pullin won six strikes against the head and Wales gave away twelve penalties to their opponents' five, yet the home team had little to offer in a game that was far from fulfilling Vivian Jenkins's wishes. David Duckham had only one of his trademark runs and once Bob Hiller had landed his first penalty that was the end of England's scoring.

John was on target with both his first-half penalties and fortuitously contributed to the game's only try midway through the second half after his deflected dropped goal was touched down for a five-yard scrum under the posts. Wales won the ball and Edwards passed to his right for J.P.R. Williams, who bulldozed past Keith Fielding and Peter Dixon to score in the corner. John converted for a 12–3 scoreline.

The final whistle produced one of those moments with which John was becoming increasingly uncomfortable. Eamonn Andrews appeared under the stand brandishing his famous red book and, after slipping into their suits and having a hurried meal at the Hilton, the whole Welsh party headed to ITV's studios to celebrate John's achievements at the recording of *This Is Your Life*.

The show was merely the latest manifestation of the celebrity status he had found thrust upon him. Since returning from New Zealand he'd been receiving sacks of letters and more and more sightseers were turning up outside his home. No one wanted to talk about anything other than rugby, yet he was desperately trying to find a way of forgetting all about it for a while. In club games, he positioned himself near the tunnel when the final whistle was imminent so that he could escape the mob. Mentally, he was wearied by trotting out the same old stories; physically, he was becoming worn down by the whirl of his existence. Invitations poured through his letter box, everything from media engagements to requests to hand out awards to boys' clubs. 'From the moment we landed back at Heathrow to the day I actually retired I don't think I had an average of even one meal a week with Jan in my house,' he said.

Part of the problem was that John continued to be affable and approachable, especially when journalists were in need of 'a line'. Peter West of *The Times* said, 'He remained the same person he was before fame was thrust upon him. There was no mock modesty with him. He knew exactly what he could do but he was never arrogant. He was always courteous, patient and helpful.'

He started warning people that he would walk away from the game if things didn't change. John had become friends with George Best after they attended a function together and had witnessed the manner in which football's biggest star had grown tired of the public glare. By the spring of 1972, Best had already performed one disappearing act from Manchester United and was about to announce from the Spanish town of Marbella that he was quitting football.[4]

John doesn't claim to have suffered anywhere near as much as Best, but certainly enough to empathise. He even did his own

---

4 Best would return to Old Trafford in September but by January 1974, aged 27, had played his last game for Manchester United before spending several years playing mostly in the North American Soccer League.

miniature version of one of his pal's walkabouts when he disappeared to Majorca after the England game, missing squad training prior to the next match against Scotland. 'The Welsh selectors had every reason to drop me,' John admits, but it was a sign of his standing that the management indulged his need for escape. His teammates showed compassion as well, John Taylor noting that even he had received 200 invitations to attend functions since the Lions tour. The break, however, proved counter-productive, merely highlighting to John the relatively carefree life he could enjoy without rugby.

Meanwhile, the selectors also showed sympathy towards Jeff Young, retaining the hooker in the team to face the Scots despite his problems against England. The argument was that his value in the scrum could not be gauged simply by keeping score of the heels. A fiery start brought an exchange of penalties between Jim Renwick and John before a flash of inspiration by Gerald Davies brought the first try. After Mervyn Davies won possession at a lineout, John's long pass missed out Bergiers and found Williams creating an overlap on the right wing. Davies's speed was too much for Alastair Biggar and his chip ahead bounced perfectly into his arms.

After conceding a 50-yard penalty, converted by Peter Brown, Wales were dealt a painful blow when Williams confronted winger Billy Steele, whose attempt to jump out of the tackle left the full-back with a broken jaw. Phil Bennett came on as a replacement. John's penalty extended the Welsh lead to 10–6 yet Scotland, despite being reduced to 14 men while Biggar was being treated for injury, took the lead when hooker Bobby Clark scored from a pass by Sandy Carmichael.

Moments later, however, Llewellyn's familiar burst from the lineout backed up the Scots against their own line and Wales emerged from the ruck in possession, Edwards forcing his way over for a converted try. It was the scrum-half's second try that has earned a place in Welsh rugby legend. Mervyn Davies stole the ball at a Scotland lineout inside his own 25 and Edwards beat the flailing arms of Rodger Arneil on the blind side. He motored over the halfway line, creating room to place a kick over full-back Arthur Brown before hacking the ball on from just inside Scotland's 25. As he and Renwick raced towards the corner of the in-goal area, where the brown dirt of the Cardiff Arms Park track was holding the ball in play, Bill McLaren was asking excitedly, 'Can he score? It would be a miracle if he could.' He did, sliding head first to touch down and emerging with the whites of his eyes blinking comically out of the paste of his facemask. 'All I was looking for was a little snipe around the blind side,' he explained later. 'I was looking for Dai Morris but he let me down for the first time ever. I was worrying about my hamstrings letting me down there.'

In the stands, his mother was also concerned about his health, mistaking the mud of the dog track for blood and fearing he had cut his head open. In his commentary position, McLaren spoke about 'the sheer magic of Gareth Edwards', while Peter West in the press box would describe it for readers of *The Times* as a try that 'rugby players still unborn will be hearing about'.

Scotland were now unravelling quickly. John kicked a penalty from 45 yards and, after Brown slung a careless pass to Arneil just inside his own half, Morris kicked ahead and tackled John Frame, allowing Young to feed Bergiers for a try near the posts. The Llanelli centre then carried the ball at speed to the 25 and Taylor's discovery that Gerald Davies was covered as he looked to pass helped him sell a dummy that deceived the defence and allowed him to cut inside to score.

John's successful conversion of those two final tries gave him fifteen points for the game. Although it was his dash with the ball in hand that had made his fame, every success he achieved in his new role of kicker served to deepen the hero worship surrounding him. 'The funny thing is that I was never first-choice goalkicker for anyone in between the time I was at Gwendraeth Grammar School and when I went on the 1971 Lions tour. At Cardiff, I was fourth choice. John Dawes said it was the kick I put over against New South Wales at Sydney at the beginning of the tour that convinced him that I had the power to become the Lions' goalkicker in the Tests.'

On that occasion John had misinterpreted Dawes's intentions and gone for goal instead of touch, but proved that even his slight 11 st. frame could generate enough strength to score from long range. John put that ability down to suppleness in his body and flexibility in his hips, enabling him to 'unwind from the ball and wind back through it with a big hip turn and big backswing of my kicking leg'.

And it was all done with the minimum of fuss. 'He just put the ball down, ran up and kicked it,' says Rowlands. 'There was no Wilkinson-like preparation.' The routine consisted of four backward steps, creating a run-up of three paces; a small shuffle to correct his position; a flick of the hands; and a relaxed approach that saw his non-kicking foot planted a few inches behind the ball – rather than right next to it in the manner demanded by the coaching manuals. It meant John was leaning back at the point of contact instead of having his head over the ball, but the technicians could hardly argue with the results.

> Bookmakers in South Wales are enjoying a boom thanks to striking miners, who are filling time and looking for extra cash. 'We have been rushed off our feet,' says one betting shop worker. 'We have been flooded with miners having a pile of small bets hoping to land the big fish. And they are winning. Their luck is in.'

Barry John's late-flourishing kicking expertise was never more perfectly demonstrated than in his final international match. His four successful penalties in a 20–6 victory against France were a record for Wales and indicate the professional rather than spectacular nature of his team's victory. The gnawing feeling of dissatisfaction that surrounded the game, however, had been largely caused by the events of the preceding seven weeks.

Wales should have visited Lansdowne Road in mid-March to play Ireland, winners at Twickenham and Paris, in what could conceivably have been a game that determined the destination of the Grand Slam. Yet in early 1972 the political situation in Ireland was at its most incendiary since the outbreak of The Troubles three years earlier. The end of January had seen 'Bloody Sunday', when British troops opened fire on protestors in Londonderry, killing 13 – plus another who would die of his injuries some months later. The IRA warned that the safety of visiting British teams and sportsmen could not be guaranteed. By the time the WRU met early in March to discuss their trip to Dublin, five women and an army priest had been killed in an IRA attack on the 16th Parachute Brigade's headquarters in Aldershot.

The Scottish Rugby Union had already declined to fulfil their game in Ireland and now the WRU sought to gauge the mood of its players. 'We had a vote,' Mervyn Davies recalls. 'We agreed we would not send a weakened team and we had a show of hands. One or two people didn't want to go. I was a single bloke in those days but some were married so I could understand it. From a personal perspective, though, it was frustrating.'

Gerald Davies and Barry Llewellyn were those who reportedly indicated an unwillingness to travel and, armed with their players' decision, the WRU hosted a meeting with their Irish counterparts. Meanwhile, they had received a letter from 30 Welshmen living in Ireland urging them not to go, and another that contained a picture of 15 white feathers, the traditional symbol of cowardice. The majority of the WRU committee agreed that it would be wrong to go to Ireland and delivered that message to the seven-man IRU delegation. WRU secretary Bill Clement explained, 'We decided reluctantly that risks to players and supporters, however small, were enough to make us resolve we would not be justified in going. We asked the Irish delegation to consider the possibility of a postponement or playing at some alternative venue.'

Talk of Cardiff, Twickenham, Murrayfield and even Brussels as alternative sites came to nothing and the Five Nations Championship would eventually go into the record books as an incomplete season with two games not played. John, denied the chance of ending his international career with a second Grand Slam, says, 'I was genuinely against cancelling the match and to this day I still cannot fathom why the WRU agreed to do so.'

The game against France, therefore, was lacking the dramatic edge that should have accompanied it. The Wales fans were also denied the exhibition of running rugby they felt their dominance allowed. Had they known it would be the last appearance of John in a Wales jersey, however, they might have been more content to enjoy the outstanding display of kicking on offer. Constantly pinned in their

Wales captain Brian Price lands his infamous punch on Ireland's
Noel Murphy at Cardiff Arms Park in 1969, part of a stormy history
between the two teams (© Colorsport)

Delme Thomas (left) is welcomed to the Welsh team for the 1969 game
against England by stand-in captain Gareth Edwards and injured skipper
Brian Price (© Central Press/Getty Images)

The inimitable Barry John glides past Ireland flanker
Fergus Slattery during the 1971 Grand Slam season (© Colorsport)

Gareth Edwards is given more good possession against Ireland by
members of his pack: (left to right) Barry Llewellyn, Dai Morris,
Denzil Williams, Mervyn Davies and Mike Roberts (© Colorsport)

Captain John Dawes is carried from the field at the Stade Colombes in Paris after his team's Grand Slam victory against France in 1971 (© Keystone/Getty Images)

Clive Rowlands, pictured shortly after becoming chairman of Welsh selectors in 1974, coached his country for five years, making the job an acceptable part of the sport (© Colorsport)

The most fearsome trio in rugby, although the Pontypool Front Row of (left to right) Graham Price, Bobby Windsor and Charlie Faulkner could also ham it up for the cameras (© Tony Duffy/Getty Images)

Pictured in 1976, comedian Max Boyce helped bring the characters of Welsh rugby into living rooms around Britain as his career took off (© Rex Features)

Winger J.J. Williams takes on Scotland with the kicking ability
that helped to make him such a scoring threat (© Colorsport)

J.P.R. Williams ensures that the 1976 Grand Slam belongs to Wales with a
last-ditch tackle on French winger Jean-Francois Gourdon (© Colorsport)

The trusty boot of Steve Fenwick, in action against England during the
Triple Crown season of 1977, gave Wales plenty of place-kicking options
(© Allsport/Getty Images)

Skipper Phil Bennett leaves Scotland's Sandy Carmichael
and Bill Gammell floundering on his way to a try at Murrayfield
as Wales clinch the 1977 Triple Crown (© Colorsport)

Hotel accommodation was often a touchy subject during the amateur era. Here J.J. Williams and Steve Fenwick share cramped conditions during the British Lions' tour of New Zealand (© Allsport/Getty Images)

Gareth Edwards beats Scotland's Jim Renwick to dive over the line at Cardiff for the final try of his international career (© Colorsport)

The unlikeliest of kickers, second-row Allan Martin, launches one of his long-range efforts at Twickenham
(© Colorsport)

Gerald Davies, pictured during a tour match in Australia, displays the speed and skill that brought him 20 Welsh tries
(© Allsport/Getty Images)

own territory, France gave up nine first-half points to John, who hit the post with another penalty attempt. Pierre Villepreux banged over two long-range efforts but the French attacks were stifled by Bergiers and Gerald Davies, who bundled Sillières into touch. It was his more familiar attacking talents that earned Wales a try ten minutes into the second half after a strike against the head. Edwards sent Lewis through a gap and Davies found just enough room to slip between two defenders. After another John penalty gave him a record 88 points for his country, John Bevan broke away from Duprat with a hand-off, kicked over Villepreux and capped his 50-yard run with the touchdown.

With the seconds ebbing away there was one final moment of drama, revealed fully only to the viewers watching at home, when Derek Quinnell won his first Welsh cap after an injury to Mervyn Davies. The cameras caught Quinnell barging through the various folks gathered in the tunnel waiting for the final whistle, while the crowd greeted his sprint onto the field with a roar. 'Swerve had had a kick in the back,' Quinnell recalls. 'The doctor was taking his time saying he was unfit and there was not long left. When you have not had a cap you never know if you might have an injury or lose form and you might never get one. That was the last place I wanted to be. I had to fight my way down the tunnel because all the policemen were waiting to cordon off the pitch. I even managed to touch the ball as well which was a bit of a miracle. If I had never played for Wales again, I would have treasured the occasion. Having played many games after that it became less important.'

So as one international career was beginning, another was over. Early in May, John announced in the *Daily Mirror*, who reportedly paid him £7,000 for the exclusive, that he was retiring from rugby. 'This is no sudden decision,' he said. 'I have been considering it for many months. I have been torn between retiring and giving it another year.'

He had decided that he could no longer combine the three roles he was expected to fulfil in his life: the family breadwinner working as a finance representative; the international rugby player expected to be in peak condition physically and mentally; and the celebrity superstar attending functions alongside the likes of Tom Jones and Prime Minister Ted Heath. 'Fame can be a great thing at first,' he argues. 'It opens restaurant doors for you and gives you privileges others do not have. But by the end I began to feel as uncomfortable as George [Best].'

John had revealed his intentions to only a small handful of people, including wife Jan and on-field partner Edwards. His successor in the Wales team, Phil Bennett, says, 'It was a shock because he was a young man but I had known Barry a long time and in a sense nothing surprised me about him. He was really laid back and rugby was an enjoyment for him. Perhaps he just wanted to relax and do whatever he wanted with his life.'

Clive Rowlands recalls, 'When he told me, it nearly broke my heart. He should have played against the All Blacks that autumn. I had no inkling at all and I said to him, "Give me one more game." But he decided he was going to make money. I think he was cashing in.' It is a view shared by J.P.R. Williams, who believes he was 'badly advised to cash in on his name'. Reports of his retirement mentioned the many commercial opportunities open to him, including writing books, working as a presenter for HTV and putting his name to sports and fashion shops. One of his most visible ventures would be a long-running role as a rugby columnist for the *Daily Express*.

Of course, the rules about amateurism meant that as soon as he began using his rugby fame to earn a living there was no going back. He admitted a few years ago, 'Yes of course I have regrets and I've probably thought about them most days since. I knew I had a good few years left at the top. But while I was reluctant to pack in a game that had given me so much, I had no option but to go through with my decision.'

John Dawes, the man who lined up alongside John and skippered him to his greatest achievements, concludes, 'We will never know why he retired because he won't tell us. He was the first superstar and there were things being offered to him that he wasn't allowed to take. I am not saying that was the reason but that was the biggest thing to affect him. It was a chance for a teacher to become a superstar worldwide. I ask him if he ever regrets it and it is a forbidden topic.'

9

GONNA MAKE YOU A STAR

'This bloody big Mercedes turns up outside the house.
It was Vince Karalius of Widnes with a cheque for
£13,000' – *J.J. Williams*

Halloween. The day when the boundaries between the worlds of the living and the dead are said to dissolve, allowing for all manner of spooky, paranormal activity. On 31 October 1972, nowhere was the mood of the supernatural being felt more strongly than in the south-west Wales industrial town of Llanelli. The touring All Blacks had arrived for what would become one of the most celebrated days in the history of Welsh club rugby.

'Llanelli is a bit of a dark town anyway and it was a dark, dry day, almost eerie,' recalls winger J.J. Williams. 'You had a sense that something special was going to happen. At the end of the match you could hardly see across the field. It was a dour, grey, hard game and the All Blacks were dark. They were grim, hard men.'

The game was part of a bygone age when a trip from New Zealand meant twenty-six matches across the British Isles (plus another four in France), rather than the whistle-stop series of three or four internationals on consecutive weekends that is the norm in the professional era. The second stop on the tour was Stradey Park. Llanelli captain Delme Thomas suggests, 'We were the first Welsh side to play them and I don't think they really expected such a hard time.'

Fly-half Phil Bennett recalled people walking around town from early morning decked out in red and white, while shops closed their doors at lunchtime and flags flew outside houses. The tone for the match was set in the dressing-room. Coach Carwyn James had given his team talk when his players assembled for lunch in a local hotel, leaving the stage for Thomas, whose address to his team is remembered by Bennett as 'putting the fear of God into anyone who wouldn't follow him to the end'. By the time Thomas had looked into the eyes of each player and asked if they were prepared to 'sacrifice everything for the next eighty minutes', Bennett was not the only one fighting back tears. 'I am not ashamed of the fact that I cried with the emotion of the moment,' he said. 'This is what I lived for, what a lot of us would seemingly have died for.'

Ray Gravell, a 21-year-old centre, recalled many years later, 'I can still remember exactly what Carwyn and Delme said, the goose pimples their words provoked.' Tom David, a powerful flanker who had recently been lured to Llanelli from Pontypridd, adds, 'Delme's speech was very emotional. He is not a noisy guy, but such a wonderful man and great captain. We were all pumped up anyway but what he said was, "This is about yourselves, your families and your friends." It was about the pride of Wales.'

With typical self-effacement, Thomas recalls, 'I only spoke the truth. We had a lot of young boys in that side, like Ray Gravell, Roy Bergiers and Derek Quinnell. All I told them was that I had been on Lions tours and won a lot of honours, but this was the most important game of my life. To beat the All Blacks on our own home ground was a great opportunity.'

It was to be another triumph for the sharp rugby brain of Carwyn James. Just as he had instructed the Lions on their tour the previous year, he ensured that Llanelli always had plenty of tacklers at the back of the All Blacks' lineouts to block off one of their favourite paths of attack. David continues, 'The build-up was immense and the tactics in the training sessions were amazing. Carwyn was one of the greatest coaches I played for and he would always say simple things to me. He asked after one training session, "Why do you run thirty yards to get involved in a ruck or maul?" I didn't want to be one of those guys standing like a seagull watching everything. He said, "Look, if we win the ball I want you between Ray Gravell and Phil Bennett to come into the line hard and straight. He could see two or three moves ahead and you could see what he was talking about. He said that if I knew it was going to be good ball I should come in outside Phil and create a situation where a big man runs at small man.'

Thomas is another who praises the planning of James, saying, 'Having coached the Lions, he knew how we could take advantage of any weakness. We prepared for the game for three or four months. Carwyn was a great tactician and said that if we could turn their forwards, they didn't like going back. Benny could put the ball on a sixpence and he pinned them back. It paid off.'

Bennett could have given Llanelli a lead after five minutes but bounced his penalty off the crossbar. Yet when All Blacks scrum-half Lindsey Colling grabbed the ball on the rebound he failed to avoid Bergiers as he bore down to block the attempted clearance. The centre then dived on the loose ball as it bounced behind the line. Bennett added the conversion and the only New Zealand reply was Joe Karam's 40-yard penalty after a lineout offence.

'We caught them cold and I think they underestimated us,' says Williams. 'They had put out their strongest team on the Saturday against the Western Counties in Gloucester and thrashed them. They gave all the other boys a run out on the Tuesday. We scored a try and it was just a brutal affair then. Games against the All Blacks in those days were always gruesome. We defended well and attacked their lineout.'

The second half was gruelling, attritional rugby, punctuated by the attempts of referee Mike Titcomb to restore order when it became too physical. According to David, 'Keith Murdoch, that most famous of all New Zealand intimidators, would have conceded it was real rugby, which by his standards was something very close to Armageddon.'

It was not, though, simply a case of Llanelli hanging onto their lead. The territorial advantage belonged to the home team and, ten minutes from time, winger Andy Hill made the score 9–3 with a fifty-yard penalty, which he called 'the crowning moment of my career'. Then Bennett repelled the final counter-attack when he fielded a

Bob Burgess kick and cleared to touch. The final whistle brought a wave of human delirium crashing onto the pitch and Llanelli's heroes were carried aloft. So long and hard was the victory celebrated that night that many local hostelries exhausted their supplies of beer, prompting Max Boyce to write of 'the day the pubs ran dry' in his ode to events at Stradey Park, called simply '9–3'. David claims, 'I think I broke the world record for lager that night. It took hours to sink in that we had beaten the best team in the world.'

> There is a boost for one of Wales's most important economic sectors with the government's award of a £400,000 grant to the Wales Tourist Board to maintain levels of advertising, publications, promotions and administration – more than double the amount it received two years ago.

The result against the All Blacks was toasted far beyond Llanelli. It stood as a symbol of the strength of Welsh club rugby, whose influence extended from the Scarlets in the west – embarking on a four-year run of success in the Welsh Cup – through the traditional powerhouse of Cardiff in the east and on into England. There, London Welsh's exciting style of play had made them the sport's show-business team, with the likes of actors Richard Burton and Hywel Bennett among the regular visitors to Old Deer Park. Every Wales player of the era has his own story of the competitive nature of club rugby and Gareth Edwards once wrote, 'Frankly, you wonder sometimes how some blokes didn't get put in jail. They would have been if they had done in the street what they used to get up to on the field.'

Prop Charlie Faulkner, one of the famed Pontypool Front Row, recalls that 'you'd learn your trade by getting some right good smacks in the face' – as Steve Fenwick, making his move into senior rugby with Bridgend at this time, confirms. 'If someone planted one on you, you weren't much of a bloke if you didn't plant him one back. In my first game for Bridgend against Aberavon, I had run into a ruck the wrong way round and my arms had got trapped. All of a sudden this hole appeared and this fist went "smack", right on my nose. My eyes were watering and as they cleared I could see it was

Billy Mainwaring, their scrum-half. I tried to get him for the rest of the game. Later, he walked over to me at the bar and said, "You all right?" I said, "I think you broke my nose." He replied, "Well, I knew you were pretty new to it, so I didn't hit you as hard as I could have."'

Fenwick describes a game some years later, by which time he and Tom David, who had returned to skipper Pontypridd, were running an industrial chemicals company. 'Prince Charles was coming down to visit Atlantic College and we got the contract to clean the pool. [Bridgend players] Ian Stephens and Geoff Davies were out of work so Tom and I got them to help. At the weekend Bridgend were playing Ponty and, as the two packs went down together, Tom's head popped up in the back row and Geoff went "crack", right in his face. Tom said, "Geoff, what are you doing? I gave you a job last week?" The answer was, "Yes, but that was last week."'

Bobby Windsor, who became his country's hooker shortly after moving to Pontypool, recalls that the referees were happy to allow the players a certain leeway. 'You had fun with them,' he explains. 'I remember playing Newbridge and we were having some problems and I said to Charlie, "Smack that bastard in the chops." The referee, John Hughes, came running over and said, "Bob, I am the only bastard on this pitch." Charlie said, "I think you're the bastard he is on about."'

Such was the interest in Welsh club rugby that Football League team Swansea City announced in 1974 they would start playing games on Sundays because they could not compete with the attraction of the local rugby team. And the depth of competition was increasing all the time.

Set in the middle of the Eastern valley, the town of Pontypool was seeing its club begin a rise through the ranks of the Welsh game, creating a force that would come to lay the foundation for Welsh forward dominance in the second half of the decade. While Llanelli were on their recruitment drive in 1972–73, Pontypool were signing Faulkner to prop alongside promising youngster Graham Price, already a Wales triallist, while in twelve months' time Windsor would trace Faulkner's journey from Cross Keys to complete the most famous front three in the history of the game. Behind them flanker Terry Cobner was already forcing consideration from the Wales selectors.

Coached from 1969 by Ray Prosser, their former Wales and British Lions prop, Pontypool were to join the core group of Llanelli, Cardiff, Swansea and London Welsh vying for superiority of the Welsh club game. Cobner recalled, 'Ray and I started at the club at the same time in the late '60s and we had finished bottom of the old Western Mail Championship the previous season. Yet within three seasons we had won the title. We were a team built on a strong work ethic, desire and an ability to get things done – whatever was required.'

Those methods, however, were the antithesis of the London Welsh school of open rugby. A ten-man game, a willingness to mix it with the opposition and fierce loyalty to each other were their defining characteristics, making them an intimidating force. Eddie Butler, the former Wales and Pontypool number 8 turned BBC commentator, admitted, 'It has to be said Pontypool could be a dirty side. Any front row who denied them their precious drive at the scrum by turning it or taking it down was liable to need medical attention.'

London Welsh would go as far as cancelling fixtures against Pontypool after an infamous game at Old Deer Park in November 1973, won comfortably by the away team after the Welsh finished with only 12 men. 'It was not the sort of game to which we are accustomed,' was the official London Welsh statement, while the Pontypool committee responded by saying they 'utterly rejected' allegations of foul play. Pontypool went as far as suggesting it was they who were breaking off relations between the two clubs, saying that 'maintenance of the club's dignity makes it impossible to consider the continuance of fixtures with London Welsh'.

Windsor adds, 'We were an aggressive physical side but you play to your strengths. There is no point in throwing the ball about if your weakness is outside the scrum. That would be bloody daft. People cancelled fixtures because they wanted to run around the field like "hoddy toddies" but we played an aggressive game of rugby, not outside the rules.'

Interestingly, London Welsh coach John Dawes, who confirmed his committee's desire to blacklist Pontypool, would soon base much of his success in charge of the national team on the play of the men against whom his club was making a stand. Faulkner says, 'John had been on the news saying we were over-robust but when he became coach of Wales he picked us. He said one thing but meant the other.' Or, as Windsor puts it, 'When we played for Wales everyone wanted us to kick England and Scotland all over the park.'

Such a breakdown of relationships between clubs illustrates the two prevailing philosophies within rugby at the time, as well as symbolising the uncompromising nature of Pontypool games. Yet Steve Fenwick recalls that, even in the heat of such dust-ups over club pride, players could be mindful of the needs of Wales. 'In between internationals we played Pontypool away. It was a bastard of a fixture. They were ruthless and games against them were like the Alamo. They would pound us for 80 minutes. It was the one game where I would tell the wife not to book anything for Saturday evening because I might be in hospital or limping back home. In this particular game we defended like hell and I fell inside a ruck. You could hear them coming and I thought, "Fucking hell, I'm in trouble." Suddenly Terry Cobner dived on top of me and shouted, "Just stay there." They kicked shit out of everyone else and Terry said, "There you go, now fuck off. See you next Saturday."'

The London Welsh–Pontypool spat was certainly not the first of its kind. Six years earlier, games between Cardiff and Neath had been put on hold following a brutal match that Edwards said had physically scared him, admitting, 'I honestly thought someone was going to be killed.' He adds, 'There was a great closeness among us as players but also a great rivalry between our clubs. It was hard to believe that you could batter yourselves to death one week and then be comrades in arms the next Saturday.'

While such rivalries could spill across the boundary of honest endeavour, there is little doubt that the intensity of the games played on a weekly basis offered ideal preparation for the elevated level of international competition. J.J. Williams says, 'Wales was so parochial that club rugby was everything. It was good quality, well organised, with big crowds and decent facilities. It contributed to the strength of the national team.'

Delme Thomas continues, 'Most of our big clubs were in a radius of 35 miles and everybody knew everybody. Llanelli played Swansea about four times a year, Neath four times and Cardiff twice. You don't get tougher games than that and it set you up for international rugby. I played against great English forwards who never got a look-in because everything was so spread out.'

The Welsh club game, with its keenly contested Merit Table and established knockout competition, soon to attract major sponsorship from Schweppes, proved that 'amateur' did not necessarily have to be a derogatory term. Conversely, England had its best players spread thinly throughout a system that still seemed more geared towards the social aspect of the sport. 'English rugby was badly refereed as well,' adds Williams. 'Fran Cotton always said, "How can we compete against you? In our club rugby, the referee blows his whistle every minute." In Wales, the game was moving and it was entertainment. We played at pace and took that into internationals. We would never win in the Midlands because the referees would whistle us off the park, but it contributed to England's downfall.'

Former Llanelli lock Stuart Gallacher says, 'We didn't realise at the time how high a level of rugby we were capable of playing. There were lots of players who unfortunately didn't win many caps because the standard around the clubs in Wales was so high. We used to play London Welsh here on Boxing Day and, in the days before health and safety, we would have 22,000 packed in.'

Aberavon prop Clive Williams adds, 'Every game was a battle. You would go up and play sides in Gwent on a Wednesday and they would all have some tough guys. I remember Wayne Evans of Pontypridd, who was only a skinny little thing but he was a pig farmer up in the hills and was as hard as anyone.'

Ebbw Vale MP and future Labour leader Michael Foot says the spread of unemployment could lead to 'decades of decay' in Wales and predicts that the proposed entry of the UK into Europe will make things worse, committing the country to 'heavy contributions to the Common Market'.

The health of the Welsh game at club and international level in the late 1960s and early '70s had a side effect: the omnipresent shadow cast across the sport by professional rugby league teams. With unemployment spreading around them, some players took the money and ran; others stayed put. But no one who made it into the Welsh team could fail to be aware of the eyes constantly being cast in their direction by what union traditionalists considered the evil empire.

It was not merely a question of playing ability. The attention on the sport in the Principality meant that a good player quickly became a household name, and professional teams were in the business of putting bums on seats as much as achieving points in the table. The debuts of David Watkins and Keith Jarrett had more than doubled the average attendance of Salford and Barrow respectively.

By the end of the 1972–73 season, the reported offer of £12,000 placed in front of John Bevan by the champion club Warrington meant the dark forces of the north had claimed yet another prize from the valleys, following the high-profile capture in recent years of men such as Watkins, Jarrett, Maurice Richards and Chico Hopkins. 'Had those players remained in Wales, it would have given us even greater strength in depth,' says Clive Rowlands, the national coach who was denied their services. 'It might have been the same players in the Test team, but you would have had all these other players on tap. But I had no qualms about them making a few shillings at the game. If you were a good shop manager in Llanelli you went to London, where the money was. It was the same thing.'

Players who signed for professional teams did so in the knowledge that they could never again be involved in the amateur game, a sanction that existed until professionalism was finally embraced in the mid-'90s. Even discussion of such matters was fraught with danger. J.P.R. Williams explains, 'We could hardly tell each other about what offers had been made because you were not even allowed to speak to rugby league teams. If you said you had spoken to a league scout you'd be professionalised.'

Although his well-publicised progress in medicine might have made him appear untouchable to some teams, there were plenty who were drawn to Williams's physical play. 'I have always quite liked the game and I would love to have played it. I had quite a few offers and my father, being an older generation, said to me, "If you play rugby league, I will never speak to you again." I first had offers when we were in Australia in 1969 and, really, if you are going to play rugby league then Australia is the place.'

Hopkins, who joined Swinton in 1972, recalls that the professional teams did a good job of laying out the opportunities as soon as a good player arrived on the Welsh scene. 'A lot of players went young,' he says. 'You knew the rugby league scouts were about and you knew where they were if you needed the money.'

When it came to the big-name players, finding the men with the cheque books was unnecessary. Backed by a comprehensive scouting system, they soon came calling. Winger J.J. Williams recalls an episode after he returned from the 1974 British Lions tour. 'I was a PE master and my wife, Jane, was a schoolteacher as well. We didn't have kids then, but I had gone four or five months without any wages on tour. This bloody big Mercedes turns up outside the house at eight o'clock in the morning. It was Vince Karalius of Widnes. I told him I had to go to school, but he said, "Before you go, here is a cheque for £13,000." The house had only cost us £4,500 brand new. I went to work and when I came back at five he was there again. This time he said, "Here is another £2,000 on top."

'It was on the news, but I told them, "No, I am not going." Later that week I was with Llanelli to play at Swansea. I walked into the clubhouse and [club secretary] Ken Jones said I wasn't playing. I said, "What do you mean?" and he told me [WRU secretary] Bill Clement had decided I had been professionalised. I reminded him I'd said no, but he said, "Yes, but you thought about it." That was enough for him – as good as taking the money. I said, "Ken, would you consider it? Of course you bloody would." It was farcical. That was the WRU acting like bloody gods and we, the players, were nothing. I didn't play that day but Carwyn sorted it out.'

Steve Fenwick was another who would discover that the professionals possessed the doggedness of private detectives. 'I came home Sunday morning to find two guys from Wakefield Trinity outside my house. Now, if I gave you the address you wouldn't find it. It's a little village with 16 houses, a pub and a church. Yet there they were. Loads of the lads had offers on the table. I always fancied it because I was always a physical player.'

Fenwick and his business partner Tom David would eventually turn professional when rugby league arrived on their doorstep in the shape of the Cardiff Blue Dragons in the early 1980s, but David was another who turned down earlier offers, most notably just after he was named in the 1974 Lions party. 'I talked to Wigan and Salford, but I came to the decision I wanted to play for Wales and the Lions. I turned down two fantastic offers, around £14,000, and then I had a call from Swinton. They were an ambitious club and wanted to offer me an awful lot of money but I didn't get involved. In the end I did enjoy rugby league and if I had my time again I would have gone earlier. If I had joined rugby league I think I would have achieved a lot more.'

Brian Price recalled the Newport players frequently receiving circulars asking about their interest in turning professional. Others would be approached outside dressing-rooms by men whose overture was to request an autograph. Billy Wood, then chairman of Wigan, admitted, 'There have been times when I have had £5,000 worth of £5 notes in a brown paper bag ready to clinch a man's signature.'

David Watkins remembered such an incident when, as an eighteen year old, he found three representatives of St Helens waiting in his living room with £5,000 cash in a briefcase. 'Dad looked round the room before saying, "Jesus Christ, where do we sign? We'll all come."' In fact it took another seven years, and a reported £16,000, before Watkins was persuaded to sign for Salford.

Eddie Waring, the BBC's voice of rugby league, explained the attraction of the established union stars. 'Welshmen cost a lot but the buying club know exactly what they're getting,' he suggested. 'The fee is a more reliable investment than the cash spent training local youngsters.'

Shortly after signing John Bevan, Warrington secretary Graham Atkinson discussed his sport's recruitment of union players. 'Every signing is a bit of a gamble,' he said. 'But a signing like Bevan creates tremendous interest and when we play on Friday nights we pull in a lot of union men. There's a big difference in fitness. When we signed Mike Coulman from Moseley he'd just come back from a Lions tour, but we had to send him to Manchester City to get fit.'

J.J. Williams, whose rise to prominence would be aided by Bevan's defection, says of his own decision to remain in Wales, 'I wasn't flush but I had a good job. I didn't particularly like rugby league and the place to be was in Wales. I think deep down John Bevan did have regrets, even though he was a huge success there and was suited to it.'

Phil Bennett recalled that the final offer he received from a professional team could have netted him £30,000, but he felt that rugby league 'sounds too much like hard work'. Besides, he had been frightened off by his first meeting with a scout from the north, whose battered and scarred face offered a lurid picture of the physical beating he could expect if he took the money.

Yet for a player uncertain about his long-term prospects in the Wales team, an offer to turn professional could easily turn a head. Stuart Gallacher, working as a police constable, needed to play only one game for his country in 1970 to find Bradford Northern literally knocking on his door. 'I couldn't have had a more satisfying and pleasing Wales debut but I decided within a week or so to do something else. Out of the blue these people from Bradford were there because we had no home phone. We chatted about what I could offer them as a player and what they could offer financially, which was a signing-on fee and the kind of money I would have needed to be a superintendent to earn. After I asked them to raise the ante a little bit I signed. At the time you don't think of what could have been. Carwyn James was going to be coach of the Lions and there was a possibility I could have got on the tour, but I upped sticks.'

Having turned himself into an outcast through that decision, it is ironic that Gallacher should have returned to guide Llanelli Scarlets throughout the professional era as chief executive. 'I remember the first time I went back to Stradey. I had broken a hand so we came home to family for Christmas. I went down on Boxing Day and had a less than warm reception. I thought it would not be until hell froze over that I would be back there in any official capacity. I stayed in Yorkshire for ten years then came back and opened my own business and, in 1992, I was asked if I would fancy standing for the committee. I was the first rugby league pro to stand for a club committee. I got elected and that was the start of my second career. I became chairman in 1995 and then the game turned upside down and I became chief executive.'

While history proved that not quite every man had his price, it was true that some players had a number in mind that would trigger a move. Keith Jarrett told interviewer David Parry-Jones in *The Times*, 'You know roughly where the limits lie and that is your only guide. I chose my figure and I stuck to it. When it was offered I took it straight away. No sooner had I arrived in Barrow than I was taken to meet various industrial bosses and before long had the choice of three or four good jobs. How could I possibly have turned them down?'

For those players who resisted the lure of the north, the motivating factor was the glory of pulling on the Welsh shirt and the desire to remain within a tightly knit group for whom greatness beckoned. It was certainly not any loyalty towards the Welsh Rugby Union, which in the 1970s could be a mixture of self-interest, petty-mindedness and old school tie – a description fitting many sporting governing bodies at that time. It was hardly an age of enlightened thinking and innovative administration. Making sure of their own seat on the plane to away games appeared the extent of the ambition of many committee men in all sports. As Bennett put it, 'there are some who appoint themselves as demi-gods', stating that they were motivated by the 'continuing preservation of their own prestige and importance'.

Although players were still no longer required to take third-class rail travel, as in the 1950s, the attitude of the WRU towards its players could still be archaic. Take the example of Arthur Lewis, who had to pull out of the 1971 game in Scotland because of injury 48 hours before kick-off. Instead of giving his replacement, Ian Hall, additional tickets, Lewis's allocation was taken from him, even though his family was already committed to travel arrangements.

Meanwhile, players were not given a hotel room in Cardiff on the night of home games, being expected to travel home after the post-match banquet. And heaven forbid that a player's wife might want to stay with her husband. Until the latter part of the 1970s, she would have to sneak in and share a single bed next to a snoring teammate.

'We could have been treated better,' says J.P.R. Williams, 'but you couldn't do anything about it. The committee thought they were more important than the players. We did have a good secretary in Bill Clement, who always told me to go to him if there was any problem when I was captain. If we were told the players couldn't have any more to drink, I could ask Bill to give us another case of wine and he would. The committee men don't empathise with the players because their only ambition is to be on the committee the next year.'

When he published his autobiography, *Gareth*, to coincide with his retirement in 1978, Edwards could not resist wondering why so little of the increased revenues the WRU was accruing through television, advertising and sponsorship was being reflected in the treatment of the players. 'When you play in a match which has attracted a gate worth over £150,000 you do not want to stay in a second- or third-rate hotel,' he said. 'Nor do you wish to be told that only one bottle of wine is allowed between four.'

Fenwick finds it ironic that the players were treated as amateurs, even though 'we were expected to act like professionals'. He also recalls a source of additional income being closed to them by the WRU. 'This was the amateur days when you could get £100 for wearing Adidas boots. It was a fortune then but the WRU said, "You can't do that. You have got to stop wearing Adidas." Two weeks later they signed their own contract with Adidas and we had to wear them anyway.'

J.J. Williams adds bluntly, 'The committee were prats at that time. Rules like having no wives in the hotel were shocking, but it was such a privilege to play for Wales we put up with anything – expenses not taken, poor hotels, poor transport. If we had any complaints they would be down on us like a ton of bricks. Most of us were in good jobs and were getting ourselves sorted out business-wise because of our names, so to have two couples sharing a room was farcical.'

Among Phil Bennett's fondest memories of his Wales career is the hour or so that the team would spend together after matches before having to mix with dignitaries at the official post-game function. 'It was just the team, the reserves, coaches and selectors. That hour with your mates was incredible. You were knackered and you'd all talk about your areas of the game, and you would really get to know each other. It was a very special time.' The inclusion of the selectors in that gathering is significant and J.J. Williams adds, 'We didn't talk to the committee and they didn't talk to us, but we had a good relationship with the selectors. They were around us all the time.'

Tom David, however, remembers a brutal introduction to the realities of getting your face known among the 'Big Five'. One of his favourite after-dinner stories is that of playing for the Probables in a trial at Llanelli. 'After the game I'm sitting in the changing-room, covered in mud, totally knackered and all I can think is, "Have I done enough?" Then Cliff Jones walks in and is going round, having a word with each player, and I am thinking that is one of the men who could make all my dreams come true. He came up to me, gave me a smile and a pat on the shoulder and said, "Well done, Delme."'

David also recalls the petty nature of the WRU administration after being called in to see the selectors during a squad session. Believing he was to be awarded a first cap, he was taken aback to discover that he, J.J. Williams, Bennett and Edwards were being reprimanded for accepting £25 expenses for playing for a Newport Saracens side and ordered to hand over the money. Graham Price has a similar tale after he, Faulkner and Windsor travelled to play for Major Stanley's XV against Oxford University. It was the unwritten custom for all players to claim expenses, even if they travelled together. Yet they were approached a few weeks later by Keith Rowlands, chairman of the selectors, and told that the Barbarians committee was upset. 'We were shocked by Rowlands's revelation and we could not understand how or why the Barbarians were involved,' he said. 'When you see officials and their wives enjoying tremendous hospitality and sometimes receiving gifts, you begin to wonder who are the real amateurs in our game.'

There was, allegedly, money to be made if one knew where to look, often in one's boots before kick-off or via beer coupons after the game. Fenwick recalls, 'I had offers to go to Swansea and Pontypool for very good deals, job-wise and money-wise. But I valued the quality of rugby more than anything else and absolutely loved our style of rugby in Bridgend.'

And David concludes, 'I always tell people that the difference between rugby now and back in the '70s was that I didn't have to pay income tax back then.'

10

SOLID GOLD EASY ACTION

'That to me was almost as perfect a game as you could play' – *John Dawes on the Barbarians–All Blacks match of 1973*

The immediate reward for Llanelli's show of strength against the All Blacks was captain Delme Thomas's appointment to lead his country against New Zealand when the tourists played the first international of their tour, by which time they had beaten Welsh sides Cardiff and Gwent but suffered a second defeat, against the North-West Counties in Workington. The job as successor to the previous year's captain, John Lloyd, had been earmarked for Arthur Lewis, but a hamstring injury ruled him out, offering a recall for Jim Shanklin in the centre. The selectors had clearly been watching events at Stradey Park closely and offered a first start in a Wales jersey to Derek Quinnell in the second row. Up front, Lloyd was replaced by Glyn Shaw of Neath, a self-employed coal screener who had previously been considered too tall and slight to be picked.

Shaw's selection contributed towards the 20 lb per man advantage that New Zealand enjoyed in the pack. But the power the tourists brought to bear early in the game dissipated as they ran out of steam, giving the two halves of competition very differing complexions. Driven on by the kicks of Sid Going from the base of the scrum – the preferred, yet unlovable, tactic of the All Blacks in this era – New Zealand led 13–3 at half-time. It was the kind of performance that prompted French flanker Victor Boffelli to describe Going as the 'patron saint of the All Blacks forwards'.

Wales paid for their habit of giving away penalties in key areas, of which hooker Jeff Young was the main culprit. It allowed New Zealand's Lebanese-born full-back Joe Karam to ease gently into his Test debut with six quick points after Dai Morris was caught offside and Young raised his hooking foot prematurely. 'Our preparations were the most demanding that I have ever taken part in outside a Lions tour,' said Mervyn Davies. 'We may even have overdone it. Why else would a mature side like ours have conceded two elementary penalties in the first few minutes?'

The All Blacks' only try stemmed, inevitably, from a Going up-and-under. John Bevan failed to gather cleanly and J.P.R. Williams, unable to clear, was tackled hard. The surge of the black-shirted forwards led to referee Johnny Johnson, a police superintendent, awarding a try to prop forward Keith Murdoch, even though Wales felt he had been stopped short. Bennett kicked the first Welsh points after Shanklin scissored to set up a ruck, but Karam completed the first-half scoring when Young was penalised again.

Wales finally had the chance to free their backs after 44 minutes when Edwards harassed Going. The ball went via Bennett to Bevan, whose pace and power took him past two men on a forty-yard run, concluding with the beating of Karam's attempted tackle in the corner. Bennett's penalty three minutes later reduced the deficit to 13–10, only for Karam to belt two more kicks either side of another Bennett effort. In the meantime, Wales had claimed a try after All Blacks winger Grant Batty was smothered and the resulting Welsh move ended with Williams appearing to force his way over with a final twist of his body. Johnson once again ruled against Wales.

Trailing 19–13, the momentum was with the home team and the visitors were so anxious about Davies and Bevan on the wings that they adopted spoiling tactics. Penalties for late tackles and obstructions were clearly preferable to giving their opponents an opportunity to run. Such an approach did much to tarnish the esteem in which the All Blacks were held in Wales – a nation that had always recognised a kindred spirit; two small populations united by a common love for a sport that did so much to define them.

This New Zealand team was one that only its fifteen mothers could love. From their refusal to perform the *haka*, the traditional pre-game ritual that was an integral part of their identity, to their reliance on safety-first rugby, the tour was becoming a public relations disaster. The team made a mockery of coach Bob Duff's comment that, 'We have no intention of playing ten-man rugby. I have no idea where people in Britain got that idea from.' They were developing a reputation for being surly and bad-mannered, even at official functions. Manager Ernie Todd accused the British press of mounting a campaign to discredit his team, but it was the *New Zealand Herald* that reported, 'A certain arrogance of mind in some players and a tendency towards churlishness and indiscipline have been noticeable.' The worst was yet to come.

Back on the Arms Park field, Wales opted to run after Bevan was obstructed by Duncan Hales but were engulfed by a blanket of black. Then a late tackle by Tane Norton on Gerald Davies allowed Bennett to make the score 19–16. There was one final opportunity to salvage the game after Williams was stopped by a short-arm tackle. The penalty was close to 40 yards out, to the right of the posts, but Bennett's kick never curled in enough.

Quinnell insists, 'In my view, we were the better side and were unlucky not to come away with it.' Clive Rowlands recalls, 'We should have won. There was no doubt in my mind that JPR scored the same type of try as Murdoch and we should have had two penalty tries against Batty taking out Gerald.'

Delme Thomas had looked around the dressing-room after the game and commented, 'God, boys. We had 'em.' These days he remembers what should have been the highlight of his career as 'one of the most disappointing days of my life'. He adds, 'We had the side to do it but we gave them too much scope to play their game. It was a chance that got away, one that we should have taken when you look at the side we had.'

And they would have done had Bennett been as deadly accurate at the death as Karam, who made five of his six attempts at goal compared with the Welshman's four out of seven. Such a success ratio was hardly a disgrace in his era, but the final kick had not been excessively difficult and prompted the question of whether he had succumbed to the pressure of replacing Barry John. Karam, meanwhile, had managed to shut out the Welsh crowd's jeers, a piece of audience participation that was frowned upon to the point where the stadium announcer attempted to make them desist. He, and the crowd, might as well have saved their breath. Karam explained, 'I'd hear the noise when I was placing the ball but when I was walking back and doing my run-up I was so busy concentrating that it had no effect.'

Not only had New Zealand held onto victory with tactics that were cynical – although not as questionable as those they would employ six seasons later – it turned out that they were less than gracious winners. Try scorer Murdoch was at the centre of a sequence of ugly incidents at the Angel Hotel, where he was said to have barged through autograph hunters and poured beer over a waiter before knocking a tray of glasses from his hand. Finally, he reportedly thumped security officer Peter Grant. On Monday morning, the New Zealand management reluctantly announced that Murdoch, originally selected for the next game two days later, had been sent home. In the end, he never made it further than Darwin in Australia, where he disappeared. He was finally tracked down some years later, living in the Australian outback.[5]

Welshman Tony Lewis scores an unbeaten 70 to lead England to a six-wicket victory over India at Delhi in his first Test as captain. Lewis, who skippered Glamorgan to their County Championship triumph in 1969, has been chosen to lead the MCC tour to India and Pakistan. He will make his only Test century later in the series, which England lose 2–1.

Having suffered an immediate loss after the Wales game, against Midland Counties West, the All Blacks had then gone unbeaten in 14 games, beating Scotland and England and drawing against

---

5   The incident assumed such infamy that it even became the subject of a play, *Finding Murdoch*, written by Margot McRae and first performed in New Zealand in 2007.

Ireland. They arrived back in Cardiff on the back of a 43–3 thrashing of a combined Neath and Aberavon team. Their final opponents on British soil were the Barbarians, the unofficial 'fifth Test', a game that was expected to be played in the spirit of an exhibition, but for which players on both teams had no shortage of motive. For the New Zealanders, it was an opportunity to strike back at a team that was the British Lions in all but name. John Dawes had even been brought out of international retirement to captain a line-up that contained 12 of the 1971 tourists, while Carwyn James had been invited to address the players. Meanwhile, the Barbarians' Welsh contingent had a chance for revenge after the painful defeat of almost three months earlier.

As any rugby student knows, the game was only two minutes old when Edwards scored the try that is still widely considered the best ever. For those who have been living under a rock for the past 30-odd years, here is what happened.

Bennett gathered a bouncing kick from Bruce Robertson deep in front of his own posts. Eschewing the kick to touch, he jackknifed through three sidesteps as New Zealand players floundered on their backsides. 'Brilliant. Oh, that's brilliant,' declared the voice of BBC commentator Cliff Morgan before Bennett flipped the ball left to J.P.R. Williams. It wasn't just his opponents whom Bennett had caught out. David explains, 'I was on the halfway line after Robertson kicked the high ball. All the forwards are thinking, "Thank God for that. Benny has got it and he'll just kick it to touch." But he has done his magical thing and now we are thinking, "Oh no, what is he doing?" So we have to run back in case he gets caught. Can you imagine Phil Bennett playing like that today? The coach would be screaming at him to just get rid of it.'

Bennett's move was more than a nod towards the exhibition status of the game. 'I sensed them bearing down on me and felt that if I broke we might catch them too far forward,' he said. Such a decision was one he was regularly encouraged to make at his club. 'Carwyn had said to go out and do what you do for the Scarlets,' he explains. 'He used to encourage us, "If you have the ball on your own line and you think it is on, you go." We used to play that kind of rugby, willing to counter-attack from anywhere, and scored a lot of tries at Llanelli from near our own line.'

With one piece of fancy footwork, Bennett had helped persuade the Cardiff public that he was up to the task of filling the boots of Barry John. He admits, 'It was daunting and it took a while to get the respect of the crowd. But I was lucky in that I'd had a few internationals already. I was completely different to Barry in that he was nonchalant and could glide through, whereas I was more of a dasher. I knew I had to play to a team plan, but I had to play the way that got me recognised. I was also lucky that I had played for a Llanelli side that beat the All Blacks, which was like Gillingham beating Brazil. It gave us so much confidence, pride and dignity and gave me a sense that anything was possible. The Barbarians game then helped to portray my image and it also gave me the confidence to say, "Yes, you can take people on."'

Half held by winger Bryan Williams, JPR moved the ball on to English hooker John Pullin, who in turn fed Dawes. A subtle dummy, delivered at speed, and the move was progressing into All Blacks territory. 'David, Tom David. The halfway line. Brilliant! By Quinnell,' continued Morgan, his voice rising towards crescendo as the Llanelli giant stooped to reach David's pass, delivered as he was tackled. Quinnell's instinct was to give a pass accurate enough to reach John Bevan on the left touchline. As he did so it was Edwards, like a 200 metres sprinter, who took the ball in full stride, covered the final 30 metres and dived spectacularly into the corner. 'This is Gareth Edwards,' yelled Morgan. 'A dramatic start. What a score!' Words that, to rugby fans this day, resonate every bit as much as Kenneth Wolstenholme's iconic 'It is now!' as Geoff Hurst provided the *coup de grâce* at Wembley in 1966.

That it might not even have been the most exhilarating passage of play in the game says much about the quality of the rugby that day. Tries by Bevan and J.P.R. Williams, both completed with a demonstration of their strength and determination, came at the end of moves in which the ball passed back and forth across the field with the ease of a parcel in a children's party game. Yet the All Blacks, down 17–0 at half-time, deserve their share of credit for a memorable occasion. They battled back to 23–11 by sharing in the kind of open rugby they'd bottled up throughout the tour. They had even performed the *haka* before kick-off.

The Welsh crowd not only had great deeds by their established heroes to cheer, but saw intriguing performances by Quinnell and uncapped Llanelli teammate David. Their places in the back row were down to the absence of Andy Ripley and Mervyn Davies, whose attack of flu on the day elevated David from the replacements' bench. 'So I am there with all the legends of the game and, to be honest, I absolutely crapped myself,' David recalls. Quinnell, as well as playing a key role in the first try, helped set up Bevan's score and looked at home within the free flow of the game. David rose to immediate cult status through a run-in with Batty. Explosive of feet and temperament and top scorer on the tour with nineteen tries, including two in this game, Batty's droopy moustache gave him a somewhat sour demeanour that did nothing to endear him to opposing fans. There were lusty cheers when David floored him with a tackle that, while not deliberately late, was late nonetheless. 'He came at me like a kamikaze,' is David's recollection of what happened next. 'If I'd thumped him I would have looked like a bully because I was so much bigger. So I ruffled his hair and said, "Now cool down son, get on with the game, you little boy." It's better to take the mick out of people rather than punch hell out of them.'

More than three and a half decades after the game, David continues to enjoy a higher profile among the players of his era than many who earned far more than his four Wales caps. It is perhaps due a little to his distinctive appearance on the field – think of a tall Captain Pugwash on a weight-training regime – and partly down to an engaging personality. David believes it is mostly down to his good fortune in being in the Barbarians line-up on that famous day. 'I was lucky in that I played for Llanelli and we beat New Zealand, which is a rarity, and then I played for the Barbarians in a legendary game and was involved in that try. It is shown so much that they all think I am still playing!'

The success of Quinnell and David was another feather in the cap of Carwyn James, who had played a large part in getting them involved in the Baa-baas game following their success against the tourists at Stradey Park. 'Both were feared by the All Blacks and everyone knew it,' he stated.

A footnote to David's memorable day was an unlikely encounter in a hotel bar after the game. 'I hadn't played for a couple of weeks because of a knee injury and the previous Saturday Carwyn suggested I get a game for a local side to get some fitness – nothing to do with the Barbarians. I played in the centre for Kivenny in a game in Gloucester. I was a giant compared with this boy I was up against and I scored a couple of tries. After the Barbarians, these two guys came up and one said, "I have got to ask you something and tell you a story." It was the guy I had played against in Gloucester. He had been standing near the touchline and when we ran out he said to his mate, "Here, that Tom David plays for Kivenny." The other guy said, "No, it says in the programme he plays for Llanelli," and they had an argument about it.'

David also remembers that it was only when he and a few colleagues saw highlights on television that they began to get a full appreciation of the historic nature of the game. 'There was a lot of emotion that night. It was packed everywhere and people were coming up to us and saying, "It was great when you did this or that," but you couldn't remember half of it. You couldn't take it all in. I remember having a drink with Benny and his wife, Pat, and we were saying, "What was all the fuss about?"'

Well into a new century, the Barbarians–All Blacks still stands as an apogee for the game of rugby. The fact that it was, strictly speaking, a friendly is less important than what it stood for: the grinding, intimidating All Blacks bullies being taken apart by the plucky, Corinthian-spirited Brits. The allegories are endless.

Events at Cardiff Arms Park stimulated casual rugby viewers in the same way that the radiant Brazilians had brought living rooms to light three years earlier as they danced their samba around Italy in the World Cup final. There are even similarities in the two moves that continue to symbolise those two games. Just as rugby's greatest try began with a counter-attack from deep, so the goal that many believe is football's finest, Brazil's fourth, was launched by midfielder

Clodoaldo tripping Bennett-like past four Italians inside his own half. In both cases the ball moved effortlessly through various teammates and was finished with a spectacular flourish out wide, the charge of Edwards down the Barbarians' left mirrored by the emphatic arrival of Carlos Alberto on the right of Brazil's attack.

In his book, *Inverting the Pyramid*, Jonathan Wilson describes the Brazilian success as being a last fling for such carefree, attacking football. So the Barbarians–All Blacks was, in some ways, for rugby. In his last major game as a player, Dawes marshalled one final, sustained display of brilliance from a back division that – supplemented by a couple of British Lions – reprised and surpassed the virtuosity his Grand Slam unit had achieved two years earlier. There has been no game to capture the imagination in such a way since. Today's professional international rugby is far too serious for such frippery, while the age of countries playing ten or more internationals every year has devalued the place of the Barbarians in the sport's calendar. A game between the Baa-baas and a major touring team is now an irrelevance, whereas the 1973 game was a genuine fifth Test for the All Blacks. The unspoken commitment to an expansive style of play took nothing away from the intensity and determination of the participants or the passionate desire of the Cardiff crowd to see their team win.

Dawes recalls, 'The quality of the game was unbelievable. I don't think we dropped the ball. The All Blacks played their part and played a looser game and there was a stage just after half-time when, had Kirkpatrick scored, they could have been in the lead and won the game. Actually, I was most pleased for David Duckham. He had never done well against Wales for England because he never got the ball. He played just as he had for the Lions and showed the Welsh fans what he could do. It was a great compliment that they all called him Dai after that. I am sure that gave him great satisfaction.'

In the years to follow, with Dawes in charge as coach, Wales would still be able to call upon many of the greatest backs ever to play the game and would continue to produce moments of breathtaking quality. But their dominance would stem from an overpowering, technically superior set of forwards. The view of JPR, who believes that the backs of the early decade and the forwards of the latter years would form the greatest of all Welsh teams, goes generally undisputed. Tom David asserts, 'Take it from me, what happened in the '70s was down to the forwards. They used to hammer nearly every country in the scrum and set a platform. There were some magical players behind the scrum but nobody ever seems to mention the dominance of the forwards. The Welsh pack used to demoralise other teams up front.'

11

YOU CAN DO MAGIC

'Do you need talent or dedication? The answer is that
you need both. One doesn't go without the other and we
have all seen individuals who have had plenty of either
but have not made it' – *Gareth Edwards*

There is no need for a double-take, no trying to drag up recognition
from the depth of memory when the familiar face of Gareth
Edwards appears. Like sporting heroes such as Henry Cooper and
Bobby Charlton, the man generally hailed as rugby's greatest player
has been away from television screens so infrequently that we
have watched him pass through middle age before our eyes. Long
before the 'reality TV' exploits of Phil Tufnell, Austin Healey, Mark
Ramprakash and numerous other sportsmen, men such as Edwards,
Charlton and Cooper were blazing a trail with *A Question of Sport*,
Superstars and *Pro-Celebrity Golf*, a prime-time format where light-
entertainment giants such as Bruce Forsyth and Ronnie Corbett
collided with Tony Jacklin and Lee Trevino in an explosion of wise-
cracks and lurid knitwear.[6]

Thanks to Edwards's ongoing public profile and the filmed
preservation of so many of his greatest moments, his genius on the
field has endured well into the new century. When the Welsh Rugby

---

6 Thirty years later these shows are considered relevant enough slices of
culture, if not sporting excellence, to merit repeat runs alongside European
Cup finals and Ashes Tests on ESPN Classic.

Union's website asked users to vote for the country's greatest player of all time, many of those who elevated him to first place would not have been born when he retired from rugby. The prompting of fathers and frequent re-runs of his most famous tries were all the evidence a new generation needed.

It was typical of Edwards that, even as 1973's rugby public buzzed about the best game most of them had seen, it was his try that inspired much of the talk after that Barbarians–All Blacks contest. His contribution to the rest of the game had been modest compared with the eye-popping exploits of Phil Bennett, J.P.R. Williams and David Duckham. Yet, referring to the try, Tom David says with affection, 'The ball went through all those hands and who scores in the corner? "Golden Bollocks" Gareth!'

Maybe all he'd had to do was run bloody fast and dive into the corner; and maybe the final pass from Derek Quinnell had been intended for John Bevan. But without Edwards's intervention there would have been no try. Bevan was barely moving at that point and his lack of momentum would have made him a sitting target for tacklers. Edwards's sheer speed, his determination to make up the ground and the breathtaking manner of his finish fashioned yet another addition to his expanding highlights collection. All commentator Cliff Morgan could manage in the aftermath was, 'Oh, that fellow Edwards,' with a sigh that sounded positively post-coital.

That fellow had been a boy in the Swansea valley mining village of Gwaun-cae-Gurwen, where one of the annual highlights of his childhood was the new rugby jersey he received each Christmas. At Pontadarwe Technical College, a school that afforded sport the same importance as Edwards gave it in his own life, he fell under the influence of teacher Bill Samuel, who advised him to abandon the 'Brylcreem position' of centre.

Even though he must have discussed such topics thousands of times over the years, Edwards gives his interviewer the courtesy of thoughtful, considered answers rather than a handful of glib throwaway lines as he recalls the defining factors of his rugby career. 'Bill took me under his wing and guided me,' he explains. 'I wanted to be a centre because I loved running with the ball but he said,

"You can forget that. Your best pal is twice your size and already played for Wales Under-15s so you have no chance of being better than him."

'I was content as long as I was doing sport. I got as much pleasure from scoring a goal as scoring a try so I wasn't bothered about making choices at that time. One day Bill said, "I have thought about it. You will make a scrum-half. It's the only place you will get a game for the valley Under–15 side and that position is made for you. You are quick, you can kick and you are a gymnast, so I am going to teach you." He spent time after school trying to teach me to pass and other skills.'

As well as critiquing every aspect of his rugby game, Samuel also realised that the boy who won the Welsh schools long jump, hurdles, discus and pole vault titles and attracted the attention of Swansea's football scouts deserved a more dedicated environment for his talent. His persistent letter writing earned his protégé a place at Millfield, the school of sporting excellence in Somerset.

'Bill had prepared me well and Millfield gave me more opportunity to practise, to become stronger and faster, and it gave me the stage on which to perform. My previous school was a small one with not enough good players so we struggled to fulfil a fixture list. Millfield gave me chance to play against the better schools in England with a lot of media attention. All of a sudden my name was noticed and opportunities presented themselves. I got a Welsh schoolboys cap and that brings you to the attention of those involved in the game.'

There was also the unusual experience of wearing an England jersey when he represented the national schools team in the 200 metres hurdles at the British Championships in Belfast. As he walked out in his tracksuit, Wales Schools rugby teammates Allan Martin and J.J. Williams fell in line beside him, whispering 'traitor' in his ear.

Returning to Cardiff College of Education, he quickly won a place in the Cardiff club's first team and earned a Welsh trial appearance late in 1966. Criticised for the way he put the ball into the scrum, he missed out on a place against Australia but played in a second trial, only to be held in reserve for the games against Scotland and Ireland. His debut came in a defeat in Paris and he retained his place for the home win against England – as he would for every game over the next 11 seasons. 'I had the good fortune to play my first two games with David Watkins, who was a very experienced outside-half and was a great help,' Edwards says. 'He realised my passing wasn't as strong as it could be and said what was important was that we didn't give opportunities to the opposition.'

By the time of the first Wales game of 1968, Barry John had joined him at Cardiff as well as in the national team. John recalls his partner being 'prone to mood swings', seized upon by the ruthlessness of the dressing-room, who reminded him how well his understudy, Chico Hopkins, was performing. On tour, Edwards could become a little introspective because of injury or a bad performance, but any doubt or dissatisfaction was directed at himself. It didn't last long, though, as team camaraderie, the role of choirmaster or a request to slip into his Buddy Holly routine would snap him out of it.

There were two memorable milestones in 1968, his selection to captain the team against Scotland at the age of twenty, making him his country's youngest leader, and a place on the British Lions tour of South Africa. It was in the clear, windless air of that country that Edwards felt he finally got his passing up to the required standard. 'It was suspect to start with, predominantly because I had not been a scrum-half at first. I really developed it in South Africa, where I had three months of working with people of the calibre of Barry and Mike Gibson. I did a hamstring during the tour and for the last three weeks or so, instead of kicking and punting, I spent my time passing the ball. I had more confidence after that.'

He still preferred not to spin pass out of his left hand, opting to adjust the position of his feet to turn his back to the forwards so that he could use his right. It did little to detract from his game. Besides, it was his rugby brain, his nose for the try-line and his devastating tactical kicking that would mark him out from his contemporaries.

'I must have kicked the ball since I can remember, when I was only about four,' he explains. 'I was kicking a ball for hours on the road or in the park with my friends. There wouldn't be a moment when I was not doing it. If we were gossiping on the roadside we would keep a tennis ball or football up in the air while we talked.

I would kick it up as many times as I could and if it went on the ground your mate would have it. No one said we should do it but we were forever competing and what we didn't realise was that we were honing our skills.

'Then we would go to the park and play kicking to touch. Wherever the ball went into touch you had to take a kick back and if you were on the right touchline you had to kick with the left foot and vice versa. The idea was to push your opponent back to the goal-line. Today it is all coordinated and organised but, for us, it wasn't part of a specific task, it was just fun. We would be playing as the street lights came on. You would take a clod from the gutter and be kicking for goal until your father said it was time for bed. When that happened, you would take the last kick at goal against England – two minutes to go and two points in it. You'd do the commentary and if you missed it, the kick had to be taken again.

'I developed the rolling kick because after the new Australian rule came in you had to find some kind of compensation and change your approach. The fact I had spent hours with that tennis ball educated my foot so that the skill was there. Performing is all about balance, touch and feel and I was able to adapt to controlling the kick once you weren't allowed to kick to touch.'

According to former Wales coach Clive Rowlands, 'Gareth worked and worked at his game. He could put those long raking kicks into the corner, making them bounce just enough. I have never seen anyone do it better. He was able to change his game and his angles.'

Along with his knack for spectacular long-distance tries, Edwards's legendary upper body strength – John remembers trying on his jacket and being swamped by it – helped him score many times from the base of the scrum, propelling him towards the Welsh record of 20 tries he shared with Gerald Davies at the time of their retirement. And it was all done with such an air of confidence. At most breaks in play Edwards could be seen standing straight-backed with hands on hips, a pose that mixed relaxed nonchalance with purposeful determination.

His ability to pin the opposition with a boot that had the accuracy of radar set up many of his own scoring opportunities. J.J. Williams, partly with tongue in cheek, says, 'Gareth did too much kicking, but we wanted to get down there near the line. JPR and I would be shouting at him all the time. We used to say, "I hope Gareth scores early today because then we'll get a bloody pass."'

Additional scrutiny inevitably fell upon Edwards when he lost his long-term halfback partner, Barry John, and Phil Bennett took his place. J.P.R. Williams believes that Edwards's quality ensured there was an 'easy transition', saying, 'I think Gareth helped Benny a hell of a lot. From being subservient to Barry, he became senior to Benny. His own game benefited because he took on an extra responsibility. He had an iffy Lions tour in 1971 because Sid Going gave him a difficult time but by the 1974 tour he was magnificent. In the first Test he kicked South Africa to death and in the second Test he span the ball and ran riot. He was in his element. In 1974, the backs' coaching sessions were taken by Gareth and me. We trusted Gareth so we did what he said.'

John disagrees that he had a more dominant role in their partnership. 'Gareth and I never competed against each other. There was no senior partner as such. Having said that, if Gareth had taken a couple of wrong options I would put my hands behind my back and point to my number 10 as if to say, "I can see what is going on better. Give the ball to me and I will make the decisions."'

Rowlands, however, believes in Williams's theory. 'In a partnership one player is dominant over the other,' he says. 'I was dominant over Dai Watkins, Barry was dominant over Gareth and Gareth was dominant over Phil. Someone has to make the big decision at some point. We didn't work it out, it just happened. Gareth became an outstanding kicker and I think that took pressure off Phil.'

Edwards himself says, 'In all probability my game did change. Barry was the dominant player because he was two years older, although we never looked upon each other in that way. But my job was to get good ball to Barry so that everything could function. My age made me more of an apprentice in the first couple of years with Barry. Playing with Phil had a completely different feel because his style was as a darting, staccato player who preferred the ball where he could run onto it. Barry quite often loved the ball standing still and, once he took it, he mesmerised everybody – myself included sometimes. But nobody shirked their responsibilities and I enjoyed playing with both of them.'

Whether Edwards's game really did expand without John next to him, or whether it was just that his talents could be more easily appreciated from a seat in the stands, his former partner does confess to seeing a whole new player following his retirement. 'I thought I knew Gareth's game inside out from the years we were paired together for club, country and the Lions. But it was only after retiring that I grasped how good he really was. Perhaps I had been too close and didn't realise just how powerful Gareth was; he could dump big forwards on their backsides in tackles.'

What impressed Bennett most about his scrum-half partner was the way his play evolved over the years. 'Gareth had that service that could put you away from the wing-forwards by giving you an extra yard or two, which was a great boost, but he was strong enough to work on his game. In my opinion his best rugby was in 1974 in South Africa, but later he adjusted his game magnificently as he slowed down a little to become a better kicker of the ball, and then he would strike from 10 or 15 yards. He always knew where the game was going and where the ball would be.'

Wales's first 'Fanfare for Europe' event is called off due to lack of interest. A three-day course at University College, Cardiff, on the implication of Britain's recent entry into Common Market had been aimed at civil servants, council members, businessmen and trade unionists. Course director David Gidwell warns, 'Industry in Wales has not fully woken up to the urgency to equip itself for the Common Market.'

By the time of the Barbarians game, Wales had already begun their Five Nations campaign with a ninth consecutive victory. England were beaten 25–9, although it needed a ten-point burst in the last five minutes to produce a scoreline that gave a true reflection of the superiority of the Welsh, who scored five unanswered tries. David Duckham might as well have been watching from the stand for all the opportunity he had.

This time Arthur Lewis had been fit to skipper the Welsh team. 'The captaincy was a surprise because there were a lot of senior players in the team,' he remembers. 'But because I was older I suppose I was in that category too and always used to do a lot in the training sessions, helping with the backs. I had been captain in every team I played for and having players like Gareth and Phil Bennett in the team made it easier. Everyone got on so well.'

The man who had held the post of captain a year earlier, John Lloyd, had returned to the front row in place of the crocked Barry Llewellyn. Aged only 24, the mobile Llewellyn had played his last game for his country, eventually easing himself out of the game to concentrate on his family and his business interests after only making it back to the fringes of the team as he sought a full recovery from his cartilage injury.

The kicking difficulties Bennett had experienced against New Zealand returned. He was wayward with two penalties and struck the post with a third, allowing England to take the lead with a drop by Dick Cowman. The early Welsh pressure, the product of strength in the mauls and efficiency in the rucks, finally paid off when Derek Quinnell ran powerfully after John Taylor retrieved a loose ball. When Quinnell was stopped, Edwards fed Roy Bergiers and then John Bevan blasted through three tackles.

With ten minutes left in the first half and England temporarily a man short, Jeff Young struck against the head and Bennett directed a neat kick to the right corner for Gerald Davies to touch down. After England full-back Sam Doble sent over a successful kick, Dai Morris drove inside the 25, Lloyd made a half break to the blind side and Edwards received his pass to establish a 12–6 half-time lead.

Taylor and Doble's penalties were the only points of the second half until the final five minutes. Lewis scored on crash ball, going through two tacklers; then the famous Bennett sidestep set in motion an attack from deep, with Williams carrying the ball into the England half. It passed along the Welsh line to the right wing before finding its way back for Edwards to free Bevan on the final overlap. It would be a long time, so the happy Arms Park fans thought, before they saw a try that good.

Any Welsh euphoria that remained from the thrashing of England and the Barbarians extravaganza was carried off in the Murrayfield wind a week later. Pinned back by the elements and the efforts of the home team, Wales trailed 10–0 before half-time, Colin Telfer dummying his way over for the first try and then flat-footing the defence with a blindside break to set up winger Billy Steele. Penalties by Taylor and Bennett reduced the deficit before the interval, but the Wales backs displayed a hint of tiredness after recent big games. Another Bennett kick was all they had to show for their endeavours, which relied too strongly on the tactic of Williams creating an overlap. Scotland's defence prevailed against such predictability.

The Welsh team's 10–9 defeat was particularly disappointing considering the disarray in which they had found their opponents, whose much-changed team included the naming of Ian McLauchlan as captain for the first time and a sixth halfback pairing in consecutive internationals. Lewis complained, 'McLauchlan's plan was to disrupt our scrummaging. The referee kept penalising Gareth for not putting the ball in quickly but the scrum was slewing around and Scotland should have been penalised.'

The Queen unveils a memorial plaque and opens a £350,000 community centre in Aberfan, the town where 147 people, including 116 children, died in a coal tip avalanche in 1966. The four-storey centre stands on ground where a number of houses were destroyed in the disaster.

The loss in Edinburgh turned out to be typical of the pattern of inconsistency that endured over the remainder of the season and all of the next as the Welsh team went into a period of metamorphosis. Over a spell of two years between the start of 1973 and 1975, a total of nineteen players would win their first caps. For the game against Ireland, however, it was an old favourite, Mike Roberts, who was brought back to the second row, having continued to fight a battle with his weight. His good work in the loose would justify his recall and Quinnell, by now playing most of his club rugby in the back row, was discarded. The selectors would revolve him in and out of the squad over the next four years before he became a permanent, dominant force at number 8.

It is a question of debate whether Quinnell's versatility to play any one of three positions enabled him to win more caps than he otherwise might, or if it merely prevented the selectors allowing him to make one position his own. 'I wouldn't say with hindsight that I would have done anything different,' he remarks. 'All through my career, I was either fortunate enough to be able to play two or three positions, or perhaps not so fortunate. At Llanelli I played alongside Delme for a while and then Stuart Gallacher came through and he and I chopped and changed a little bit. It was a question of fitting in where I was most needed.' Which for now, the Welsh selectors decided, was back on the sidelines.

The other change to the team beaten at Murrayfield would be a portent of a permanent state of affairs, with the injured John Bevan – replaced by Jim Shanklin – never to wear the Welsh shirt again.

Phil Bennett was the notable contributor to a 16–12 victory that hardly set Cardiff pulses racing. There was deftness about his kicking early on and he gave glimpses of his ability to instigate a running game as events progressed. His two penalties gave Wales a 6–3 lead at the end of a first half in which Ireland's carelessness prevented them harvesting the crop of their possession advantage. Bennett launched the attack that finally produced a home try when he beat three men after taking a kick from Tom Grace inside his 25. Eventually Morris found Edwards, who squeezed down the blindside before beating two tacklers and feeding inside for Shanklin to finish.

The second try came after Wales spoiled an Ireland scrum. Bennett switched play to the right and Edwards passed to Lewis, who scissored with Gerald Davies. Edwards, meanwhile, had found room on the outside and accepted a pass to complete the move, with Bennett converting. Ireland's Mike Gibson emerged from a crowd of players to touch down for Ireland's only try.

Edwards, who had given an impressive performance, was about to be handed the captaincy of his country once more. First named as skipper five years earlier against Scotland, and again two games later, he held the job in 1970 for three matches. For the final game of the 1973 season against France he was in charge again. A sense clearly existed that a player who was so influential in his execution of the pivotal scrum-half duties was a natural to take the role of team leader. That, at least, was the theory. 'I have learned a lot since those early days,' was the player's response to the latest developments. 'If I can't do it now I never can.' There is an argument that maybe he never could.

John Taylor is far from being alone in believing that Edwards was affected by captaincy. He felt that the need to distance himself, metaphorically at least, from the hub of the action meant that Edwards was no longer able to use the instincts that were the cornerstone of his game. J.P.R. Williams adds, 'Gareth originally had the captaincy too early. He was far too young. He wasn't a natural captain, but who is? Good captains are not always the best players; the best ones are those who can see what is going wrong with the lesser players.'

Whether Edwards was the right captain or not, he was unable to prevent a 12–3 defeat in Paris, a result that helped the Five Nations table finish as a five-way tie after ten victories for the home teams.[7] The most disappointing aspect for Wales was the deterioration in the effectiveness of the Edwards–Bennett combination and their unimpressive personal performances. The training sessions aimed at eliminating Bennett's tendency to cramp his backs by going sideways did not appear to be having the desired effect. The situation was not helped by Edwards introducing a longer-range spin pass, seen by some as being a less productive platform than his previous shorter delivery. It was even a poor pass by Edwards that led to the dropped goal with which French fly-half Jean-Pierre Romeu added to his earlier penalties for a 9–0 lead.

Wales had originally left out previous skipper Lewis in favour of Keith Hughes and dropped flankers Morris and Taylor for the more muscular Llanelli duo of Quinnell and Tom David. 'In the 1970s, it was very difficult to break into the side because they were winning everything,' recalls David, whose move from Pontypridd was clearly paying off. 'It was fairly parochial selection back then. You had the big

---

7 Depending on which history book one reads, the season is either recorded as a five-way or awarded to Scotland by virtue of scoring most points.

teams like Cardiff, Newport, Llanelli and Swansea, while Pontypridd was an unfashionable club.' In the end it was Taylor who partnered David after Quinnell went down with flu, while Lewis was recalled when Hughes broke his jaw in a club game. France had made ten changes to the team beaten in their previous game at Twickenham but played with more cohesion than Wales, whose only points were from Bennett's drop with six minutes remaining. Romeu kicked a further penalty for the victorious home side.

Another new cap was earned when J.J. Williams replaced the injured Lewis late on. He had enough time to give a glimpse of the future by almost scoring with the kind of run and chip ahead that would be seen so often in years to come. He would have further opportunity to make his mark on a post-season tour of Canada, a trip that was seen as vital in sorting out the uncertainties within the team, especially in the back division.

Predictably, all five games were won, including a 58–20 victory in the unofficial international in Toronto. Williams played in that game for the injured Gerald Davies and scored a try, while Hughes and David grabbed two each. Aberavon second-row forward Allan Martin celebrated his first taste of being part of an international squad by kicking eight conversions and four penalties in a 76–6 thrashing of Alberta and the team ended the tour with a tally of 288 points scored against 41 conceded. Quite what relevance that would have when Wales returned to real action was anyone's guess.

12

BORN TO RUN

'JJ was a fly-half playing on the wing. He trained as an athlete would train and he ran like an athlete. His kick ahead, he had it off better than any player I have ever seen' – *Clive Rowlands*

The bright, spacious kitchen in which John James Williams is making tea is adorned with the kind of memorabilia you'd expect in the home of an international sportsman; photographs, jerseys and the like. Yet these are not rugby-related items. They mark the achievements of JJ's son, Rhys, a European Championship silver and bronze medallist who, but for a broken bone in his foot, would have been one of Britain's 400-metres hurdlers in the Beijing Olympics. Williams senior has his own souvenirs dotted around the walls elsewhere in his home on the outskirts of Bridgend. In among the various Wales and British Lions artefacts is his own piece of track and field history. The vest he wore for Wales in the Commonwealth Games is not only a clue to the source of his son's particular sporting genes, it is also a reminder of the alternate sporting path that delayed Williams's entrance to international rugby until he was nearly 25, several years after many of his teenage contemporaries.

'I was an international outside-half as a schoolboy,' he explains, seating himself at a high breakfast counter from which you can look out the window and catch the blue glint of the swimming pool. 'When I went to Cardiff College to be a teacher, Lynn Davies was a lecturer there and he got me massively interested in athletics. I concentrated on it for a little less than three years and played no rugby.'

Under the guidance of the man who had won the long jump at the 1964 Tokyo Olympics, Williams went to the 1970 Commonwealth Games in Edinburgh, recording a personal best in the 100 metres, and ran for Great Britain in the World Student Games. Still possessing the figure of an athlete, although his flowing brown locks are now short and nearly white, he admits, 'I was never going to be a world-class sprinter. I was Division Two compared to someone like Linford Christie. In hindsight, perhaps I should have gone back to rugby sooner. I missed an opportunity with the 1971 Lions tour, but I was being dragged both ways by the college. I wanted to give athletics a go and I did as well as I possibly could. I could have ended up as quite a good 400 metres runner, but rugby was always in my blood. I came from the valleys [the Maesteg village of Nantyffyllon] and my brother Peter played second-row for Maesteg and Bridgend for ten years.'

Having returned to play for Bridgend, where he scored 100 tries in 92 games, he decided that a move to Llanelli would further his career. 'Bridgend were massively successful in the '60s but weren't getting representation in the Wales squad. I scored 40 tries in a season and was not mentioned. I liked the style Llanelli played, I was frustrated at Bridgend and my wife was from west Wales, so I thought, "Let's try it." It was the best thing I ever did. We were professional in our approach, although there was no money involved – despite the big joke that the car park was funding the players. But the attitude of our coaches, Carwyn James and Norman Gale, was fantastic and we were superbly fit.'

By the end of his first season at Stradey Park, Williams had made his Welsh debut and was picked for the tour of Canada. 'The original plan when we went there was to move Gerald Davies back into the centre, with John Bevan on the left wing and me on the right. But centre play had changed since Gerald played there and he didn't like it. And then, all of a sudden, John went to rugby league and it never materialised.'

Instead, Williams simply slotted into Bevan's place on the left wing and, despite his preference for the right, he became a fixture there for the next six seasons, winning selection for two Lions tours along the way. One of the most familiar sights in rugby during that period was that of Williams using the skills he once applied as a fly-half and a sprinter, chipping the ball beyond an opposing full-back or winger before gathering in to score.

Six members of Cymdeithas yr Iaith Gymraeg, the Welsh Language Society, stage a 36-hour sit-in at the BBC studio in Cardiff as part of an ongoing campaign to increase the amount of Welsh content on television. Another 30 protestors invade HTV's studios.

J.J. Williams scored one of the tries as Wales began their 1973–74 season with a workout against the Japanese touring team. They cruised to a 62–14 victory in the unofficial international at Cardiff, but the two Japanese tries, scored by right-wing Itoh, were cheered just as lustily by the 35,000 crowd as any of the eleven run in by the home team. Phil Bennett and Keith Hughes scored two each, while uncapped hooker Bobby Windsor, recently moved to Pontypool, crawled over the try-line and emerged kissing the ball triumphantly. Bennett's nine conversions took his points tally to twenty-six, more than any Welshman had ever scored against another country. Clive Shell made an appearance at scrum-half and John Taylor captained the team in the absence of Gareth Edwards. It turned out to be the equivalent of a golden handshake for the London Welsh flanker because when Australia pitched up at the Arms Park a few weeks later he was out of the side.

Wales again won by a big margin and the Australians, making an eight-game journey around England and Wales, failed to breach the home team's defence. Edwards was back as captain – although Shell would win a first cap when the skipper's hamstring gave out in injury time – and saw his team lead 12–0 at half-time through four Bennett penalties. It had been a surprisingly nervous Wales performance, as if conscious of not having beaten a major touring team at home for 15 years. The forwards dominated the rucks and lineouts and Windsor, succeeding the often-criticised Jeff Young, marked his full debut with three strikes against the head.

The second half was a different, brighter story. A scintillating piece of adventure led to the first try, with J.P.R. Williams and Gerald Davies, now a Cardiff player, galloping from the shadow of their own posts and the ball passing through numerous hands before Windsor's hack went into touch a couple of yards from the Australian line. With the crowd still on their feet, Quinnell took the ball into a maul and Dai Morris emerged to score on the short side. Quinnell and David were relishing the opportunity to run at their opponents and link up with their backs and Williams set up an overlap for Davies to score the second try. The final score rounded off a perfect day for Windsor, who ran in from the 22[8] after Hughes cut inside and found support from Glyn Shaw and David.

The 1974 Five Nations season was to be the last of Clive Rowlands's reign as coach. In January, he offered his resignation to the WRU, which announced its intention to identify a successor in time for him to assist in the final two games. Depending on one's outlook, it was either a campaign in which the only defeat came in controversial circumstances, thus robbing Wales of another championship, or it was a season of diminishing returns in which an unimpressive opening-game victory was followed by three matches without a win.

Before the games began, Wales had spent a week fearing that the career of Phil Bennett could be at a premature end. Suffering from back pain, he was shocked when hospital doctors in Swansea told him to prepare for the worst following a spinal examination. Further opinion was sought at Liverpool's Royal Southern Hospital, where he was told that the risk to his health was only marginally greater than that of any other player. He was immediately back in training and fit for the start of the championship.

A dour 6–0 success in the opening match against Scotland in Cardiff was something of a reality check after scoring 86 points against the autumn tourists. The only try of the game heralded the

8 This was the year that rugby went metric, with the 25-yard line replaced by a new equivalent.

start of the distinguished international career of Pontypool flanker Terry Cobner. His place on this occasion was down to a shoulder injury to Tom David, but it was never to be seriously threatened, fitness permitting, over the next five years. Cobner, named Welsh Player of the Year by the end of the season, was celebrating his 28th birthday on the day of the game. His chance of playing for his country had appeared to be vanishing as quickly as his hair, a physical trait he believed made the selectors even less likely to select him. His appearance gave him an avuncular air, but opponents around the world would discover that he was no soft touch.

It had been ten years since he had first worn a Wales jersey, picked for the national schools side while at West Monmouth Grammar, which later produced Graham Price. While training as a teacher at Madeley College in Stoke-on-Trent, he played club rugby for Walsall, but was back in Wales by the late 1960s to join Pontypool, helping their rapid ascent. 'He was a very difficult opponent because he was short but very strong,' says David, denied more caps for Wales by Cobner's excellence. 'I had a lot of respect for him.'

The triumphant moment of his debut arrived in the 22nd minute. Edwards advanced to the blindside after a Welsh heel against the head, Bennett fed Gerald Davies and he cut inside two defenders. As he was stopped short of the line, he flipped the ball to the conveniently placed Cobner. The overall performance of the back row, where Mervyn Davies had been asked to lead the pack, was the most satisfactory aspect of a victory that was preserved by a couple of trademark JPR tackles. Wales, with the direct Ian Hall picked in the centre to complement the more delicate Hughes, had their attacking ambitions undermined by seeing Bennett constantly back tracking to retrieve long Scottish kicks.

Had Dublin offered less blustery conditions, Ireland's Tony Ensor might have kicked Wales to defeat in their next game. Instead, the Five Nations' run of 15 consecutive home victories came to a halt when the Welsh snatched a 9–9 draw, courtesy of Bennett's late penalty. The Irish full-back hit the target with only three of nine attempts and the home side were left debating the decision to play Mike Quinn at fly-half instead of specialist kicker Barry McGann.

The Welsh selectors, meanwhile, had given first caps to London Welsh winger Clive Rees, following the withdrawal of Gerald Davies with a hamstring injury, and to Cardiff centre Alex Finlayson. Hughes had asked to be left out to concentrate on his medical studies, but Finlayson's 27 tries in the season for his club would probably have earned him selection anyway. Quinnell was dropped from the second row for Swansea's Geoff Wheel, a factory production engineer who had only taken up serious rugby two years earlier.

Wales spent much of the game on the back foot. Before Bennett kicked his equalising penalty out of the mud on the left side of the field, their only six points had come in the first half after Bennett switched play and JPR set up J.J. Williams outside him.

The inconsistent performance of the Welsh team was mirrored by uncertainty among the selectors, who changed both second-row forwards for the home game against France. Quinnell and Cardiff's Ian Robinson came in, while Neath's Walter Williams only retained his place up front when Barry Llewellyn's potential return was thwarted by a dose of flu. Bennett came close to missing the game because of a similar ailment, but declared himself fit on the morning of the game. He had been told he could catch pneumonia if he took the field and John Bevan had already been informed he was starting – and Keith James summoned as a replacement – when Bennett changed his mind and stated his intention to play. 'I felt sorry for John and Keith, who must have thought I was a real jerk,' admitted Bennett, forced to spend the next four days in bed. His performance betrayed his lack of health and it was only after two kicks were charged down that he began to settle by connecting with a penalty. He failed to spark his midfield and a try for Jean-Pierre Lux, far too easily executed, helped France towards a 7–3 lead. By the time half-time approached it was 13–9, a Bennett penalty and Edwards's dropped goal cancelled out by two successes for French stand-off Jean-Pierre Romeu.

Slender, with a fulsome moustache and thick dark hair, Romeu needed only the beige raincoat to complete the Inspector Clouseau look. There was no buffoonery about his play, though, as he skilfully kept the ball close to his pack, where second-rows Alain Estève, the

'Beast of Beziers', and Elie Cester were threatened in their dominance only by Mervyn Davies. It was the ability of J.J. Williams to extricate himself from an apparent dead end that sent Wales in on level terms. By the time the ball had meandered its way along the line to him 40 yards out, Williams appeared to be running out of room. A quick grubber kick changed all that. Racing outside Roland Bertranne, he bounced the ball off his knee from the 22, leaving full-back Jean-Michel Aguirre for dead and taking advantage of a perfect bounce to ground the ball.

When Williams speaks, his delivery is quick and direct, reflecting his style of play. Explaining the origins of his trademark move, he points out, 'I was a right winger but I had to play on the left. I can kick the ball with both feet but I couldn't sidestep as well off my left as off my right, so I had to chip ahead. That is more or less how it came about. It was an obvious ploy half the time. I scored so many tries from it. Typically, some of the Welsh people thought I should take on the full-back, but I thought that if I chipped it I would definitely score. I used to practise kicking a lot as an outside-half, so it was easy. I find it quite bewildering when professional players can't do it. You have to know when to accelerate and decelerate, to wait for the bounce and control it.'

But his move against France was not to be the launch pad for victory, even after Bennett's third penalty with ten minutes to go gave Wales the lead. The final statement of the game was made by Romeu, who dropped a goal after number eight Walter Spanghero jumped to win possession. The 16–16 scoreline meant Wales's run of consecutive Five Nations wins at Cardiff had ended at 11, but the season's results meant that Clive Rowlands could still win the championship in his final game in charge at Twickenham.

An old Rowlands stalwart, Delme Thomas, was back for his own international farewell. Although only 31, he had announced his retirement before the season but had been persuaded back by Llanelli on Boxing Day to fill their need for a lineout jumper. So well had he performed that he would earn one more cap, at the expense of Quinnell. Swansea's Roger Blyth won his first cap at full-back, courtesy of JPR's aching knee ligaments.

England's only point of the season had been a draw against France, but as the sun above the Twickenham stands cast long shadows across the pitch, it was the home forwards who shone, despite the efforts of Windsor in winning six strikes against the head and losing only two. English locks Roger Uttley and Chris Ralston even showed their handling skills before David Duckham cut in from the right to open the scoring after ten minutes. Five minutes later, a penalty by fly-half Alan Old stretched the lead to seven points.

The opportunism of Mervyn Davies brought Wales back into the game when he seized on an untidy tap by Ralston, kicking ahead and diving on the ball for a try converted by Bennett, whose 40-yard penalty produced a 9–7 half-time lead. It could have been a greater cushion had J.J. Williams held onto a vital pass, but England were back in front 13–9 after the stork-like figure of number eight Andy Ripley picked up at the base of the scrum and charged across the line.

Now came two pieces of officiating by Irish referee John West that helped ensure Wales were beaten by England for the first time in eleven years. First, Bennett broke into space and was about to send Gerald Davies in for a try when West blew to bring play back for an obstruction perpetrated by the English. Bennett's penalty was scant consolation for the loss of a possible six points. Then, after Old had kicked England's lead to 16–12, Wales got the ball to Williams on the wing. He kicked ahead and, in the opinion of most people in the stadium and watching on television, beat Duckham and Peter Squires in the race to touch the ball down. West was apparently too far away to give the try, even though television replays supported the claims of the Welsh players, who were incensed enough to mount a football-style protest.

Would-be conspiracy theorists pointed out that the result of the game, West's first international appointment, guaranteed that Ireland won the championship, although no one seriously believed that the Five Nations was open to the kind of corruption rife in European club football around that time. Instead, Max Boyce captured the prevailing Welsh mood by writing of a charitable home for 'blind Irish referees', while West went on to a distinguished 15-year career in international rugby.

J.J. Williams is unforgiving. 'It was farcical,' he argues. 'I scored the try, looked back and he was on the halfway line. I had even winded myself by landing on the point of the ball. Duckham and Squires both said, "No try." Bastards. We ragged the English boys for four months on the Lions tour. I felt sorry for Clive that he went out on a losing note. Back in the hotel we presented Clive with a tankard and he was bloody heartbroken.' Mervyn Davies believes the earlier failure to apply the advantage law was the more critical moment and said of his outgoing coach, 'I can't recall ever seeing a man quite so angry after a rugby match.'

Victory would have prevented the reign of Rowlands ending with three years without an outright championship after three had been won in the first three years. Yet it might also have given a false sense of the health of the team over the previous couple of seasons. Davies sensed that Rowlands was 'undoubtedly tired and drained of ideas' and felt that the 'fire in the belly had burned low'.

Rowlands admits, 'I think six years was too long as an amateur coach. I should have gone after four or five but somebody had to be there during the transition. Some of the games we lost were bloody close and we should have beaten the All Blacks. That was my biggest disappointment.'

Davies also believes that the pressure Bennett felt in succeeding Barry John was contributing to his inconsistency and affecting the Welsh performance. Ironically, it was the one game that Wales lost during the season – the finale at Twickenham – in which Bennett gave one of his best performances and took his points total for the international season to thirty-six.

Volunteers are needed to man Cardiff's ambulances during a 24-hour strike by 90 staff, whose claim for an extra efficiency payment of £2 per week is being resisted by the local health authority. The volunteers are required to have a driving licence and first-aid experience, but union representative George Jones scoffs, 'Many of them just want the glory of the driving the ambulances.'

When it came to selection for the British Lions tour of South Africa, Phil Bennett had done enough to earn selection in the fly-half position, along with England's Alan Old. Bennett was one of nine Welshmen chosen for captain Willie John McBride's party, the reduction on the numbers of 1971 reflecting the transitional period in which Wales found themselves.[9] J.P.R. Williams, Gareth Edwards and Mervyn Davies were the only Wales representatives remaining from the previous tour. Joining them were wingers J.J. Williams and Clive Rees, who benefited from Gerald Davies's unavailability, centre Roy Bergiers and forwards Bobby Windsor and Tom David.

Rugby was by now the only major sport not to have isolated South Africa and those picked for the tour found their participation in such a controversial event being questioned. The Wales Against Apartheid Campaign had written to a dozen top players asking them to refuse to tour. The letters, whose signatories included future Labour leader Neil Kinnock, urged the players to 'follow the bold lead already taken by a few of your colleagues' and to 'show the world Wales does reject apartheid'.

Flanker John Taylor might have refused to face the Springboks at home four years earlier, but turning down a selection that represented the scaling of a peak in their sport was beyond most players. Mervyn Davies explains, 'Some people demonstrated against us and said we shouldn't go, but I told John Taylor, "You went in 1968 and didn't make yourself available after that. You have been there and seen it first hand. Let me go and when I have seen it maybe I will think the same."' The final comment that Davies makes on the subject, though, is the most accurate reflection of the state of mind of most players: 'I just wanted to play rugby.'

David, whose dilemma before accepting his invitation was his various offers to play rugby league, was one of the most unexpected selections. 'A lot of people said I had a great chance but you never believe things like that,' he says. 'All those established players in their national sides were playing well. Hearing I was picked was the most

---

9 On a related note, *Rugby World* magazine failed to name a single Welshman among its top five players of the year, a stark contrast to only two years earlier when four of the nominees were from Wales.

magical phone call of my life. But then one of my biggest regrets was that after playing the first three games I pulled a hamstring. I missed five games and was out of the Test team.'

While the accomplishments of the 1971 party in New Zealand, and the style in which they were achieved, may stand at the peak of all Lions tours in terms of romance and success against the odds, nothing can match the simple ruthlessness of the results of the 1974 team. Under the management of Alun Thomas, a former Wales player, selector and tour manager, and the guidance of the Irish duo of coach Syd Millar and captain Willie John McBride, 21 of the 22 games were won, with only a draw in the fourth and final Test denying the Lions a perfect record.

According to Bennett, the foundation for the tour's success was laid in the first nine days of training at Stilfontein, a venue that resembled 'a wet Saturday night at Maesteg's bus station'. The preparation was so intense that he recalls the forwards 'nearly reduced to tears'. David adds, 'A lot was down to the quality of the training. We had the two best trainers and the two worst together in what we called pods. In mine, there was Andy Ripley and J.P.R. Williams – a 400 metres runner and the fittest full-back in the world – and then there was me and Bobby Windsor, who were not the best trainers. But it worked.'

Among the Welsh contingent, the tour helped the trio of JPR, Edwards and Davies confirm their standing as the best in the world in their positions. Bennett felt he saw Edwards achieve a greater maturity in his game as the Test series progressed, while he himself took the opportunity offered by the injury to fly-half rival Old. His 26 Test points and overall tour tally of 103 saw him move further out of the shadow cast by Barry John's reputation.

J.J. Williams rounded off his first full season of international rugby by elevating himself into the elite of the game. After the first Test had been won 12–3 courtesy of Welsh boots – three Bennett penalties and an Edwards drop – Williams scored two tries in each of the second and third Tests as the Lions unleashed a quality of rugby to which the Springboks had no answer, recording final scores of 28–9 and 26–9.

'The tour was huge for my game, without realising it at the time,' says Williams. 'I didn't start well because I picked up a knee injury and then we didn't move the ball much. It was all about the up-and-under. The whole party was fast and we used to do horrendous sprint sessions, even for me. We did 300- and 400-metre reps and Fergus Slattery would stand next to me in every session. If I took it easy he would beat me. Some people can't handle the intensity of rugby every day while you are on tour, but I loved it. I wasn't playing many matches but then I scored six tries in one game [the 97–0 win against South-West Districts] and that helped me get into the Test team. By the second Test we had a bit of supremacy, Gareth started kicking into the box and I scored a couple of tries. In the third Test we were confident enough to move the ball out and some of our moves were a bit modern for them.'

By the time the final game was drawn 13–13 in Johannesburg – where Slattery had a late attempt ruled out and J.J. Williams was tackled two yards short of a dramatic winner – the tour had achieved a level of infamy because of the frequent outbreaks of violence. The Lions gave as good as they got, invoking their '99' call, a battle-cry intended to combat the home team's reputation for rough play and fears about the leniency of the South African referees. At the first hint of trouble, the call would go up and the Lions would wade in as a unit, working on the principle that no referee was likely to send off the whole team. 'Confrontation was everything,' J.J. Williams says. 'They wanted to sort us out before first Test and we were determined to do it to them. It was quite brutal.'

Most notably, the series boiled over in the third Test in Port Elizabeth, the 'Battle of Boet Erasmus Stadium', where the South Africans became increasingly uninterested in fair play as the series slipped away from them. J.P.R. Williams's remoteness from the heat of the forward battle was not going to prevent him from fulfilling his responsibility to his teammates. Hair worn in a headband, adding to the air of a tribal warrior, the sight of JPR racing half the length of the field and launching himself, fists swinging, into the fray turned him into public enemy number one. 'It was a one-in, all-in philosophy,' he explains, although admitting that the particular incident is 'not something I am proud of'.

Skipper McBride adds, 'JPR was a bit different. He would have liked to have played in the forwards and he loved the hard stuff. We would have the odd thug come out and try to take out one of our key players and my attitude was, "We're not going to have this. We will sort it out ourselves and get back to playing rugby." The South Africans realised you don't mess about with these guys and there is no point getting mixed up with them. JPR loved taking people on and when this was suggested to him he wanted to know if he could sort out three or four of them in one go.'

After throwing a couple of rabbit punches at Natal's Tommy Bedford in a later game – retaliation for having his hair pulled and his head kicked – Williams was even described by the local media as 'the biggest thug' ever to tour their country. But it earned him even greater respect among his teammates. 'You would go and fight tigers with JPR,' recalls Windsor. 'Flipping roll on, he would die for you and he would die for the team. If anyone gave you too much rough play you always made sure you got the bastards back.'

In Wales, disparaging comments about their heroes were dismissed as bad grace on behalf of a losing team. Fans were far more interested in toasting the success of the six Welsh representatives who played in all four Tests – Edwards, Bennett, Davies, Windsor and the two Williamses. Such achievement also whetted the appetite for the next season of internationals, with J.J. Williams recalling, 'I couldn't wait to start playing for Wales again and take on the players I had been on the Lions tour with.'

13

================

ALL THE YOUNG DUDES

'We were just told to go out and play our normal game.
We'd had a good run-out in the Welsh trial, where the
Probables had scored about 40 points, and we took that
confidence into the French match. We dominated them'
– *Graham Price*

Wales had no more influential journalist during the period
covered by this book than John Brinley George Thomas, the
long-time sports editor of the Cardiff-based *Western Mail*. JBG, it
was thought, could get a player into the Wales team with an aptly
penned phrase. When it came to the subject of the new national
coach, he laid out his demands. 'Coaching should concentrate on
new attacking ploys or the rehabilitation of the standard methods,'
he wrote. 'One expects to see the Welsh midfield players moving
ahead from their Twickenham display, providing there is an
improvement in the forward play.'

In other words, he was demanding innovation, yet a concentration
on the fundamentals of the game; increased productivity of the backs,
while building a stronger platform within the pack. Not much to
ask for really.

Thomas's demands sum up the expectations with which the new
coach could expect to be saddled. The three men who had declared
their willingness to bear such a burden were former captain John
Dawes, Lions coach Carwyn James and Newbridge's David Harries.

It quickly became a two-horse race between the first two, yet Dawes explains that James's candidacy had taken him by surprise.

'By 1971, I had been involved with the Wales squad for a long time and I was 31. There were rumours that when Clive Rowlands finished I would be offered the job. I had thought Carwyn would take over and then I would follow, but Carwyn got himself involved in Plaid Cymru, which some people didn't like. It seemed clear I would follow Clive so I thought I would have a break from international rugby. I retired as an international player and stayed on as a coach for London Welsh. I knew what was coming and that I would be spending a lot of time up and down between London and Wales. I was eventually appointed by a committee meeting, but Carwyn's name was mentioned as well. I thought he had already been blown out. Had I known he was still interested I might have said, "Don't consider me." I could have waited.'

James's downfall, according to some sources, was his notion that the coach should have sole control of selection. Such an idea, which would have spelt the end of the 'Big Five', was akin to an American professing a sneaking admiration for communism during the age of McCarthyism. Dawes can't vouch for the exact sequence of events but says, 'What Carwyn wanted was no interference. He couldn't say that in Wales without being condemned. It was the WRU prerogative to appoint the coach and selectors.'

James would end up in exile, coaching in Italy. Delme Thomas, his captain at Llanelli, says, 'I have great respect for both men but I would have loved to see Carwyn as Wales coach. He was one of the best, but the Welsh set-up didn't want him. He wanted to run it himself. In that respect he was 20 years ahead of his day.'

Those familiar with Dawes and predecessor Rowlands understood that they would be experiencing a very different approach. J.P.R. Williams believes that the time was right for such a change, saying, 'Clive was a great coach, a totally opposite kind of coach to John. It worked for a while but when Clive finished everyone had had enough of the ranting and raving and smashed doors and wanted another way of thinking. Clive's time had come to an end and John was a bit cooler.'

Gareth Edwards adds, 'Clive had been all about emotion and was good at pinpointing the basics of the game, but year on year everybody else improved and spent a bit more time preparing. Therefore, you had to counter that by working a bit more yourself and John was the man for that. He had always been a very shrewd tactician. But he still didn't try to over-complicate our approach. He emphasised that they were our decisions on the field. We would go in with a plan but he knew we might have to change it.'

Dawes admits he could never have emulated Rowlands because 'I never had that motivating capability.' He continues, 'I saw that if I was going to develop as a coach it would be along the Carwyn line: get them playing as you know they can play.' His desire to improve techniques would be aided by the improvement in facilities at Afan Lido. New grass pitches meant that the sands were used less frequently, while squad sessions reflected a thoughtful teaching environment rather than resembling an army assault course.

Edward Nevin, a leading professor at University College, Swansea, says that 'only incurable optimists could fail to view the [economic] scene in anything other than dismal terms'. He warns that colliery closures now make Wales too dependent on the general British economy for providing local employment opportunities.

With a new coach came a new captain. John Dawes was in the camp of those who felt that leadership placed too great a burden on Gareth Edwards. 'I felt that as captain he would try too much himself and take more responsibility, especially when things went wrong. He was getting bogged down and it affected his judgement. I thought, "How am I going to take the captaincy off him?"'

Dawes needed an experienced player whose respect among teammates was beyond question. And no one was revered more than Mervyn Davies. Tom David purrs when he recalls, 'His bravery was unquestioned. Everywhere you went, that guy went over the top. He was always there at rucks and mauls and he would take so many kickings it was not true. But he wouldn't whinge, he would just get up.'

Dawes continues, 'Merv became the obvious person and the first one I told was Gareth. He was very, very disappointed but I explained and he accepted it because it was Mervyn. What could have been a problem didn't arise.'

Without any hint that the subject rankles with him, Edwards offers an objective view of the issue of whether the captaincy adversely affected his game. 'I wasn't aware of it,' he says, 'although possibly it did. I never felt as if it was a burden, although I had some of my better games when I didn't have the captaincy. Possibly, when I was ready to have the captaincy they took it away from me. But I was very proud to have been nominated in the first place.'

Davies, meanwhile, had become one of the most recognisable personalities in the team, a dark, drooping moustache adding an air of lugubriousness to his other distinctive physical attributes. And he felt that his game was evolving, assuming a greater responsibility for setting an attacking tempo. He recalls, 'When John Taylor and Dai Morris departed, people like Terry Cobner and Trevor Evans were totally different players at flanker. I was senior and now I could dictate to them. I said, "Right, I am going forward and you can hang back a little bit." They were dogged and could do the dirty work I was doing before. Quite often with a ruck ball situation, I used to be the man on the ground, but now I was receiving the ball and making a few yards – showboating if you like.'

Having played under Dawes for so many years at club and international level, Davies found a certain comfort in becoming his on-field lieutenant when he was offered the position after leading the Probables in the season's trial. 'John was running my life from the age of about 22. My only time away from him was with the Lions in 1974. He had a massive influence on my attitude towards the game.'

The captain and coach's deep understanding of each other's philosophies and foibles meant they were well suited, like an old married couple. Dawes knew he could trust Davies to carry his instructions onto the field, while Mervyn was happy to relinquish some of the captain's traditional tactical duties to a coach who epitomised the new thinking in the sport. 'Gareth had been captain for the third time in his career and he tried to do everything, basically,' Davies says. 'The coach needs his man as a go-between him and players and my relationship with John had gone on for years. It seemed the logical choice to have someone he knew to pass on instructions.'

Explaining the demarcation of duties, Davies continues, 'Three-quarters of an hour before the game the coach was gone. Then it is down to you as captain, although for me the worst part was speaking at the dinner afterwards. You had to be responsible for carrying out the coach's wishes but if things weren't going right you had to have enough self-confidence to think, "Let's change it." Most of the time that didn't need to happen and the most important decision was who was kicking at goal. I used to say to Phil Bennett and Steve Fenwick, "Which one of you is it today?" They used to take it in turns.'

J.J. Williams adds, 'Mervyn had the respect of everyone and he knew the game. As soon as we stepped on the field, Mervyn took over, although he had people like Gareth and Phil behind him controlling events.'

Of course, there would be occasional differences of opinion. Davies, a pragmatist in his approach to rugby, had accepted the captaincy by telling Dawes, the romantic, 'I will take Wales on the pitch to win. Club games are for fun; at international level victory is the aim. Nobody should expect to see Wales playing like performing seals under me.'

Davies explains, 'If 50,000 people turned up to watch, that was their business. Once we had established a winning lead, then they could hope for some exhibition stuff, but my first instruction to the backs would always be, "We'll give you the ball – use it to get points on the board." We would come off the field winning by about 20 or 30 points and John would say it was not good enough. He was joking but there was a serious edge to it. He'd say, "Let's improve on that, go higher each time and aim for perfection."'

Dawes expands on that by saying, 'My philosophy was that I wanted to win well, whether it was by one point or twenty. We would not mind if they scored four tries as long as we scored five or six. Merv was his own man and if he tended to play a little bit tighter it was because he felt we had not done enough up front to release the backs. He was a little more cautious than I might have been, but he wanted to be sure of it.'

The first Welsh commercial radio station, Swansea Sound, is finally launched, despite a several-month hiatus caused by the three-day week restrictions, which has delayed the delivery of equipment to the £112,000 studios. The station has been recruiting local on-air talent, learning from the experience of Radio Clyde, whose imported presenters struggled with the pronunciation of local place names.

Before Mervyn Davies was named to take his place at the head of the Welsh team, the first game of the international campaign was a fixture against Tonga, the highlight of a ten-game tour that began with a win against East Wales before turning into a series of defeats. With no caps on offer and Wales selecting only those who had not gone to South Africa with the Lions, Gerald Davies took charge of a 26–7 win. Bridgend's Steve Fenwick and Llanelli's Ray Gravell teamed up in the centre of a senior Welsh team for the first time, with Alex Finlayson scoring twice from the wing and Aberavon's John Bevan and Swansea's Trevor Evans getting eye-catching tries from fly-half and flanker respectively. Echoing Japan's visit a year earlier, the most enthusiastically received score was the 45-yard run by Tongan winger Talilotu.

The next game was more serious, but not as much as a game against the All Blacks would usually be. Having agreed to tour Ireland to support the Irish Rugby Union's centenary celebrations, New Zealand had also scheduled a visit to Wales. Strangely, though, their game against the home nation would be on a Wednesday afternoon and, despite being against a full-strength team, would not have full international status. It seems incongruous now, when so many caps are awarded for fleeting appearances as substitutes against even minor nations, that a full-blooded 80 minutes against the fiercest scrummagers in the world was not considered sufficient to earn a first cap for new prop forward Charlie Faulkner.

As a consequence, Welsh preparation was non-existent. J.J. Williams recalls, 'It was all a bit last-minute. JPR came back from America for the game and we didn't even have a squad session.' It was not enough to deter a capacity crowd calling in sick or taking the day off in order to watch Wales, led for the last time by Edwards, go down 12–3. Phil Bennett missed five of his six attempts at goal, while the home pack was constantly back-pedalling and Ian Kirkpatrick scored the only try of a generally unsatisfactory occasion.[10]

As 1975 dawned, Davies was confirmed as Welsh captain and Dawes was faced with his first real test, an opening Five Nations contest in Paris. If the coach and selectors, who now included Clive Rowlands, wanted to make a statement to mark a new era, they did so emphatically by picking six uncapped players among the total of nine changes from the last full international. Davies admits that the influx of new men assisted in establishing 'his' team. 'The hardest part of being captain is that one minute you are an individual in a team and next minute you are in charge. It is difficult not to be one of the boys. You have to take a step back and change your mindset. I did it consciously because I had to take the role seriously. I had an air of authority with the new players, which helped.'

Bobby Windsor adds, 'When we first all played together in Paris, Mervyn was brilliant. He settled everyone down and, of course, he was a rock-hard man himself. In those days, when you got the ball and went down it was like being in a combine harvester, but Mervyn led from the front. And John Dawes was nice and easy as a coach, no hollering and shouting. He would just talk to you plain and simple and tell you when things were not as they should be; all calm and collected.'

There had clearly been a whiff of magic in the room when the selectors met in Cardiff's Angel Hotel to pick a team that would provide the foundation for the next half-decade of achievement. The most eye-catching decision, especially to those not paying close attention to the season in Wales, was the preference of the bearded, stocky figure of Bevan in the number 10 shirt, which had appeared

10 The tour ended with another Barbarians contest, this one at Twickenham, where Mervyn Davies scored the equalising try in a 13–13 draw.

destined to belong to Bennett for some years. The Llanelli man's miserable game against New Zealand had weighed more heavily in the minds of the 'Big Five' than his summer heroics with the Lions and it was Bevan who had been picked for the Probables in the final trial, helping them to a 44–6 win against Bennett's Possibles. One reporter pointed out that Bevan had enjoyed an afternoon in an 'armchair' compared with Bennett's day in the 'hot seat'.

Dawes decided he wanted the less static play and greater ability to release the backs that Bevan could offer. A physical education teacher at Neath Grammar School and former Welsh Schools cap at Under-15 and Under-19 levels, Bevan was to be compensated for the heartbreak of that late exclusion from the Australia game a year earlier. 'That was my biggest disappointment,' he said. 'To get so near was exciting enough, but then to drop out was extremely sad.'

Meanwhile, Trevor Evans was rewarded for his efforts in the two unofficial internationals by retaining his place at flanker. The announced team was also notable for the introduction of two combinations that would serve Wales so well in future years. In the centre, Fenwick and Gravell, having been overlooked for the now-injured Ian Hall and Roy Bergiers against the All Blacks, were given the chance to bring their complementary qualities of guile and vigour to bear on Five Nations opposition. At prop, Faulkner and tight-head Graham Price were given debut caps, flanking their clubmate Windsor and bringing the Pontypool Front Row to public prominence. 'They are all my boys,' said their club coach, Ray Prosser. 'I nearly cried with joy when I heard they were selected.'

The selections solved a mystery that had taxed the more experienced players during quiet moments in South Africa. J.J. Williams explains, 'We had the nucleus of a team but we needed more. We often sat on the Lions tour and said, "Where are we going to get the ball from? We need some scrummaging." Bobby said to us, "I have got just the guy in Charlie Faulkner, to which we replied, "Who is he?"'

That question was answered by the events of a famous January afternoon, although the day began inauspiciously for the new Welsh skipper. Davies's nerves about his pre-match team talk had prompted him to script his address. 'Carefully and laboriously I wrote down every single thing I planned to say, complete with underlinings and exclamation marks,' he recalled. Yet when it was time to step forward, his cue card was nowhere to be found, forcing him to ad-lib: a method he never changed.

His words seemed to have the desired effect and within four minutes one of the new men had screamed his arrival in international rugby. Edwards gathered the ball from a two-man line and his hurried attempt at a dropped goal sliced towards the corner, where the misjudgement of French centre Jean-Pierre Lux allowed the blond figure of Fenwick a reward for his persistence in following up the kick.

'I was absolutely gobsmacked,' he remembers, the moustache that accompanied him throughout most of his Wales career now conspicuously absent above a smile that rarely takes its leave. 'Paris was the most difficult place you could go for your debut, but I scored after four minutes – a marvellous try from a yard! I was still trying to get over the noise and everything and then Merv gave me the kick. I was so chuffed about the try I didn't give a shit about the conversion and it nearly hit the corner flag.

'Bertranne in the French centre had played about 30 games and Ray and I were getting our first caps. We were shitting ourselves. Over all the noise before kick-off I heard one voice. It was Bertranne. "Hey, Fenwick. Me . . . swoosh." [Makes swerving motion with his hand.] My arse was going, but I went, "Me . . . smack." [Punches his palm.]'

Fenwick remains a hearty soul who, while discussing his route into the Wales team, breaks off at regular intervals to crack jokes with staff at the recruitment agency he runs in Cardiff. It was his arrival at Caerphilly Grammar School that represented the first step towards international rugby. 'If they caught you in the yard with a football they put a knife through it,' he says. 'I was probably a better soccer player than rugby and I would have played it had it been down to me, but you were stifled out of playing.'

Having 'started off at hooker and worked my way back', Fenwick recalls playing at flanker in a final Welsh schools trial, with future Wales winger John Bevan lining up at number 8. 'I scored three tries and I thought, "I have got to be in." Then this guy put his arm around me and said, "I don't want you to be too disappointed but you are not very big." I didn't get picked.'

When Fenwick did win an international shirt it was a white one, playing flanker and full-back for the English Colleges while studying at Borough Road College, west of London. Back in Wales for a teaching job – which put paid to plans to join his college pals at Wasps – he played in the centre for junior club Beddau. 'Then I had one game for Aberavon against Pontypridd. I was the "missed pass" all day. I said, "Can I get the ball now?" and they said, "No. Can you step back a bit?" In those days it was beer tickets, not money, and the captain came round to me and said, "Ah, you won't be here next week," and didn't give me a ticket. Half an hour later they asked me to play against Northampton and I said, "No. You can sod off." I went to Bridgend, where they were playing attractive rugby. Things happened quickly and in no time I was in the Wales training squad. I had quite a good game against Cardiff's Alex Finlayson and I was picked for Wales B. Then I was in the team. One minute I had been watching Gareth and JPR as a student and next minute I was in there.'

Having made an impact after only four minutes, Fenwick would remain a fixture in the Welsh midfield over the course of thirty internationals. He was never a dazzling runner in the style of a Duckham or a Davies, but his consistent contribution in all areas helped those around him shine, just as John Dawes had done previously. He assesses his own strengths as, 'Reading the game, knowing when to pass and when to kick. My legs weren't fast but my brain was fairly active. I could do the basics and I did a lot of work. Every night of the week, bar one, I used to run on the roads and practise sprinting. It probably put a yard on me and made a difference between making a break or not. Nine times out of ten I would be in the right spot at the right time. I was not a sprinter like JJ, but I made a lot of fucking tries for him.'

Alongside Fenwick for the next few years, with the notable exception of the 1977 season, was a man whose passion for his country became as well known as his strong, bearded jaw and the juggernaut-style running that earned him twenty-three Wales caps and another four for the British Lions. Ray Gravell had almost failed to make it onto the field for his first international. First of all, J.J. Williams had woken in the early hours on the morning of the match to find his roommate packed and ready to head home, saying that he was too nervous. Later, after changing into his kit, Gravell disappeared to the lavatory to be sick and spent 15 minutes singing the songs of the Welsh folk musician Dafydd Iwan. He had to be pulled out and sent to the pitch by Derek Quinnell.

Such exhibitions of nerves and nationalistic pride from Gravell would become part and parcel of life in the Welsh dressing-room. Carwyn James said that 'no one more Welsh ever played for Wales', while Tom David explains, 'What Ray had, apart from his strength, speed and determination, was this enormous passion – for Llanelli and for Wales. When we had our team talk before Llanelli faced the All Blacks there was Grav with tears running down his cheek.'

Gravell explained, 'All that matters is pulling the red jersey over your head. Nothing beats playing for Wales. It is, and always has been, a privilege of the few, something to treasure for life.'

Dawes says, 'You might have some players who would lose a bit of confidence, but you knew it just took one good run and they would be back in it. Ray was a perfect example of that. He was such a worrier that he would go to pieces and you would have a job to get him on the field. It was essential for him to get involved straight away and we made sure he did. Then off he went.'

Gravell's life, tragically cut short in 2007 by a heart attack at the age of 56 following a long fight against diabetes, had begun in Kidwelly, in Carmarthenshire. It continued in Mynydd-y-Garreg, where his old road has been renamed in his honour. On the rugby field, fierce competition forced him to give up playing at scrum-half and he eventually fell under the spell of Llanelli coach James, commenting, 'I do not think I was that good a player, but Carwyn made me think I was a world-beater.'

Buoyed by such guidance, Gravell – a lineman for the South Wales Electricity Board – broke into the Wales team. There, his ability to challenge defenders head-on, tying up large numbers in the tackle, meshed perfectly with Fenwick's eye for capitalising on the gaps created by such surges. 'We hit it off because we were both unselfish players,' says Fenwick. 'We decided that we would play for each other, cover each other's mistakes. In club matches at Llanelli, Ray would smash into me and say, "You all right, Steve?" We were very physical and I don't think anybody got the better of us. We might not have been the purists' first choice, but for effectiveness it worked. If you have people like Phil Bennett, Gerald and JJ, who weren't physical, well, we had to do a lot of tackling for them.'

David recalls Gravell as a 'wonderful man' and explains, 'He was such a strong ball carrier. Every time he had the ball you knew he could stand on his feet and you could go and get it from him. Someone like Roy Bergiers, on the other hand, would go down and there would be a ruck. Ray was a smashing guy. I moved back to captain Pontypridd and we were playing Llanelli at Sardis Road. I am going through my team talk, being fairly animated and saying things like, "If you get Phil Bennett in a ruck make sure you turn him over." I am swearing and ranting and raving and in walks Ray. He says, "Tom the Bomb. What a wonderful man. Play really well for him," and he walks out.'

J.J. Williams is well placed to assess the pairing of Fenwick and Gravell inside him, saying, 'Grav was a superb player. He was not popular with some at the time because he was not the classical English centre. It was all blood and guts, but he had superb pace and his hands were good, even though Phil only used him on the crash ball. Grav would get carried away emotionally sometimes and want to kill someone instead of passing the ball out. Carwyn always used to say to him, 'Give the ball to JJ." We played a cup game against Swansea and he actually passed the ball to me over the try-line. I caught it but I was almost over the dead-ball line. "Carwyn told me to pass it," he said.

'Steve Fenwick was a nice foil for everyone, not the quickest, but his timing was superb. He needed good players around him. John Dawes had been a slightly better passer but Steve was a better kicker and a strong tackler and a grafter.'

Clive Rowlands sums up the duo by saying, 'Fenwick and Grav could create room by knocking people over in tight areas. They were good, skilful players as well, not only strong down the middle but they could put players over for tries.'

In Paris, after a few further scores – including a French try by winger Jean Francois Gourdon and a Fenwick penalty – it was a typical contribution from the new pairing in the centre that helped re-establish the visitors' lead after 32 minutes. Receiving the ball from Bevan, Gravell burst through a tackle. Fenwick then fed Gerald Davies, who cut inside and saw the ball advanced by Mervyn Davies, flipping the ball for Terry Cobner to complete the move. Fenwick converted and four minutes later Michel Taffary failed to deal with a grubber kick by J.P.R. Williams, allowing Gerald Davies to hack forward and win the race to the touchdown.

Wales's 17–7 half-time lead had been earned by their forward dominance, the basis of which was that first international gathering of the Pontypool Front Row. 'I thought we did well in Paris,' Price would say later. 'Bobby may have had some reservations: Albert Estève's punches from second row were hardly intended to improve his looks. Eventually Bobby decided enough was enough and when he got the opportunity he booted Estève in the mouth.'

Meanwhile, Edwards looked more able to take advantage of the pack's success without the worry of captaincy draped around him. His top-spin kicks punished the opposition and his try, after France had pulled back three points, was a trademark effort. The forwards ripped possession away from the French following a lineout and he seized upon the loose ball to slide past a tackle to score.

Alongside Edwards, fly-half Bevan performed neatly enough to justify his elevation, including a try-saving tackle on Taffary, and it was another of the new caps, Price, who rounded off the game with a flourish. Having teamed up with Geoff Wheel to halt French centre Jean-Pierre Lux at the Welsh 22, Price led the charge of red shirts in pursuit of the ball after Wheel hacked it downfield. J.J. Williams overtook him to scramble with Taffary for possession, but Price continued to follow up, completing his 75-yard run by picking up and flopping happily over the line. He had just enough energy to celebrate by tossing the ball into the air. 'I just followed up in support, and it didn't occur to me when I set off that I would eventually score.' But he adds generously, 'If you look at the replay, you will see that the next two men up there in support were Bobby and Charlie, who caught the ball after I threw it up.'

It was a grand way to complete a memorable first game for the new leadership team of Dawes and Davies. While the coach cautioned that 'we won't see the best of this team until March', the skipper reminded his men that they should celebrate hard, but then come quickly down to earth to prepare for the next match.

> British Railways causes a row by announcing its decision to scrap plans to make Cardiff its Western Region headquarters, a development that would have housed a 2,000-strong administration staff in a 17-storey office block near the city centre. Extreme union demands on manning and salary scales are blamed.

Against England, an unchanged Wales team was unable to win more than an even share of possession, but the combined efforts of Gareth Edwards and his back row were largely responsible for the visitors to Cardiff having little to show for their endeavours. The lusty boot of Allan Martin provided an early lead and the first try came from what was already becoming a familiar routine: Gravell took the ball on the scissors from Bevan, straightened and passed to Fenwick, and his overhead pass was run in by J.J. Williams. After another Martin success, Gravell helped set up a try as half-time beckoned. Quinnell, a 25th-minute replacement for the injured Wheel, got the ball back from a maul created by the centre's thrust and it ended up wide on the right for Gerald Davies to finish. Martin converted and it was a happy captain who gathered his team around him during the interval.

Mervyn Davies saw his team's work in terms of a three-act drama and, at 16–0, the England game was going according to the script. 'The first few minutes is about testing and feeling out the opposition,' he says. 'The second phase is about knowing where the weaknesses lie and starting to exploit them. The last bit is domination. Unlike Dawesy, I was safety first. A lot of the time I would take the kick-off and tell Phil or whoever to put the ball between the posts so it went dead and they had to drop out to us. That meant we were receiving the ball in their half and would try to stay down there for ten minutes. It used to work most times and in the last half-hour it would be safe for the fly-half to do whatever he wanted. It was one area where John and I disagreed, because I always played my rugby more negatively than positively.'

Graham Price continues, 'We had a game plan based on percentages in the first half, picking up penalties. We would gradually expand our game and in the end we saw those great tries. There was always an air of expectation and the fans knew it was going to happen, but they just didn't know when.'

On this occasion, though, Wales failed to exploit that final period against a beaten English team, unable to fulfil Dawes's vision of expansive, attacking rugby. Instead, they seemed to throttle back and a better team than their opponents might have scored more than the four points they gained via lock Nigel Horton at a lineout. It took until the 79th minute for the home team to complete their 20–4 win when the ball was worked left through Bevan, Evans, Windsor and Martin before Gravell's half-break cleared the way for Fenwick.

It might not have been a convincing second forty minutes, but after two one-sided wins with a side supposedly in a rebuilding phase, there were smiling faces all round the Arms Park as the final whistle sounded. Yet a man who, only a few weeks earlier, had appeared integral to the fortunes of this Welsh team would be wearing a furrowed brow for a few more months yet.

14

STAND BY YOUR MAN

'The way it was with selectors in those days was that if
you messed around you were out' – *J.J. Williams*

There were plenty of Welsh players in the mid-1970s whose
backgrounds equipped them to put the slings and arrows of
rugby fortune into perspective. Gerald Davies, Gareth Edwards, Ray
Gravell and many others knew all about the hardships of life in the
mines, having seen their fathers become ingrained with coal dust and
stooped by back-breaking work. They had heard tales of accidents
and fatalities deep underground.

As 1975 progressed, no one needed that wider outlook on life
more than Phil Bennett. He, perhaps more than anyone in the squad,
knew that the game of rugby should not be treated as life and death,
regardless of the cornerstone it provided for the average working
Welshman. He remembered the mental scarring inflicted upon his
father after he'd seen a work colleague boiled alive in a pit of molten
metal at the local steelworks in Llanelli. And, far more recently, he'd
had to endure his own family tragedy. But still, the twisting path his
rugby career was taking at this time offered the sternest possible test
of his level-headedness.

It was a career for which doctors originally held out little hope
after discovering that he had been weakened at birth by a gland
disorder. Born and raised in Felinfoel, a collection of cottages either
side of the Carmarthen–Llanelli road, he spent every spare moment

on the local playing field proving the worthlessness of such medical opinion. Promising at both forms of football, his rugby master at Coleshill Secondary Modern played him in every position in the backs, creating the versatility that was to serve him well early in his Wales career. Meanwhile, Cardiff City, Bristol City and West Ham showed an interest in his soccer skills and he was invited to play for Swansea's junior team.

'They had some wonderful players and it was enjoyable,' he recalls. 'Swansea asked me to play another game the next week, but my local youth rugby team was playing a match the same evening. Rugby was my number one sport by then and combining the two was crazy. It was killing me playing two games on a Saturday. I had to make a decision and I chose rugby. One regret is that I didn't go away somewhere for a week and test myself against more talented soccer players. I could run up and down all day and I might have made it as a grafter but some of those guys were geniuses with the ball and I didn't have their skills.' Despite the decision to concentrate on the oval ball, it would still be Swansea's Vetch Field where he could be found in future years when injury sidelined him from rugby duties.

Although always one of the smallest players on the field, Bennett appeared in the Welsh Schools Under–15 team and captured the attention of Llanelli, who offered him a game when short of players, and Aberavon, for whom he turned out six times. It was Llanelli where his affection lay, ever since his father had taken him as a boy to see a dramatic Scarlets victory at Swansea. After training with the club he committed himself to their cause. That was despite the shock of experiencing what he called the 'lunatic antics' overseen by fitness instructor Tom Hudson, whose sessions included tackling tree stumps.

Thus began a first-class rugby career that brought a rapid elevation to the Wales squad. His first cap owed much to the quick thinking of Llanelli teammate Norman Gale, who ripped off Bennett's tracksuit trousers after the zip stuck when he was called upon following a late injury to Gerald Davies in Paris. Further appearances were down to his ability to fill a variety of positions, which was some compensation for being part of the same generation as Barry John, the team's undisputed number ten.

Bennett explains, 'I was kept out by a genius but I trained hard and gave it my best shot and the selectors said, "Hang on, perhaps you can do a job in the centre or on the wing." The big thing was not to throw your toys out the pram if you weren't fly-half. Squad sessions were very important and I remember on one occasion we did all kinds of tests, like sprints over 20 metres and 200 metres and pull-ups. If you came out with good results the selectors would notice.'

Bennett admitted in his autobiography that he had been 'relieved' at John's early retirement, although he adds, 'I wasn't automatic to take over just because I was reserve to him. There were some good outside-halves who were going to fight for it.' The first two years during which he could consider himself a Wales regular included highs – Llanelli and the Barbarians against the All Blacks; the Lions in South Africa – and the lows of some inconsistent displays, the 1972 Test against New Zealand for example.

Two seasons later, it was another match against the All Blacks that provided a crossroads in his career. Although the early-season game against New Zealand was not considered an official international, the selectors were unforgiving of a performance in which he kicked poorly, failed to move the ball smoothly and was blamed for missing a tackle that led to the only try of the match. What the general public did not know on that day was the story that provided the backdrop to Bennett's display. Only a few days before the match, he and his wife, Pat, had lost their first-born child, Stuart, who had died after only a few hours. Bennett 'withdrew into a shell' but the couple agreed that playing in the game could provide an important release from his grief, while the selectors, aware of the situation, chose not to suggest he stand down.

Meanwhile, Bennett's livelihood was being threatened by proposed job cuts at the same steelworks that had employed his father and, as well as lingering fatigue from the Lions tour, he had a nagging knee injury. 'Playing that day was the biggest mistake of my rugby career,' he confessed. 'From the moment I stepped on the field I didn't want to know.' For several weeks, Bennett battled with the feeling that he should walk away from rugby completely. Not only had he lost his desire to drag himself to the ground, but hadn't it been rugby that had kept him thousands of miles from home throughout Pat's pregnancy?

'To have that happen to your family, which is the most important thing in your life, for Pat and I to lose a little baby boy, well, that knocked me back and knocked us back as a family,' he recalls falteringly. 'Oh God, even today I can't describe what it was like. Rugby meant very little to me for weeks and months after that. But then it was rugby, the boys urging me to come down to training, that helped me realise life had to go on.'

The unforgiving Welsh selectors promoted Aberavon's John Bevan for the new Five Nations season, preferring his ability to see openings for teammates over Bennett's more instinctive ability to create his own breaks. J.P.R. Williams says, 'John Bevan was a real outside-half. He was not flashy but he never left you in trouble.'

Steve Fenwick, who would become accustomed to playing outside both Bevan and Bennett, ventures, 'They were different guys to play alongside, but both equally talented. John would take people on physically and set things up, a back-row's dream. Phil was individually brilliant and sometimes you couldn't read his game. John would say before a scrum, "I am going that way and will take that player on." Benny would say, "Well, let's see what happens." When you played with him for a while you knew what he was going to do. Both had their pluses, but the press would always go for Phil because John was not flamboyant.'

The 20-year-old 'Centreplan' scheme to redevelop land between the heart of Cardiff and the docks as a new city centre is finally shelved. During two decades of dithering, debate and public inquiries, Cardiff City Council and their partners, Ravenseft Properties Ltd, have seen the cost of the regeneration climb many times over to an unmanageable £100 million.

After two Five Nations victories, there was no question of John Bevan losing his place for the third game of 1975, the trip to Murrayfield. In the end, he probably wished he had stayed at home. Scotland's pack proved too strong, especially in the tight, where captain Ian 'Mighty Mouse' McLauchlan was a force, using his diminutive stature to dip low and force his opposing tight-head to ease back. Mike Roberts was back in the Welsh team after Derek Quinnell dislocated a shoulder, but the pack was unable to protect their halfbacks from a torrid afternoon, while opposing scrum-half Doug Morgan forced them further back with accurate kicking and landed nine first-half points.

Bevan had little opportunity to continue the encouraging start to his international career, suffering a dislocated shoulder after 26 minutes. Six minutes later, Wales lost Fenwick with a broken jaw after he had kicked two penalties. Phil Bennett and Roger Blyth were the replacements, but the Lions fly-half never appeared to catch up with the pace of the game. His kicking was inaccurate, including a vital missed penalty from 35 yards, and his running too often took his team down dead ends. Scotland went further ahead through an Ian McGeechan drop five minutes from time, but a late Welsh lifeline materialised in injury time. Edwards ran a short penalty; Ray Gravell, Terry Cobner and J.P.R. Williams moved the ball onto Gerald Davies; and he slipped inside three men and switched the ball back for Trevor Evans to barge over. Visions of 1971 flashed in front of the eyes of many of the 104,000 crammed inside Murrayfield, but Allan Martin's conversion attempt lacked the accuracy of John Taylor's and Scotland completed a deserved 12–10 victory.

Captain Mervyn Davies recalls coach John Dawes saying only 'hard luck' in the changing-room, but adds, 'After a poor result we all knew that the next training session would find us totally committed to the idea that we were not going to have our colours lowered again.' In the next squad session, Dawes told his men, 'The Scots won through our mistakes. Some of the three-quarters dropped too many passes.'

The approach of Dawes was to invite input from all his players. 'In the next squad session we would talk about what we hadn't put into practice and why not,' he says. 'Everyone would have their say. Some would say a lot and some would say nothing.'

Bennett was fully aware of the blame being placed upon him. 'I had what I can honestly admit was a stinker. It was my worst performance for Wales and if the selectors had cut short my international career forever that afternoon I would have had no complaints.'

Yet, in the continued absence of Bevan, he was entrusted with the fly-half duties for the final game against Ireland, a match that presented the opportunity of an outright championship victory if Wales won and Scotland went down at Twickenham – which they subsequently did. Bennett, with his international career perhaps one bad performance away from termination, responded with a display that he had never bettered in a Wales jersey. Working from the solid base of a dominant pack, he prompted his team to a 32–4 victory – an overwhelming attacking exhibition that had BBC commentator Nigel Starmer-Smith gasping, 'One wonders how they ever lost a game this year.'

Bennett, who kicked expertly, ran with intimidating intent and was involved in most of the game's highlights. His thirteenth-minute penalty was one of only two first-half scores, the second coming on the half-hour when Windsor retrieved the ball from a ruck and found Edwards, who broke for the line, skipped out of one attempted tackle and squeezed between two more men to touch down. The starting point for that try had been Ireland's inability to give scrum-half John Moloney clean ball against the ferocity of the Welsh pack, where Geoff Wheel had returned from injury.

The try that opened the second-half scoring was out of the Barbarians' back catalogue, with 13 individual contributions. J.P.R. Williams fielded a kick inside his own half, Gerald Davies took the ball on the scissors and Terry Cobner, Edwards and Martin continued the momentum to set up a maul. Wheel to Edwards, a diagonal run, Bennett on at speed to Roy Bergiers – deputising for Fenwick – and another maul was formed. This time the ball was worked to the right through Edwards, Bennett and Gravell before Davies dived into the corner. Stunning stuff.

Bennett, who had converted both tries, landed another penalty before three more scores took Wales to their biggest win over Ireland since 1907 – an inauspicious way for Willie John McBride to exit the international game. Yet even he recalls with fondness that 'it was a privilege to play against those Wales teams'. He adds, 'Individually, they were tremendously gifted players, but they were also a team. When you think of Gareth Edwards and Barry John, JPR and Gerald Davies, my God! And that's without mentioning their forwards. You couldn't fail to admire them.'

Skipping forward with confidence, Bennett earned the admiration of the Arms Park by creating a break for J.J. Williams, who passed to Windsor on the charge. As full-back Tony Ensor made the tackle, Faulkner jogged up in support to take the ball over the line. Bergiers then tied up the Irish backs in a maul, allowing Edwards, Bennett and JPR to outman the opposition and set up J.J. Williams. Finally, Bergiers beat the tackle of Mike Gibson and sped past two more green shirts for a try after a move that once again featured the running of Bennett, who kicked the conversion. The exhibition rugby went a touch too far when Edwards attempted a blind reverse pass to Bennett and Willie Duggan intercepted to score. But, apart from leaving the perfectionist J.P.R. Williams ranting at his scrum-half's casualness, it mattered little. Not only had Wales become champions in Dawes's first season as coach, they had clinched the title in the grand manner he craved.

> Having qualified for the last eight of football's European Championship, Wales turn down an invitation to stage the home leg of next spring's quarter-final at Wembley, where capacity could be double that of Cardiff's Ninian Park. Welsh FA secretary Trevor Morris says, 'It would be treason.'

That autumn's trip to Japan was as notable for high jinx off the pitch as events on it, such as the night when Phil Bennett, Allan Martin and Graham Price came close to arrest after 'borrowing' a set of bicycles. The tour did, however, help develop team spirit among a relatively new combination of players and gave John Dawes the opportunity to learn more about some of the fringe figures.

It was also a chance for some of the newer faces to stamp their personalities upon experienced teammates, as Steve Fenwick recalls.

'I remember Mervyn having his fag before kick-off and saying, "You. Go and get me some tie-ups." I said, "Fucking get your own tie-ups, Merv. I don't get anyone's tie-ups." He still thought of me as a new boy and thought I was being stroppy. But we always had good team spirit. We had a good mix with six or seven new players and some who had been there a few years. They were super heroes to some of us, but we found out they were only as good as we were.'

It was a full-strength squad that won all five games in Japan, including victories of 56–12 and 82–6 in the unofficial Tests. In the second of those, Bennett scored two tries, two penalties and ten conversions. Back home, proof that Bennett had retained his place ahead of a fully fit Bevan in the pecking order was provided by the announcement of the team to play Australia a few days before Christmas. Life was good again. He felt that the summer speed work he had done with the Carmarthen Harriers athletics club had furthered his game, while the happiest occurrence of all had been the safe arrival in late November of his son Steven. But then events took another turn.

The day before the Australia game, he was forced to withdraw from the side because of a foot injury he had suffered during a Welsh Cup game, in which he'd been a reluctant participant because it coincided with Pat's return from hospital with the new baby. 'Carwyn James asked me to play because they were desperate, down to the bare bones,' he says. 'A guy landed on my right foot and we put stitches in it. I felt I couldn't do Wales justice.'

But on the Monday after the international, Bennett turned out for his club against Bath at Stradey Park. 'I said to two or three of the committee that I wanted to play. They said, "Phil, you can't play. You dropped out of the Wales game." But I was confident I could run and I had good guys outside of me to do the kicking. I had one of my best games. I was running like a lunatic. I don't think the selectors were very pleased to see me running around like a two year old on the Monday evening, but I was an amateur and I wanted to enjoy myself.'

In the meantime, Wales had not done too badly without him against a team whose only international success on their tour would be in the final game against Ireland. Earlier in their trip, the Wallabies had been beaten by Cardiff and held to a high-scoring draw by a Llanelli side who would win their fourth straight Welsh Cup during this season.

On their way to a 28–3 victory, Wales were dominant in the lineout and effective in wheeling the scrum whenever Australia looked like winning the ball. Mervyn Davies and Trevor Evans were outstanding in the loose and Gareth Edwards had a clinically effective game, while Bevan was once again solid and the defence never gave their opponents a sight of the try-line.

A scrappy opening featured some schoolboy-like miscues and a warning for both sets of forwards for rough play. Clive Rees, called up because of Gerald Davies's sore hamstring, seemed to be impeded as he raced to touch down before Fenwick scored with a mis-hit penalty. The try that gave Wales a 9–3 half-time lead resulted from Edwards sending a nonchalant kick over his shoulder into the left corner, creating pressure from which Wales won a five-yard scrum. When the ball squirted out, Edwards picked up and, with fantastic pace over the first two or three yards, brushed past full-back Paul McLean to score.

The absence of Davies gave J.J. Williams the opportunity to demonstrate how effective he could be in his preferred position on the right-wing and he took it emphatically with three second-half tries. 'There were some who said I shouldn't be in the team at all, that I had lost my zip,' he said. 'So I went out there to show them.' The first try came after 51 minutes when Bevan created an overlap by looping outside Gravell's surge.

After Allan Martin tidied up at a lineout to set up Bevan's drop, the full force of the Wales attacking game was unleashed. With 11 minutes left, a tapped penalty from deep launched a flowing move that was only ended by an ankle tap on Rees inside the 22. From the lineout, Edwards hoisted a high kick, Fenwick and Mervyn Davies pressured McLean and the ball ended up with Evans, who attacked the line and gave J.J. Williams another run into the corner. Williams completed his hat-trick in the final seconds after Evans picked up on the run at the back of a lineout and passed to Gravell. Once the ball was in the hands of Williams there was no stopping him: a chip ahead from the 22, another touch to push the ball over the line, and a successful race to complete the score as fans spilled onto the pitch.

And so to the Welsh national team trial, even more of an anomaly since a full international had been played two weeks earlier. Quite what the selectors expected to glean from this scuffle was a mystery. When the teams were named, the line-up that had faced Australia was selected en bloc for the Probables, while Bennett was asked to lead the opposition. He played a club game against Penarth on New Year's Day, two days before the trial, but then pulled out with what was reported as an ankle injury. Swansea's Dave Richards was called up and more eyebrows were raised in Bennett's direction.

On the evening after the trial, Bennett's phone rang and he found *Daily Mail* journalist Peter Jackson informing him that John Bevan had been named for the opening Five Nations game against England, with Richards on the replacements' bench. Bennett had officially gone from being first-choice for his country to, at best, third in line. John Dawes confirmed as much, while also attempting to diffuse rumours that Bennett's demotion was the selectors showing their disapproval of his recent absences. Dawes said it was 'purely a matter of straightforward selection', and added, 'We were very impressed by Bevan's performance against Australia, but so were we by the efforts of Richards in the trial. It follows that at the moment Bennett rates as our number three and I am sure we have made the right decision.'

In the *Western Mail*, J.B.G. Thomas described Bennett's omission as 'ungracious on the part of the selectors' and said he was sure the injury was genuine. 'His word has to be accepted,' he stated. It is worth noting, however, that by the time Bennett wrote his autobiography, *Everywhere for Wales*, in 1980 he appeared to have forgotten the reason that was given at the time and said that he had been suffering from flu. He summed up his attitude to the trial games by writing, 'Hardly anyone wants to play in them . . . it's not surprising that Wales suffers a chronic attack of influenza around trial time.'

Dawes would later comment that he and the selectors erred in not telling Bennett that he had not even been named as a replacement because they thought his mindset was not suited to coming off the bench. Bennett described the situation as a 'Welsh Watergate cover-up' and would comment, 'I have never understood why a member of the Big Five didn't have the common courtesy to give me a ring to explain why I had been dropped. I had no doubt that my withdrawal from the Australian match and the final trial had caused my relegation.'

Events more than 30 years old can clearly be clouded by time and when interviewed for this book Dawes recalled that Bennett had, in fact, been kept informed. 'Bevan was a different type of fly-half and could make better use of the three-quarters. Phil hated the bench and would rather not be involved at all. We didn't want Benny as replacement because of what had happened in Scotland. He was told all this beforehand. He was disappointed but happy with the scenario.'

The recollection of team captain Davies focuses on Bennett's argument that he had been given a public dressing down. 'I am not privy to this day to exactly what happened but basically that was a discipline thing,' he ventures. 'He played for Llanelli when he said he was carrying an injury, although John Dawes would also say that at the time John was distributing the ball better than Phil.'

Bennett's Llanelli teammate, J.J. Williams, has this view of the episode. 'He was always a bit of a strange one, Phil. He would sometimes not turn up for squad sessions and was never a great trainer anyway, although he became one in his later years. Earlier he was hopeless – a fatty boy. John Bevan was pushing and John Dawes liked him. There were a lot of arguments in those days, especially among the London Welsh boys, that Phil wasn't taking his club form into internationals. In the end, Phil left himself wide open and they dropped him. But it became a bit farcical in the end.'

Williams is referring to the final twist in the story, which came with the Twickenham game only six days away. Bennett was preparing for a Sunday with his family when Llanelli secretary Handel Rogers, the WRU president, phoned up and asked him to report immediately to that day's squad session because both Bevan (elbow) and Richards (hamstring) were injured. From out of the blue, he was back in the team, and Max Boyce would chronicle events in a song called 'The Divine Intervention'. However, Bennett recalls none of the selectors being able to look him in the eye when he arrived at Afan Lido.

The drama all served to feed the Welsh rugby writers' need for a big story in the build-up to the new season, but a legacy of the episode was the decision that only chairman of selectors Clive Rowlands would speak to the media before games, a policy designed to protect players uncomfortable with the attention of reporters. 'The players felt they didn't want to be bothered going into an important match,' Rowlands explained. Davies felt that the Bennett saga highlighted a more serious issue: the pressure placed upon players to turn out for their clubs, sometimes to the detriment of Wales. 'Clubs want their top men to appear as often as possible in the interests of winning rugby and attracting customers through the turnstiles. Committees should give some thought to players' feelings and allow them full recovery time from injuries.'

Davies was uncomfortable that he had not been more fully informed about the selectors' intentions. He was less concerned about which of Bennett or Bevan was selected – he had confidence in both – but 'as captain I needed to know well in advance and with certainty which one it was to be for he would probably have to control tactics behind the scrum, call the moves for the backs and maybe function as vice-captain. So I was irritated by the selectors' lack of conviction.'

Davies also went on record saying that, if the selectors wanted to discipline Bennett, 'Why did they not do it privately, while covering themselves with a general statement that they were not satisfied with his general fitness?'

If the WRU's communication with their captain left something to be desired, such lack of direct contact with the troops was typical of the time. Steve Fenwick even remembers, 'I'd be driving through the Rhondda and the press would know the team before you and you'd see newspaper signs saying, "Four Welsh stars dropped". Sometimes you couldn't stop and you'd be driving home thinking, "Fucking hell, is that me?"'

To conclude this particular narrative by returning to its central character, Bennett sums it up like this. 'Anything that happened to me after what had happened in the previous year was put in perspective. By then, we'd had a little boy, and that meant more to me than anything in the world. Yes, you get hurt by being dropped but it pales against what is happening in your family life. Rugby was still massively important, but you prioritise things and your family is everything.'

15

═══

THE BIGGER THEY COME,
THE HARDER THEY FALL

'When I'd had 110 stones of the French pack coming at me, I sometimes stood up from a scrum and wondered which planet I was on. I felt like I'd been caught up in a bomb blast' – *Bobby Windsor*

The champions who are revered and loved the most are those whose achievements have been magnified by the presence of an arch-rival; an opponent against whom they have been forced to slug it out over 15 rounds or strain every sinew in a race for the tape. Nothing elevates a winner to greater heights than the broad shoulders of a worthy adversary. Just as the legend of Martina Navratilova, for example, is richer for the presence of Chris Evert, so the feats of the Welsh team in European rugby during the 1970s would have resonated less had France not consistently played Joe Frazier to their Muhammad Ali.

All three Wales Grand Slams of the period were clinched by wins in their final game against the French. In three other seasons covered by this book, France were the only team to prevent Wales winning all their Five Nations games. Scotland, meanwhile, were the only home nation to manage more than a solitary victory over the Welsh.

The denouement of the 1976 Five Nations season was the French visit to Cardiff. With the Triple Crown already secure, Wales were one win away from a record-equalling seventh Grand Slam. Victory for the visitors would leave them needing to beat England at home in their final game to claim their own clean sweep. 'France was always the big game,' says Mervyn Davies. 'They were the best side, apart from Wales. They had a massive pack and all the talent to link it together.'

Steve Fenwick explains, 'France was always my favourite game because I was a fan of that fantastic flair and subtlety of handling and interplay between the forwards and backs. To watch a French side on song is the best sight in rugby. My hero had been their centre, Joe Maso, and I remember a charity game in Glasgow where he gave me his entire kit. There was never more than a few points in our games – it was always hammer and tongs and they were the hardest side to beat. Any player will tell you that once you are 20 points up you lose your appetite; it is the real close games, where you have to pull out all the stops, that you want to be involved in and that you train for.'

France had evolved from the team Wales beat to win the 1971 Grand Slam. They were no longer personified by dashing three-quarters, but by the musketeers occupying the back row and the tiny firebrand marshalling them from scrum-half. Jacques Fouroux, 'Le Petit General', seems an impossible figure in today's bulked up game, 5ft 5in. of passion with a chip on his shoulder almost as big. There was no more incongruous sight than him barking instructions up at the 6ft 6in. number 8 Jean-Pierre Bastiat. Strong around the base of the scrum, he worked energetically to make breaks and set up possession for his powerful pack, a tactic that earned him the disfavour of those with leanings towards the traditional expansive style of French rugby.

Any lack of adventure could be excused, however, by the dominance his forwards enjoyed over most opponents and the springboard that was provided by the back row of Bastiat, Jean-Pierre Rives and Jean-Claude Skrela. By the time France arrived in Cardiff, they'd helped make short work of Ireland and Scotland.

There was no greater admirer of the French breakaway trio than J.P.R. Williams, who was a frustrated flank forward in any case. 'They had a great back row,' he enthuses. 'They were one of the best of all time and, boy, Rives was hard. But France are still the biggest enigmas in rugby. When they are on song they are the best players in the world, but they are so temperamental that you can upset them quite easily. We did that with big hits early in the midfield with guys like Arthur Lewis and Ray Gravell.'

Several weeks before the France showdown, Wales had gone into the first game of the campaign on the back of considerable uncertainty over their personnel. Not only had the Phil Bennett–John Bevan situation been played out very publicly, but Gerald Davies, Ray Gravell and the entire front row had been passed fit only in the final few days before facing England. Graham Price recalled Welsh medical officer Gordon Rowley helpfully prodding the wrong side of Bobby Windsor's injured ribs in his fitness test, while Price himself went through the painful twists and turns of his examination in the knowledge that physio Gerry Lewis was asking him to perform only exercises within his physical capabilities.

Aberavon prop Clive Williams, one of those waiting in the wings, recalls, 'Those Pontypool Front Row boys wouldn't give anything away. Bobby had injured his ribs against us, but they would play through injury and it was very difficult to get them out. They were always viewed as a unit so even if one of them had a bad game they would all still be picked. It made it difficult for others to break in.'

On this occasion, the tight forwards had to settle for an even share of the play against England. The decisive advantage enjoyed by the Welsh was in their loose play and the ability of J.P.R. Williams to ensure they made better use of their possession. England's efforts in the scrum and in defence were let down by their inability to think up a route to the try-line.

Gareth Edwards, brutally efficient with his kicking, scored on 17 minutes after England won a scrum deep in their own territory. A mix-up between scrum-half Mike Lampkowski and Andy Ripley saw the ball clunk off the number 8's heel, allowing the alert Edwards to pick up and drop over the line. Fenwick converted for a 6–0 lead. Then Ripley was caught laughably offside after Edwards fielded a clearance and Allan Martin's hefty boot from the touchline increased the Wales lead. In between two penalties by England's bearded, cricketing full-back Alastair Hignell, Wales scored another try after Mervyn Davies did well to pick up at the base of a disrupted scrum. The ball went along the line, missing JPR when he joined the attack, but as J.J. Williams was being forced out of bounds it was his namesake he found with an inside pass and the full-back powered through two tackles.

The game remained at 15–6 until Hignell pulled England to within a converted try in the 76th minute, but Wales were safe three minutes later. Edwards dropped off the scrum to take a pass by Davies, and Bennett fed inside to J.P.R. Williams on the scissors. With a full head of steam there was no way he was going to be stopped by Tony Neary. The only impediment to his clear run was when David Duckham's attempted tackle clattered him into the posts as he went over the line.

Fenwick recalls, 'Sometimes JPR would just give you a shout and come into the line and very often, especially against England, we would practise moves. Against someone like John Horton at fly-half we just put someone into a gap close to him.'

Having played with seven stitches in his left cheek, Williams emerged from his try-scoring endeavours needing seven more in the right and gave his post-match *Grandstand* interview looking like a walking autopsy. There was no doubt that he was the story of the day. He had made an important barging tackle on Hignell during a period of English pressure and, in becoming the first Wales full-back to score two tries in a game, had taken his total in international rugby to four – all of them at Twickenham. He admits that those games contained extra spice for him. 'I was living in England most of the time I played for Wales and all my mates were English. You feel more Welsh in London than you do living at home, so it felt more important to do well in those matches.'

Despite the individual satisfaction felt by Williams, those in charge of the Wales team were less than effusive about the collective quality of the performance. John Dawes warned, 'We will not win the title if we continue to play like that.'

It was J.J. Williams who seemed to have set his alarm earliest when Scotland visited Cardiff two weeks later, winning the second-minute race to touch the ball down after Andy Irvine and Billy Steele collided in trying to field Bennett's kick to the corner. Watching his opposite number, J.P.R. Williams always felt he was being wasted in the number 15 shirt. 'It is a tragedy Scotland never turned Andy Irvine into a three-quarter. A brilliant runner, he would have graced the centre or wing. But at full-back he lacked the basic confidence under the high ball and in the tackle.'

It was moments like Scotland's equalising try, when Irvine finished off a move by ducking below the attempted tackles of Gerald Davies and Bennett, that prompted such a conclusion – although Irvine appeared to be pushed into touch before grounding the ball. It was only one aspect of a refereeing performance from forty-eight-year-old Frenchman Andre Cuny that was unsatisfactory. His refusal to apply a stricter interpretation of the rules of foul play in the forwards undermined the game and created a nasty undercurrent. Then, his stubborn refusal to leave his first international after injuring his calf meant that he struggled to keep up with the play. He was 50 yards away when he failed to see J.P.R. Williams taken out illegally by Alastair Cranston as he readied himself to receive a certain scoring pass. It is not often that a stadium has been united in its chants of, 'Off, off, off' – all aimed this time at Dr Cuny.

Wales stretched away after two Bennett penalties had given them a 12–6 half-time lead. JPR and Fenwick were key Welsh performers, both defensively and offensively, with the full-back's foray into the line setting up the ruck that led to Fenwick's dropped goal. Then Fenwick crashed into Irvine as he took Bennett's hoisted kick and Wales spun the ball across the field to Gerald Davies. When he went down under a tackle he found Evans peeling around the outside for an unchallenged ten-yard dash to the line. The final try followed Windsor's heel against the head, but there still appeared little threat when the ball came back slowly from a subsequent maul and Bennett passed to Edwards. It was all a bit static, but a dummy and a burst of acceleration left Edwards with nothing but green in front of him and he scored from 25 yards.

Injury to Terry Cobner prevented Wales naming the same team for the third match running and offered Tom David a third cap. 'That was how tough the game was at that time,' David says with resignation. 'The selectors were just picking a team that was winning every week. Once you were out of the side it was very difficult to get back in.'

Reports leading up to the game suggested that some of the Welsh players had more important things to worry about than the fact that none of them had ever won at Lansdowne Road. Several received death threats in letters posted in Dublin, although, unlike 1972, there was no hint of a boycott of the game.

Until the final 20 minutes, there was no guarantee that Wales would come away with their first win in Ireland for 12 years. Mervyn Davies needed all his leadership qualities to keep his pack on top and he was aided by outstanding performances by Geoff Wheel and Price in the tight and a marauding display by Evans on the fringes. As always against the Irish, things got a little fraught and, in an incident that would resonate a year later, Wheel had to be calmed down by Windsor as he threatened Irish prop Phil O'Callaghan.

The luxury that skipper Davies enjoyed in being able to call on a variety of able kickers was demonstrated when Martin connected from 50 yards, and a more functional effort by Bennett gave Wales a 6–0 lead. Ironically, the first try stemmed from a 20th-minute penalty that Martin completely messed up, Gerald Davies advancing quickly to charge down a clearance and following up to score. Bennett also seemed to have lost his radar, banging his conversion against the crossbar, but after Barry McGann's three kicks had brought Ireland back to 10–9 at half-time it was Bennett's boot that stretched that lead back to seven points with only thirteen minutes remaining.

'We've cracked them; let's enjoy ourselves now,' was Mervyn Davies's instruction. With that, Wales unleashed the kind of irresistible sequence of play that elevated this team above one capable of winning only hard-fought, functional games – as per the captain's pragmatic blueprint – into a side that could soar on the wings of John Dawes's beautiful vision. Within the space of six minutes they scored three tries, eighteen points, and were one step away from the Grand Slam.

J.J. Williams says, '1976 was our best period and I think we hit the high spot in Ireland away. They were always difficult in those days and had some very good players. They had recently won the championship and I think that was our best game.' Edwards is in accord with that view, commenting, 'We played possibly the finest 20 minutes of rugby in the whole decade. The quality of the attacking rugby even had the Irish fans standing and applauding.'

Irish full-back Ensor failed to make his mark as he caught Bennett's kick and was swamped by red jerseys. The ball was wrestled back, J.P.R. Williams made a timely arrival on the scene and Gerald Davies was the spare man who scored in the corner. Three minutes on, Wheel charged through after Ireland tapped back at a lineout, creating an opportunity for his team to win second phase ball. From then it was all Edwards, attacking the blindside, kicking ahead twice and capitalising on a favourable bounce. Finally, another show of Welsh dominance. Mervyn Davies palmed back, Edwards passed to Bennett going right and Gravell took the ball on. Looping outside his centre, Bennett received the ball again, dummied to Gerald Davies and headed for the line to score his first international try. There could be no doubt left about his rightful claim to the number 10 jersey. As Dawes states, 'From 1976, Phil began to assert his authority and became a natural leader.'

The Welsh steel industry is in disarray after the British Steel Corporation announces proposals to save £170 million in 1976 through job losses and a reduction in weekend working. A strike of 1,000 employees at Port Talbot closes the plant for three weeks, laying off 10,000 workers, while 4,000 are on strike at Trostre and Velindre. Work resumes when it is agreed that job cuts will be phased in through voluntary redundancies.

Gareth Edwards's record 45th Welsh cap was marked by his emergence at the head of an unchanged team as the Arms Park congregation rose in anticipation of the Grand Slam decider against France. Sheepishly, Edwards turned to toss the ball to a colleague only to discover that they had allowed him to run out alone. He was left flipping ball from hand to hand, the only sign of discomfort he displayed all afternoon. With Wales making more mistakes than in any previous game of the season, he produced his best strategic kicking to stop France taking advantage of such sloppiness.

The Welsh forwards struggled against the mighty Bastiat, whose colleagues were in no mood for taking prisoners. Tom David sets the scene from inside the scrum. 'The French side was always very talented and had flair, but very physical. Once we got on the floor they used to leave a few calling cards, I can tell you. You can't do anything now because you are off or caught on video and they can cite you. Linesmen then couldn't get involved and rucking the player was an accepted situation. Don't get me wrong, I would be doing the same. It wasn't cheap shots; it was just one of those things. If you fell the wrong way in a ruck you used to just count to ten because you knew you were going to get a real leathering. No one said, "Excuse me, let me get my slippers," or "You shouldn't be there." Your back would be like a zebra crossing.'

Hooker Bobby Windsor recalls, 'I played against France five times and had my nose broken five times. They would put the boot through from the second row. When the scrum-half passed, everyone watched the ball and that is when their second rows would step out and boot you in the chops. Flippin' heck. Then after the game they were brilliant and would take us all out.' Quickly reeling off the eight names of the French pack, Windsor adds, 'That is going to be put on my headstone. It was like facing the A-Team. You had to fight fire with fire. If you got away 50–50 you had done well. When you scrummaged against France and charged at them from ten feet away, you couldn't have been in more danger than that.'

Tight-head prop Robert Paparemborde, 'The Bear of the Pyrenees', was a judo black belt, while loose-head Gerard Cholley was a former heavyweight boxer and, at 19st., frequently played like one. On this occasion he stopped short of flooring the four men he once famously achieved in a game against Scotland. 'Pricey had his eyes gouged by Cholley,' Charlie Faulkner points out, forgetting to add that Price had his revenge by biting his opponent's thumb. 'You had to give some back against France,' he adds. 'If you didn't retaliate or hold your own they would walk all over you and give you a good kicking while they did it.'

Several times tempers were barely kept in check, with Price on the receiving end of more rough stuff – eventually to be replaced by Cardiff's Mike Knill, who performed creditably – and Mervyn Davies reduced to limping around on a worsening calf injury. The skipper had suffered a broken blood vessel after being stepped on, but was determined to remain at the helm. Bennett would comment, 'I'm convinced, had he gone off the field, we would have had to settle for a Triple Crown.'

Outside the mayhem of the scrum, the Welsh midfield was tentative. If this Grand Slam was to be won, it would be done so on pride and resolve as much as technical excellence. France were handed the lead after only five minutes when their backs quickly closed down their opposite numbers as they tried to run out of defence. This was why Davies always preached safety first in the early stages. Fenwick was tackled and, as he tried to hold up the ball for a teammate, he fumbled it into the grasp of Jean-Pierre Romeu, who passed to the right for the powerful winger Jean-Francois Gourdon. A conversion from wide gave Romeu his hundredth point in international rugby, although he would miss three penalties later in the contest.

Edwards teased the French deep men with his kicking and Bennett reduced the lead after a lineout offence. Wales's new record-breaker had more tricks up his sleeve, launching a try-scoring move with one of his reverse passes after Davies palmed back from a twentieth-minute lineout. Wheel charged into the defence on the peel and, once Edwards had switched the play, Gravell made a half break, Bennett threw a long pass to Fenwick and J.J. Williams sped into the corner before bouncing up to celebrate a Welsh lead. Another French indiscretion gave Bennett three more points and Martin poked a long touchline kick towards the posts. 'It looks a funny one,' Bill McLaren informed his viewers, but the visitors weren't laughing as they faced up to the fact they had conceded 13 unanswered points.

Romeu made it 13–9 before half-time after Wales obstructed and the home side were denied an early second-half score after Mervyn Davies and J.J. Williams threatened. The pressure, only partially eased by Fouroux's kick to touch, led to further scoring after Edwards flipped the ball to Bennett – that trick pass again – and the fly-half was tackled late by Bastiat. Too injured to take the kick, Bennett gave Fenwick the responsibility and was given a reassuring smile and thumbs-up by his colleague as the ball sailed over.

France weren't done. Gerald Davies hoisted infield and several teammates were offside as they converged on Skrela. The unlikeliest-looking of all kickers, Bastiat, was called forward to attempt the penalty from inside his own half, but his tree-trunk legs, topped by high shorts, barely got the ball inside the 25. A Welsh clearance was instantly booted back and J.P.R. Williams for once couldn't handle it cleanly. Bastiat, Romeu and Pecune combined, Aguirre kicked ahead and winger Jean-Luc Averous was ruled to have beaten JPR to the ball in the in-goal area. Williams looked pleadingly at the referee's back as he walked away, Bennett stood with hands on his head and Mervyn offered a calming gesture to his players. Meanwhile, the television audience was watching a replay showing Williams getting his hand on the ball at least at the same time as his opponent. Even now Williams sounds aggrieved when he says, 'That wasn't a try.' But he adds, 'I think one of the best things about rugby is that if you argue with the referee you are penalised. Everyone knows things go against you, but you bite your tongue and take the rough with the smooth.'

Ten minutes from time, France were whistled for offside at a maul and Fenwick slotted over a penalty from the left of the field. Now it was 19–13, but again the visitors rallied. One of the most iconic moments of the Welsh rugby era was needed to maintain their advantage. Fouroux tapped a penalty, Skrela moved the ball to Gourdon in full flight and he was one step away from a try in the corner when the figure of J.P.R. Williams, with even less regard for his own safety than usual, hurtled into view and barged him into touch, clenching his fists in celebration. 'That tackle would be illegal now,' he smiles. 'Whether it would be a sending off or yellow card I am not sure, but you would still do it because he will score if you tackle him properly. His momentum will take him over. I knew that was a Grand Slam tackle.'

There were still some anxious moments for a Welsh crowd beside themselves with the tension and torture of the moment. Bertranne kicked for Averous in the corner and when the bounce eluded him Aguirre slid in among four Welsh jerseys and claimed the try. This time the ruling went for Wales, with the Frenchman failing to achieve clear downward pressure as Fenwick challenged him. With the final seconds about to expire, Martin barged into Gourdon as he called for a mark and, as France strove to keep the ball in play, the whistle sounded on a Welsh Grand Slam.

None had given a more heroic performance than Mervyn Davies, crippled by his injury yet still winning his share of lineout ball while urging his men to greater effort. 'I was glad that our Grand Slam culminated with a victory for which we had to drive ourselves to the utmost. I was proud of the way the boys knuckled down and remained calm in the face of a furious offensive by the French. The second half seemed endless.'

Recalling the previous Grand Slam team of five years earlier, Davies concludes, 'The '76 side probably was a better team. We had a better pack of forwards because, even in the early '70s, we weren't particularly dominant up front; our strength was our three-quarters. By 1976, we had probably the strongest pack Wales had ever put out so we could dominate possession for long periods, yet we still had the same quality behind the scrum.'

The win marked the completion of the transition undergone since the Barry John-inspired team of 1971. While key men remained – JPR, Edwards, Gerald and Mervyn Davies – the personnel around them had changed. Yet, with the exception of the influx of new caps in Paris a year earlier, the overhaul of the team had been gradual rather than revolutionary. 'It was like a club side,' says the captain. 'The team did change, but like a tropical rainforest. Barry went and Phil just carried on. The squad system helped keep the success going.'

Dawes adds, 'We carried on as it had been 1971. I treated everyone in the same way I had as captain and I expected from them exactly what I had expected all along. Newcomers saw this and fell into that group. All of a sudden we had a new team, all tarred with the same brush.'

The contribution of Dawes himself should not be underestimated. Kevin Bowring, who became team coach two decades later, says, 'Everybody these days thinks of the Welsh coaching job as the poisoned chalice, with the passion, the fervour and what it means to people. John handled it superbly and was one of the most impressive rugby brains I have ever met. When I was national coach I asked him to be an adviser because he was such a terrific rugby thinker.'

The facts of the season are that Wales equalled England's record of 13 Triple Crowns and 7 Grand Slams, while their total of 102 points eclipsed their previous best of 88 in 1910. J.J. Williams sums up the campaign by suggesting, 'It took a year with John Dawes coaching but I think the '76 Grand Slam is possibly Wales's greatest-ever team. Earlier, we had started our squad sessions and gone to Japan and Mervyn said, "We have seven games this season," – which was a lot in those days – "and we are going to win them all." And we did. We had some experienced British Lions and some boys who were now in their second year in the team. We had superb leaders and vital people in vital positions; like the hardness of the Pontypool Front Row and Terry Cobner, who was ruthless. We had good coaching, good organisation and we were happy.'

Wrexham, the first Third Division club to reach the last eight of a European competition, narrowly miss out on a place in semi-finals of the Cup-Winners' Cup when they draw 1–1 at home with eventual winners Anderlecht, after losing 1–0 in Belgium in the first leg.

There was one worrying footnote to the victory over France – made more chilling now by knowledge of events at Hillsborough thirteen years later. During the game at the National Stadium against Scotland, 40 people had required medical attention and more than 400 fans had spilled onto the pitch surrounds because of overcrowding in the lower section of the West Terrace. WRU secretary Bill Clement said it was possible that too many people had been allowed to make cash payment to gain entry at the turnstile, but also pointed out that an excessive number were pressing to get to the front when there was room at the back of the terracing.

One fan, M.J. Slater, said, 'The terraces became crowded around the entrances, making it impossible to move up or sideways. It was an unnerving experience.'

Despite promises that the issue would be addressed for the visit of France, another 30 spectators were treated by medical workers when a similar crush occurred. Fans had been urged to arrive early and make their way to the top of the standing area, but Clement spoke of people 'deliberately pushing down to the front and then climbing the barrier'. To its credit, the *Western Mail* was not content in its leader column to simply laud its victorious team. Instead it pointed out, 'After the Scottish match we warned the WRU that the situation held too many dangers for complacency to be tolerated. Saturday's events prove that the action taken does not measure up to the problem.'

The underlying cause was, of course, the sheer determination of the Welsh public to see their team close-up. It was more than a simple desire to watch great sport. Rugby was the religion to which the people turned in times of trouble and, in the mid-1970s, they needed their gods more than ever.

16

FANFARE FOR THE COMMON MAN

'It was like a breath of fresh air for Wales when we won. Coming back home on Sunday morning was amazing. It meant everything to the people and everybody was happy' – *John Dawes*

Wales had won the Grand Slam for the second time in five years. For most people in the country it was a shaft of joy breaking through a landscape of gloom and hardship. There were some, though, for whom even the highest level of achievement in European rugby was not good enough.

Steve Fenwick says, 'It got to the stage where, because we were winning a lot of the time, we would get criticised for not winning by enough. I can understand that. There was this blind faith in Wales, whatever the circumstances.' And captain Mervyn Davies adds, 'Some people expected rather too much of us at times and thought we should have run the ball from everywhere.'

At the heart of it all was not a desire to knock down those whom the public and media had built up. That was, and remains, an English trait. This was simply a sign of the importance of the national rugby team's fortunes in the lives of the Welsh people. The sport had long formed an important part of their identity; now the results were a source of pride and joy in increasingly difficult times for the working man and his community. As times got harder, it sometimes seemed that the emotional elevation that was needed to lift the nation above the strikes and the shutdowns became even greater.

It was a pressure that the players understood. 'The price of failure in Wales is high,' Phil Bennett wrote at the end of his playing days. 'No other nation honours its rugby players with so much diligent attention and no other crowd accepts its defeats so grudgingly.' Yet even comments like that were born of empathy rather than resentment.

The players knew that fans appreciated it was their own people out on the pitch. The men wearing red jerseys weren't the remote millionaires that footballers, and some 21st-century rugby players, would become. 'They knew you were one of them,' recalls Bobby Windsor. 'I had to take a double shift off from the steelworks to go to squad training. That would have been 16 hours' pay. The fans understood it because they were your workmates. In 1974, I was still getting around on a pushbike and a local garage gave me the loan of a car free of charge. I had it for a week and then Bill Clement said I had to give it back otherwise I would be professionalised. We worked from 7 a.m. to 5 p.m., then we'd go home and pick up our kit and go off training. We never saw the missus or kids.'

Some of the Welsh squad had just as many worries about employment as those cheering them on. Bennett, for example, worked at various times on a building site, as a glorified debt collector for an oil company and for British Leyland before being made redundant at the end of a third spell at his local steelworks. At that point, in the summer of 1975, he publicly pondered moving to South Africa, saying, 'The thought of emigrating arose after my tour to South Africa with the Lions. Several of the players were approached there and the offers were good ones. I would rather stay in Wales if I could get the right job.' That job, a position with Courage Breweries, arrived via an early-morning call to his hotel in Tokyo during the tour of Japan. By the end of his rugby career he was trying to make a go of running his own sports store. 'The Welsh rugby international is by no means offered a golden spoon to feed him,' he would note in his autobiography.

The biggest star of the early '70s, Barry John, was a miner's son who had grown up fully recognising the shadow of tragedy that loomed permanently over that profession. He had seen the suffering of his father after an explosion at his colliery killed several workers. Many Welsh fans had been touched by similar events over the years. Meanwhile, Tom David's memory of his drinking colleagues paying for his father to travel to see his debut game in Paris further illustrates that the Welsh support emanated from the same clubs and pubs where the players spent their time. The fans didn't rely on *Titbits* – the *Heat* magazine of its day – to see where their heroes were spending their nights out.

A victory for Wales, therefore, especially one achieved with style, was a victory for the common man. It was a blow struck, not just against old enemies, but against the adversity that had been creeping over the Principality in the previous 20 years and had accelerated just as the nation's golden rugby generation had been maturing.

As well as the widespread problems of post-Second World War austerity, the end of conflict in Europe had found Wales seeking ways of halting the increase in unemployment that had plagued the country between the wars as industrial development had regressed. The focus was on widening the range of activities upon which the economy was built, so that not so much was vested in the traditional worlds of mining and steel. Although the war had brought forced economic expansion in some areas of Wales, the decline had continued in the south, the rugby heartland. The tinplate industry had only 10,000 workers by 1945, as opposed to 25,000 before the war. The collieries of south Wales had employed 136,000 in 1938, but only 112,000 six years later.

The first ten years after the war brought renewed prosperity and a vast reduction in the numbers out of work. Government assistance led to the establishment of factories and the development of a buoyant manufacturing industry, including a new trading estate in Bridgend that offered 30,000 jobs. Ports such as Swansea and Barry were thriving and a new period of stability was arriving in collieries and steelworks. The entering of the mines into public ownership signalled the death of the old barons, improved labour relations and created an environment in which there would be no major work stoppage until

1972. The Steel Board was constituted in 1951, nationalising the iron and steel industries and adding further to a happier outlook among the working people of Wales. By 1955, unemployment was down to the relatively low level of just over 13,000 and private industry was looking at the valleys as fertile land. The success of the Welsh rugby team, led by the likes of John Gwilliam and Bleddyn Williams, seemed like a natural, inevitable reflection of the wider improving health of the nation.

Yet two decades later, the achievements of Mervyn Davies's men would be seen as an antidote to the national ailments of industrial unrest and mounting social deprivation.

The mid-1950s proved to have been a high point for Wales, economically if not on the rugby field. As the cycle of boom and bust turned to the disadvantage of the country, a period of recession hit in the latter years of the decade. And so unemployment numbers began a new climb. The National Coal Board embarked on a series of pit closures, with 23 collieries ceasing operation in the final three years of the '50s. It was the start of an inexorable shrinking of the industry. In 1960, there were still 106,000 employed in the Welsh mines; by 1970, following approximately ten pit closures a year, that number was a little above 30,000. Between the nationalisation of the industry in 1947 and the fuel crisis of 1974 in the wake of the Arab–Israeli war, 150 collieries sent their last men underground.

Meanwhile, those growing oil prices had increased the importance of the remaining mines and workers felt it was time to make a stand for an improved standard of living. During the strikes in the industry between 1972 and 1974, Welsh miners lined up alongside those from Yorkshire and Scotland as the most militant in Britain in their demand for a 60 per cent wage rise. Despite a brief revival in the mid-'70s, when more mine workers were recruited, the final year of the decade would see the NCB call for ten more Welsh pits to be closed, including Maerdy, the last remaining colliery in the Rhondda valley.

Such developments meant more than mere unemployment statistics. The Welsh workforce shifted geographically as the industrial centre of many Welsh communities disappeared. That often meant a fundamental change in lifestyle, even if the displaced miner managed to find new employment. The north Wales coalfield, which had six collieries in the 1960s but was down to two a few years later, saw much of its workforce cross the border into England, while the southern population drifted from the mining valleys into areas like Newport and Cardiff, where many of the new employment prospects could be found.

The 1960 Local Employment Act was designed to create such opportunities by enticing private industries such as chemicals, artificial fabrics and engineering to the region via tax and rates concessions. The motor car industry was established locally with the Rover plant in Cardiff and the Fisher/Ludlow body works at Llanelli, while the building of the BP refinery in Milford Haven was representative of a growth in the oil industry. Service industries, such as the passport office, arrived in Wales.

Boosted by such activity, the Welsh economy had achieved something of a resurgence by the late 1960s. But the extent to which that revival would be maintained in the new decade was selective and isolated. It certainly did not extend into the heartland of Welsh working life. Rather, the decline in the steelworks mirrored that of its coal-mining brother. After the boom of the '50s and '60s, when demand had been high for steel in the manufacture of cars and other goods, the '70s were a story of contraction. The Ebbw Vale works was closed after years of financial loss. Ebbw Vale's MP was Michael Foot, Labour's Secretary of State for Employment and future party leader, while many Cardiff constituents of Prime Minister James Callaghan would lose their jobs when the East Moors works ceased production. In 1976, the Welsh Development Agency was set up with a £100 million fighting fund, a sum that was increased in 1978 as a result of the Labour government's desire to preserve the support of Plaid Cymru in the House of Commons.

What this shrinking and shifting of the working population meant for the Wales rugby team was that their results and performances took on a greater significance beyond the cosy confines of their sport. As former Wales forward Eddie Butler put it in a 2007 BBC documentary, 'The Welsh side of the 1970s represented the aspirations of the Welsh mining communities.'

Phil Bennett recalls, 'I hated the build-up to games, the Friday nights at the cinema and the Saturday morning team talk, because I was so nervous and didn't want to let the country down. You'd see all the people coming to watch us and you'd think, "My God, we have to win for them."'

John Dawes adds, 'In Wales, because of this passion and intimacy, you felt that if you lost you had let people down. It was a gut feeling, something you would take home with you. The next day when you were going home and going your separate ways, that is the loneliest time and that is when the hurt of losing gets to you most.'

The starkest of all the economic statistics is that by the time the 1976 Grand Slam had been achieved, the country had lost 100,000 jobs in the previous 12 years. On the most basic level, then, there was a huge need for something to which the people of Wales could cling; a source of pride, inspiration and solace. It was a huge burden to place on players who, unlike their highly paid counterparts in other sports, had their own everyday jobs to hold down and families and mortgages to fret about. Mervyn Davies says, 'The expectation of victory and the pressure of the Welsh public was always there and fortunately, most of the time, we didn't disappoint them. There was a tendency to think, "Let's try not to lose today," although we managed to be more positive than that and the coaches managed to bring out absolute confidence in our ability.'

The downsizing of the mining and steel industries meant that local communities at the heart of Welsh life were being eroded. Amid the fragmentation as workers moved to find new jobs, it was the national sport that kept communities together or helped integrate many people into new ones. The population, with their more detached lifestyles, needed that common bond. Rugby had always been important, of course, but with villages and towns dissipating, it was increasingly the national team that became the focus. Mass popular entertainment was taking over from the smaller outlets, such as miners' lodges and church Sunday schools. The shared experience of a Five Nations international, either watched with 50,000 others in the Arms Park or viewed on television and dissected over a beer, assumed perhaps a disproportionate importance.

British society in general had been feeling and showing the effects of early-'70s malaises such as industrial unrest, three-day weeks, power cuts, inflation, an increasingly violent society and mainland terrorism. Bernard Donaghue, a close aide of Prime Minister Harold Wilson, noted, 'The psychology of our people is in such an appalling – I fear irretrievable – state. Meanness has replaced generosity. Envy has replaced endeavour. Malice is the most common motivation.' While that might have held true for much of the population on many days of the week, Donaghue had clearly not been in Wales on a Five Nations day. For a few hours, those growing used to having wedges driven between them could pull together in the same direction and, assuming the result went their way, everything was smiles, optimism and brotherly love. Unless, of course, you were wearing an England shirt.

Kevin Bowring, an up-and-coming player with Neath in the 1970s and a future Wales team coach, says, 'The magnificent effect of that Welsh team brought the whole country together. You knew the players and some people worked close to them. And on a rugby level you have to remember that Wales is very tribal in its rivalry between teams, with all that fervour and passion, but the national team gelled everyone together.'

Welsh historian Kenneth O. Morgan has an interesting perspective on the Welsh obsession with rugby, suggesting that perhaps it stopped the population becoming more militant about the state of their nation. Plaid Cymru had won its first Westminster seat in 1966 and, by 1974, support for Wales's own political party had grown enough for them to return two MPs in the February General Election and a further one – the significant recapturing of Carmarthen – when the country went to the polls again in October. Yet Morgan pondered on 'whether the heady excitement of international days at Cardiff Arms Park, with its emotional cascades of hymn-singing, did not blunt the passion for a more solid and political form of national self-expression'. Instead, he said, 'Beating the English through skill with an oval leather ball appeared to be satisfaction enough.'

Yet once such gratifying results began to arrive and individual Welsh heroes like Barry John, Gareth Edwards and J.P.R. Williams emerged, even more was required of them. 'The biggest pressure was to win by a lot of points,' says Williams. 'People expected us to win and, by and large, we usually did. But we would come off having won by quite a few points and still be criticised.'

Steve Fenwick adds, 'If you start winning, you are judged at a higher level. It became difficult for the players. The press could turn you inside out. Before the Ireland game over there in 1978, the papers were saying that this was my last chance. I was not playing well, not doing this and that. Then I scored 16 points and they said my place was never in doubt. People had short memories.'

According to J.J. Williams, 'There was more pressure on us than ever. If we only won 12–9, well, crikey that was not good enough. I remember someone asking me what my hardest game was. I always said, "The last one," because it was getting harder every game.'

Rugby, as the Welsh national sport, was always going to attract most of the attention of the media and public, especially with the team in the ascendancy. Ieuan Evans, who would be inspired by the 1970s Welsh team to lead his country some years later, says, 'We are a country of only three million people so when the team had so much success it was very easy for it to become a focal point, a means for Wales to be punching above its weight and doing so with total ease. It gave the country identity.'

Meanwhile, other sporting heroes who could have shared some of the burden of national responsibility were thin on Welsh ground. There had been individual champions in the 1960s such as Olympic long jumper Lynn Davies and world featherweight champion Howard Winstone, while David Broome, one of Britain's greatest-ever show jumpers, had been world champion in 1970. On the cricket field, Glamorgan had gone unbeaten in winning the County Championship in 1969, yet Welsh soccer success had been non-existent since they were beaten by a Pelé goal in the last eight of the 1958 World Cup. A brief flirtation with qualification for the finals of the 1976 European Championship finals was never likely to turn the heads of a rugby-adoring public.

Evans was a typically impressionable child at the time and recalls, as a nine year old, being taken to watch the Barbarians–All Blacks game in 1973 by his father John. 'After the first two minutes, well, if that didn't turn you onto rugby and excite you and stimulate you, then nothing would. It was mostly Welsh players that day and their team was sprinkled with stardust. What an introduction.' Yet it was an absentee that day who inspired the future Welsh captain more than any other player. 'My great hero was Gerald Davies. He came from the bottom of our village and he went to the same school as me. I always wanted to be Gerald Davies.'

That affinity with someone who was virtually from the same street was a common theme. Fans who turned up for the big games had often first seen those stars playing for their local school or junior club before following their progress into first-class rugby. Frequently, their first trip to Cardiff Arms Park had been to see a local player who had been picked for an important youth game.

Bonds were strengthened further by the housing of the team for home games in the Angel Hotel, across the road from Cardiff Arms Park and at the heart of the fans' match-day gathering. Players would descend the circular staircases, fight their way through the crowded lobby and walk beneath the arched hotel entrance into the throng. 'We walked over individually or in groups of two or three and got to the changing-room about ninety minutes before kick-off,' Dawes explains. 'They closed Queen Street and St Mary Street and we walked through all the people. They all knew you, but a week earlier in Swansea or Llanelli they wouldn't have a clue who you were. Now they would all be patting you on the back. The closeness of it made it special. It was a physical thing as well, having to go through them. You felt a belonging to them and that you had to do well for them.'

J.P.R. Williams was protected from the weight of the Welsh public by a medical career that kept him in London until he moved back to his current home in 1976. 'I was very fortunate to live in London most of the time because the players in Wales lived in a goldfish bowl. I don't think I could have withstood that as a young person. Nobody knew me in London. It was when I got recognised in Oxford Street that I thought it was time to go home. Gavin Henson has had to go through that same problem. He is a celebrity and it is very difficult to deal with when you are young. Whatever you do is wrong.'

Mervyn Davies had been another of the London Welsh contingent in the early '70s, but his return to Swansea in 1972 put him back among a population who were far more likely to recognise his distinctive figure than the average Englishman would notice, say, Andy Ripley. 'Too much enthusiasm is better than too little, so we all put up with it,' he said. 'But I have often envied Englishmen or Scots who can slink off into the comparative anonymity in London or Edinburgh after a beating.'

As Welsh pride continued to feed more voraciously off its rugby team in times of social and economic hardship, other cultural symbols were being clutched closer to the heart. From the 1970s, increasing numbers of people began learning the Welsh language and the effect of prompting by Plaid Cymru and the Welsh Language Society was to get the BBC to set a level of seven hours of programming in the national tongue per week. Elsewhere, the popularity of folk singer and political campaigner Dafydd Iwan extended far beyond the record collection of Ray Gravell.

Even the world of entertainment, though, could lead back to rugby, as in the case of Max Boyce, whose increasing nationwide success went hand in hand with the Welsh players about whom he sang and spoke with such passion and reverence. His stage persona might have been a caricature of a typical Wales rugby fan – his ego after victory as oversized as the leak he carried onstage – but his elevation into the elite group of British performers was another Welsh triumph.

He not only helped project the Wales team into living rooms and made them part of a wider British popular culture, he helped the Welsh public identify even more closely with their boys, strengthening the belief that the team truly belonged to them. 'I was on national television at the time and had a massive audience,' he recalls. 'Some of the songs introduced new people to the game and players, but that was just an accident because of the power of television.'

What was not an accident, however, was the amount of rugby content in his performances. Anyone tracing the history of the game in Wales in the 1970s could do worse than delve into Boyce's back catalogue of songs, where various important characters, events and matches are immortalised. 'I was just a social commentator really,' he continues. 'I came via the folk clubs and I was writing about whatever was going on in Britain; life as I knew it. Rugby is such a part of the social fabric of south Wales and particularly the valleys that it was inevitable that I wrote about the success of rugby at the time.'

Along with portraits of their heroes, Boyce offered Welsh fans miniature slices of their lives, describing journeys to Murrayfield and Twickenham in stories that, while exaggerated, were easily identified by those who regularly set off from their villages on such crusades. 'People recognised the truth in the songs. They captured the imagination. I had experienced "The Scottish Trip", which you had to in order to write about it. Man's best work in whatever field is always of his personal experience. It did help me that the team was successful, but some of the songs that were equally well known were coal-mining ballads. The mines were being closed down and it was a very emotive time. The press, though, gave the rugby songs more prominence.'

Such was Boyce's synonymy with the national team that when he earned a gold disc for his breakthrough album, *Live at Treorchy Rugby Club*, released in 1974, it was presented to him on the Arms Park field before an international against Australia, which he said was 'like winning my first cap for Wales'.

That was the day when 'Hymns and Arias' first reverberated around the stadium. They are still singing it 35 years later at the Millennium Stadium. 'I was being presented with the gold disc and while Frank Bough was interviewing me for *Grandstand* the crowd behind me started singing,' he remembers proudly. 'Then it spread to the rest of the ground, which was an overwhelming experience. No new song had been sung there for a hundred years probably. As a singer-songwriter, that is the perfect legacy. When a song is embraced by the people like that it is something you can't buy, something no one can give you. Nothing can compare to hearing 75,000 people singing your song 35 years after it was written and people coming up to you and shaking your hand as you walk round the ground.'

In the same year as Boyce's album release, BBC2 featured two plays on one weekend focusing on the impact of rugby on the lives of the Welsh people. On the eve of the Wales–Scotland international, the station aired Gwyn Thomas's *Up and Under*, which showed the effect of an ex-international's reputation on his son's efforts at his local club. Two days later, Ewart Alexander's *Dummy Run*, much of it filmed inside the National Stadium, centred on the reunion of a group of former internationals.

In 1978, the anti-climactic nature of Wales's game in France the previous year was captured by BBC Wales in a one-hour comedy called *Grand Slam*, written by Glenwyn Parry and starring Windsor Davies, fresh from *It Ain't Half Hot Mum*, and Oscar-winner Hugh Griffith. The story follows a group of Welsh fans whose wild weekend in Paris includes rekindling old flames, igniting new ones and, in the case of Davies, missing most of the game while locked in a police cell in his underwear. The denouement of the piece, which has achieved cult status among Welsh fans familiar with such experiences, is the late-arriving Davies lamenting his heroes' lost Grand Slam. Genuine Parc des Princes footage is interspersed with the drama, including the Welsh players arriving at the stadium and examining the field before the game.

In fact, the chaos of the fictional weekend had extended into real life. When supporters learned that several members of the Welsh team had missed their flight home it was another sign that these boys were no elitists, just a down-to-earth bunch who liked a good time as much as their faithful, if sometimes demanding, fans.

17

ANARCHY IN THE UK

'It was not a violent match but it lacked control from
the referee downwards' – *Wales selector Keith Rowlands*

While the people of Wales were still revelling in the latest Grand
Slam, the celebrations were suddenly, brutally, halted by a
near-tragic turn of events. Leading Swansea in a Welsh Cup semi-
final against Pontypool in Cardiff, Mervyn Davies collapsed as he
made an innocuous-looking run in support of his backs. As the eyes
of the crowd followed the passage of the ball, barely anyone even
noticed. It was only when teammates wondered why the captain was
not celebrating their try that attention was brought to the prone
figure. Later, Davies would recall having felt out of sorts before the
game, short of energy and lacking in interest in what should have
been one of the highlights of the season. Yet nothing could have
warned him about the calamity about to strike.

At Cardiff Royal Infirmary, he was placed on a resuscitator before
being transferred to the University of Wales Teaching Hospital, where
it was discovered that he had suffered a brain haemorrhage. When
neurosurgeon Robert Weeks announced the next morning that Davies
was 'fighting for his life', the nation held its breath and said its
prayers. For two weeks, in the middle of which an operation was
performed, every news bulletin was monitored for updates on the
skipper's condition. At last, the crisis abated. He would never play
again, but he was out of danger.

When a life has almost been lost, the fact that a rugby career must end hardly seems like the end of the world. Certainly, Davies himself has lived since retirement without bitterness or regret over missed opportunities. 'Not many people play international sport as captain of their country and win a prize like the Grand Slam,' he says. 'The biggest disappointments were not beating New Zealand in a Welsh jersey, not captaining the 1977 Lions and just the way it all ended. But you take solace in the fact you have done everything else.'

After 38 internationals, Wales would need a number 8 jersey to fit a new man at the start of their 1976–77 campaign. The player who would eventually make the shirt his own was hardly a stranger to the team. Six years after playing his first Test in the red of the British Lions, Derek Quinnell would finally have a place to call his own in the Welsh side. Since touring as an uncapped Lion he had won eight Welsh caps, mostly in the second row, but would soon become a fixture at his preferred position, anchoring the back row for the next four years.

He remembers, 'When I came back from that Lions tour, the guys I was competing against for Wales were all guys I'd been to New Zealand with. We had far more depth than today and we had great talent at the top end. It was frustrating to be in and out but you become philosophical about it. It was not until Swerve had his brain haemorrhage that I had a run of games at number 8, which I enjoyed. But I would rather have seen Swerve out there because he was such a good friend of mine.'

Quinnell knew all about the pressure of being asked to fill the shirt of a prematurely retired hero, having seen Llanelli teammate Phil Bennett's elevation to Barry John's outside-half position. The circumstances of Davies's withdrawal from the sport increased Quinnell's gratitude that it was he who was asked to perform the task of succeeding him. 'He was such a good pal and I was very thankful it was me who was doing it. I know he must have felt it horribly not to play again, but I hope he felt slightly less bad due to the fact that I was there in his stead. Even so, it must have been horrific for him. He was one of the most influential players in the game.'

ANARCHY IN THE UK

Rhymney Valley District Council prepares for war by appointing cash and carry owner Bob Adams as Wartime District Food Distribution Officer, unsurprisingly the first such appointment in Wales. 'I'm not exactly making any plans in advance,' he says, 'but I would be ready.'

The first match of the new season, in October 1976, was not considered a full international, but Wales knew all about the threat that could be posed by their opponents. When they had last met Argentina in 1968, a weakened Welsh team had lost a two-game series in Buenos Aires. But few expected the full-strength Grand Slam winners to be relying on Phil Bennett's injury-time penalty to save them from embarrassment when the Pumas visited Cardiff Arms Park.

Argentina unleashed some exciting attacking play, led by a fly-half, Hugo Porta, who might have been the most talented player in his position in world rugby. He proved a threat with the ball at his feet, manoeuvring the Welsh forwards around the field, and in his hands, frequently breaking out of defence. Wales appeared to have the game won after taking a 17–6 lead through tries by Gerald Davies and Edwards, but Argentina rallied before winger Varela's penalty in injury time produced a shock 19–17 scoreline. But with two additional minutes played, Pumas centre Travaglini was guilty of one of those rushes of blood that British sports fans had come to recognise from his country's soccer players. His short-arm tackle on J.P.R. Williams conceded a penalty and the nature of the celebration between Bennett, Williams and Ray Gravell betrayed Welsh relief at their victory after Bennett slotted the ball between the posts. 'It was one of the hardest matches I have ever played,' was Graham Price's verdict. 'Argentina deserved to beat us.'

Terry Cobner had been the victorious Welsh captain, but when illness sidelined him for the beginning of the Five Nations season, another leader was required. Bennett was at home over New Year when Edwards called him to announce, 'Llongyfarchiadau' – 'congratulations'. Bennett thought his halfback partner was offering seasonal greetings until Edwards explained that Bennett had been appointed captain.

Without underestimating Bennett's ability or subsequent achievements as skipper, J.J. Williams suggests that at that time 'it wasn't that difficult a job to do'. He explains, 'The team talk was done by coaches and the captain didn't have to talk to the press because the coaches wouldn't allow it. But Phil thrived on being captain of Wales, as he did as captain of Llanelli.'

Bennett's first game in charge would be against Ireland, the side against whom he had played some of his best games in a Wales shirt. The selectors' main concern was the back row, where Mervyn Davies had clearly been missed against Argentina, although perhaps that was an inevitable reaction given his omnipresence in previous years. Quinnell had been number 8 for that game but now he lost out to Newport's Jeff Squire, who had played most of his career as a flanker. Cobner's place went to Clive Burgess of Ebbw Vale, who had only taken up rugby at 20 after leaving the merchant navy and had since earned the nickname 'The Steel Claw'. In the front row, the Indian summer of Charlie Faulkner's career seemed to have been halted when Glyn Shaw was selected at loose-head, while David Burcher replaced the injured Ray Gravell, who would end up a season-long absentee.

Bennett 'managed to string together a few sentences' for his team talk, but had no idea that his first game in charge would confront him with an issue never yet encountered by any of his predecessors. Ireland were leading through a Mike Gibson penalty with three minutes left in the first half when the old enmity between these Celtic rivals spilled over once more, with Wheel trading punches with Irish number 8 Willie Duggan. Wheel got in a roundhouse blow and Duggan went down, although in a somewhat delayed manner reminiscent of Noel Murphy eight years earlier. Referee Norman Sanson ignored Bennett's appeal for leniency and made the two combatants the first players to be sent off in Five Nations history.

Bennett believed the incident 'looked worse than it was – just a punch and a slap', but Sanson explained that he had already given the players a warning. Bennett suspected that a recent IRB directive instructing officials to eradicate dirty play had left Sanson with little choice and Wheel departed the field close to tears. Condemnation of the players' action would be widespread, yet the Scottish official did not escape unscathed. Many felt he had exacerbated the ill feeling by failing to take a firmer grip early on in what one Sunday newspaper called 'a primeval affair'.

Gibson's penalty gave Ireland a 6–0 lead, which he restored to 9–6 after Bennett had kicked the game back to parity, but the visitors appeared to be the team affected more by the dismissals. They missed Duggan in the lineout and Wales overwhelmed them in the final quarter of the match to win 25–9. They found pace and purpose and took the lead after Edwards raised a kick and saw his team win possession. Edwards moved the ball left to Fenwick, who halted in mid-stride and switched back to Bennett. He set off on a side-stepping break to feed Burcher, whose pass as he was tackled was gathered up by Gerald Davies for a try. Nine minutes later, Wales won a scrum close to the line, Fenwick took the ball on a miss move and J.P.R. Williams entered the play to barge through two tacklers under the posts, launching the ball skyward to celebrate the novelty of scoring against someone other than England.

Quinnell, a replacement for the injured Evans, peeled from a lineout to set up Fenwick to score with a dropped goal via the crossbar before Wales launched a rapid counter attack. Bennett passed to Williams, who ran from inside his own 22, and Davies took the ball on. Bergiers got it to Bennett and J.J. Williams kicked beyond Irish winger Tom Grace only for the referee to rule he had been beaten to the touch. Wales regained possession from the drop, and Davies wormed his way towards the posts to set up Burgess, who galloped the final ten yards for a debut try.

It was the last scene of a final act made more impressive by the mediocrity of the early exchanges; a performance demonstrative of the way that this team could suddenly deliver a series of killer lines. Bennett, notably, was praised for refusing to deviate from the outline of attacking play that he and Dawes had prepared.

Novelist John L. Hughes's latest book, *Before the Crying Ends*, aims to show a slice of real Welsh life, rather than the approved tourist board image. A former shop owner in Clifnydd, Hughes depicts a violent, seedy world, saying, 'I draw from fact. Life at the level I am writing about is nasty.'

It was only the second game of the season but the Welsh trip to Paris was again considered to be a possible Grand Slam decider. Wales were without Wheel, banned for four weeks by the WRU (as opposed to the two-week suspension given by the Irish to Duggan), and the injured Evans. Quinnell and Cobner took their places.

It was clear from the start that this occasion belonged to France, narrow winners at Twickenham two weeks earlier. Their forwards displayed deft handling to go with their size and fury, while Wales took only one of the first twelve lineouts and required strong defence, plus the charity of the French backs, to remain in touch. Bennett would say that Wales 'simply weren't clued up for the game' and was critical of the continued selection of Shaw, who struggled against the fearsome Robert Paparemborde. Price says, 'Glyn was more mobile and was a great player in some ways, but he wasn't really an equivalent to Charlie. Our deficiencies were exposed and Bobby had to keep knocking the ball back with his head and I collapsed every scrum.'

A pair of Fenwick penalties actually had Wales 6–3 ahead early in the second half, but they lost Gerald Davies after a high tackle by Jean-Pierre Bastiat, one of several indiscretions by the French forwards. It was clear to see, some commented, why they had refused Norman Sanson as referee. France went ahead when they wheeled a scrum close to the Welsh line and Jean-Claude Skrela picked up. Romeu converted and four minutes later Jean-Michel Aguirre began a move on the left and winger Dominique Harize finished it off on the right. An exchange of penalties between Fenwick and Romeu rounded off a 16–9 French victory that prompted hundreds of complaint calls to BBC Wales. The callers' beef had not, however, been the problems of the pack. The country had been unable to see events clearly because of constant interference on pictures and poor sound quality.

Having seen the Grand Slam slip away, Wales went into a game four weeks later that would eventually determine the destination of the Triple Crown. England arrived in Cardiff with the kind of optimism they'd rarely experienced during the previous decade. Victories over Scotland and Ireland, plus the close game against France, had some observers, particularly those based in London's newspaper offices, believing that this could be England's day. Even Irish skipper Tom Grace warned, 'England's pack will take Wales apart.'

Pondering his pre-game address, Bennett decided that such reports offered him a theme and took a nationalistic approach. 'Look at what they have done to Wales,' he implored his men. 'They have taken our coal, our water, our steel. We have been exploited, raped, controlled and punished by the English.' Clive Rowlands would have been proud, although Bennett recalled it later with a tinge of embarrassment.

Aberavon's Clive Williams had taken the front-row berth previously occupied by Shaw – soon heading to rugby league – after Charlie Faulkner was recalled and then forced to withdraw with a shoulder injury. 'We had a Welsh training session on the Thursday, and on Friday I was in because Charlie hadn't responded to treatment,' recalls Williams, who had feared that a four-week suspension for being sent off at Pontypool in January had undermined his international chances. 'I was ready to go up to Porthcawl to the local club when I got a phone call. The great thing about the Pontypool boys was that they were ruthless. Even though Bobby [Windsor] was best mates with Charlie, he just got on with it and made me feel part of it.'

Windsor adds, 'We missed Charlie and felt for him but Clive was a strong lad, a very good prop and a great bloke. He did a very good job. Every club had a good front row in those days. There were lots of people who could have stepped into our shoes.' Edwards would describe Williams as 'an absolute revelation' and 'the cornerstone' of the pack.

Meanwhile, Quinnell moved to number 8 to accommodate the return of Wheel, who was no stranger to bouncing back from disciplinary problems. He had been suspended for six weeks during 1972–73 for offences in games against Blackheath and Coventry. 'You don't have to be a heavyweight champion to succeed at rugby and so I set out to prove I was not a dirty player,' he said a few years later.

A former centre-half for Swansea City reserves, he had turned away from the round ball during the summer of 1970 after being invited to train with his local club, Mumbles. A few months later he made his first-class debut for Swansea. 'I was getting a bit heavy for soccer and didn't believe I was good enough to make the big time. Yet soccer did help me to get springs in my legs and I was strong enough to survive in the rucks and mauls.'

At more than 16st. and over 6ft 4in., Wheel proved to be a formidable presence in the Welsh second row after his debut in 1974. Loose-head prop Faulkner, who spent several years with Wheel's hand up his shorts in international games, says, 'Geoff would give me everything. He was a good second-row and he could get around the pitch as well. I would say to him, "OK, Geoff, let's go for it now." He had good timing and we spent a lot of time on the scrummage machines as well as doing a lot of live scrummaging together.'

Wheel's comeback against England, combined with the other changes, helped to produce a far more efficient performance from the pack, with Allan Martin combining his lineout expertise with a valuable contribution in the loose. The Wheel–Martin partnership was one of the stabilising forces of the team through the second half of the 1970s. Martin, who would win thirty-four caps and become a two-time British Lion, had come to national prominence during 1973–74 when he played his first three internationals and smashed the Aberavon club record with 285 points. 'They were two good boys,' states Windsor. 'Geoff's main strength was his strength, while Allan was a complete footballer. He was a superb lineout forward, perhaps not as abrasive as Geoff, but that is what you look at in a good partnership. Geoff would chuck people about and Allan was a superb athlete getting the ball. It was the sort mix you needed. You always find that the front jumper is more abrasive than the middle jumper. That is how it should be.'

Clive Williams, who played club rugby with both men at Swansea and Aberavon, adds, 'They were totally different sorts of forward. Allan played way above his talent and was a great athlete. Kicking goals was unheard of for a second-row. Then Geoff was a real boiler house, so they worked well together.'

On this occasion, their team fell behind when Alastair Hignell kicked two penalties, but Wales applied pressure through J.P.R.

Williams, who was held up on a crash ball, and Edwards, whose clever kick forced winger Mike Slemen to carry over his own line. England kept all their forwards engaged to prevent a pushover try and Edwards capitalised by bursting through Slemen's tackle to score on the blindside.

Two attacks launched from deep by JPR whipped the Cardiff crowd into frenzy, although neither ended with a breach of the England line. First, the full-back fielded Slemen's clearance and scissored with Gerald Davies, who sidestepped his way past four players into English territory. After John Horton cleared back into the Welsh half, JPR charged into them again.

Fenwick kicked a penalty before half-time and added another following a Hignell reply after the break. Then came JPR's customary moment of glory against the English. Edwards reverse passed to Bennett, who combined with Burcher to set up Williams's entry into the line. He faked towards the outside before cutting inside to score. Full-time: 14–9, meaning that the trip to Edinburgh offered Wales an opportunity to win successive Triple Crowns for the first time since 1909.

That it was achieved in a game in which their forwards struggled against Scotland's pack, who covered technical shortcomings with sheer enthusiasm, was a testament to the Welsh powers of counter-attack. Scotland were adventurous in possession but also sloppy, which meant the only score they had to show for their first-half pressure was a dropped goal in the first minute by Ian McGeechan, a left-footed thump on the run. Bennett's 45-yard penalty produced a half-time score of 3–3.

Scotland made a fast start after the interval, winning a scrum and releasing Jim Renwick. His balding, moustachioed appearance made him look more like a pernickety park-keeper than an accomplished international centre but his burst took him beyond the initial wave of Welsh defence. As Bennett caught him, he passed to Irvine and the full-back muscled his way behind the posts. On 50 minutes, the game was tied at 9–9 after Edwards, who had missed Welsh squad training the previous Sunday to film the *World Superstars* competition in America, wrong-footed the defence by shaping to pass right before going left to Bennett. J.P.R. Williams joined the line and J.J. Williams took advantage of the overlap.

Wales gained control with two bursts of counter-attacking play. McGeechan dummied and danced his way inside the 22 but his pass was grabbed at full stretch by Fenwick, who kicked to near the home team's posts. Morgan cleared into touch but the Scots were penalised for holding back a red shirt, giving Bennett an easy kick.

Four minutes later, Bennett was at the business end of a scintillating try that was one of the highlights of the Welsh rugby decade. Scotland probed down the left and Irvine kicked to the 22, where J.P.R. Williams fell on the ball and jumped up to propel Fenwick into attack. He then moved the ball to Davies in a central position. 'What was he doing there?' purred commentator Bill McLaren as the winger broke tackles and performed hand-offs in the style of the centre he once was. Davies found Bennett, who released Burcher on the right. As the move gathered pace, Burcher lobbed inside to Fenwick, who moved the ball with sleight of hand to Bennett about 30 yards out. An extravagant sidestep saw him bisect two Scots, who were left looking up from the turf as he raced away and slid under the posts. Bennett's first season as Wales captain had ended in a suitable moment of crescendo. Four years after setting up Edwards's famous Barbarians try, he had scored one of his own that would take its place in rugby's hall of fame.

The 18–9 final score did more than put another Triple Crown into the Welsh team's ledger of achievement; it meant that Bennett earned the chance to lead the British Lions in New Zealand. Proudly and eagerly, he accepted. Yet before an arduous slog through a wretchedly sodden New Zealand winter was over, he realised his heart had pushed him into a role for which his head knew he was ill-suited. There were others 'better equipped than I to deal with the all-engulfing pressures', he would admit.

He felt that his own form suffered through the demands of leadership, coupled with homesickness, while J.J. Williams believes that the experience wounded him so deeply that it contributed to his disappearance from international rugby less than a year later. 'In hindsight, the captain should have been someone like Fran Cotton. It affected Phil's mood and his game and, although he bounced back in 1978, he retired far too early. After the experience of New Zealand, he wanted to go out on top.'

Bennett's squad had been denied the presence of J.P.R. Williams and Gareth Edwards, whose careers and families came before another three-month commitment to rugby. There was, however, the comforting presence of John Dawes, whose achievements with Wales and his triumphant leadership of the Lions six years earlier made him the only realistic choice to fill the coaching role under Scottish manager George Burrell.

It was not to be the crowning glory of Dawes's career, however. 'Wet,' is how he sums up the tour. 'We'd had one boggy pitch in 1971 and in training we never got wet. In '77, it never stopped raining and it was depressing. That got to us more than anything and you could see the players' body language. Well before the end of the tour they'd had enough and wanted to go home. In the pack we murdered New Zealand but we had a halfback problem. We didn't have the best players, or they didn't play well, and they got at Benny. In the second Test, all the flanker did was late tackle him and you could see it was predetermined. It knocked the stuffing out of him. Those conditions were not his forte. He was a top of the ground player.'

Despite the notable absences, there was an overwhelming Welsh presence in the tour party once again. Of the original selections, Geoff Wheel withdrew after suffering what was described as a 'minor heart disturbance' in a late-season club game, but by the time Jeff Squire, Charlie Faulkner and scrum-half Alun Lewis had flown out as replacements it meant that 18 Welshmen appeared in Lions jerseys during the 26-match tour. Remarkably, Bennett, Steve Fenwick and J.J. Williams were the only national team regulars among the nine Wales backs involved in the tour. They were joined by fly-half John Bevan, Newport three-quarters David Burcher and Gareth Evans, Neath winger Elgan Rees and scrum-halves Brynmoor Williams and Lewis. Despite being uncapped for their country, both Williams and Evans would play in three Tests. The line-up of Welsh forwards had fewer surprises: front-row men Price, Windsor and Clive Williams (later joined by Faulkner); Cobner, Evans, Quinnell and replacement Squire in the back row; and lock forward Martin.

There was no repeat of the triumph of 1971, although the Lions did pull level at 1–1 in the series when they followed a try-less 16–12 defeat in the first Test with a 13–9 victory in Christchurch. J.J. Williams scored the only try of the game, adding to three Bennett penalties. Defeats by 19–7 and 10–9, however, concluded a disappointing series, in which the Lions were never able to select a settled side and crossed the All Blacks' line only twice. Creditably, the provincial games produced 20 wins in 21 games.

By the time the party returned to Britain, the esteem in which coach Dawes and skipper Bennett had been held had taken a knock, not just for the results in the Test matches, but because of the atmosphere of mistrust that had developed between the tourists and the media. Naturally, that meant that the projection of the tour leaders to the rugby public was less than flattering.

Bennett had been unhappy when what he believed was an off-the-record assessment of the All Blacks' weaknesses appeared in print. Meanwhile, Dawes increasingly kept the press at arm's length, much to their annoyance. The situation degenerated further when Carwyn James, Barry John and Mervyn Davies arrived as paid pundits mid-way through the tour and failed to offer the backing that Dawes, perhaps naively, expected to receive from his former comrades. Access to the squad for the journalist corps was all but shut down completely. The Welsh correspondents could not help draw attention to the difference from the last time they had toured with Dawes – albeit in more relaxed circumstances in Japan – when daily press conferences had been conducted over coffee and sherry.

Within the squad itself, Bennett felt that Dawes was correct in turning to Terry Cobner to take charge of the forwards but felt that the responsibility could have been handed to him even earlier. 'I have yet to be convinced that three-quarters who become coaches have the slightest idea what forward play is all about,' he said later.

Going into the first Test on the back of a shock defeat to the New Zealand Universities side, Bennett suffered a shoulder injury that impeded him for the rest of the tour, but he saw his team respond with a win in a second Test that was notable for the brutality of the action. It was contested, according to the Lions skipper, by teams who 'had little respect for the basics of rugby'. With Cobner sidelined by a virus, the third Test was lost and Bennett chastised himself by saying, 'I kicked and passed like a novice.' The series was unable to be won and Bennett admitted that he 'felt a failure as captain'. Brynmoor Williams and Quinnell joined the absentees for the final Test in Auckland, where the Lions led 9–3 at half-time before being held scoreless after the break and losing by a single point. The All Blacks' winning try stemmed from a misdirected kick by Bennett.

Ironically, the victorious All Blacks took such a pounding in the series from the Lions' well-drilled forwards that they lobbied successfully for changes in the scrummage laws. As Windsor noted, 'Their scrummage was so wrecked that they put only three men in the scrum and didn't try to contest them. Then they wanted it all changed. They said the scrummage was dangerous and needed weakening.'

The New Zealanders called for a ban on some of the Lions' preferred techniques, such as pulling opponents as low as possible. In the All Blacks' defence, concerns over such practice had also been aired in Wales a year earlier after two junior club players suffered broken necks in the front row. At that time former hooker Jeff Young's retirement because of spinal compression had been cited, his consultant having said, 'It was as if he had run at full speed into a brick wall with his head down.'

Yet to many, it simply sounded like the All Blacks were whining for mummy and, for a group of men from Pontypool in particular, it was music to their cauliflower ears.

18

LIVING ON THE FRONT LINE

'If Gerald Davies were to write a book on his philosophy
of rugby, it would read like a poetry book. If Charlie
[Faulkner] and Bobby [Windsor] did one, it would
be like an autobiography of Ronnie and Reggie Kray'
– *Graham Price*

The British Lions might have been beaten but there was one
moment in New Zealand that sits among the career highlights
of three of their number. 'When Charlie Faulkner came out on tour,'
states Bobby Windsor, 'that topped the lot off.' Faulkner's arrival for
injured prop Clive Williams meant that the Pontypool Front Row
had advanced from club to country to Lions, the first time such a
thing had happened.

When he received the call, Faulkner had been planning his return
to first-class rugby after missing the end of the 1977 season with
a separated shoulder. 'It was the worst injury I'd had but I knew I
would come back once the shoulder settled. When Clive did his knee
ligaments I was on a coaching course in north Wales somewhere.
Next thing I am in New Zealand. I had worked to get fit and did
a lot of boxing training and mountain running.'

If there was anyone more proud than the three men themselves
when they took the field together against the Counties-Thames
Valley team, it was Pontypool coach and former Lions prop Ray
Prosser. 'He was the biggest factor in our success,' says Windsor.

'He knew the importance of the front row. He brought us together and coached us in how to play as a unit. The front row is a world of its own and we learned more from him than we ever did from anyone else.'

Graham Price was the first of the trio to work with Prosser, having been the only one to have begun his playing career at Pontypool. Born in Moascar, in Egypt, while his father was posted there as a sergeant major, he settled at the age of six in the town with which he became synonymous. He played rugby at West Monmouth Grammar School and won selection for the Wales Schools Under–19s, as well as becoming the country's best schoolboy shot putter in 1970. By that time he had already made his first-team debut for Pontypool and his stars became fully aligned when Prosser was appointed club coach at the end of the 1969–70 season.

'Pross used to say to us, "Find what you are good at and concentrate on that,"' says Price, who also remembers an early lesson in the hard facts of front-row life. 'I had come from the local grammar school, where you could show your opponent who was boss by giving him a stern look. I was a bit intimidating to them. In one of my first club games the opposition shoved my head up my arse and when Ray asked what had happened I said, "They were breaking all the scrummaging laws." He just said, "Out there you make up your own laws."'

Acknowledging his luck in having Prosser as his mentor, he adds, 'He would bollock you, but only if he knew he could get more out of you. If he didn't bollock you, it was a bad sign. He would persevere with a young player and push him to the limits if he considered he had potential.'

Price would become acknowledged as one of the best tight-head prop forwards in the world during an eight-year international career, but it was only the arrival of Faulkner from Cross Keys for the 1972–73 season that saw him moving permanently to that position, having sometimes occupied the loose-head berth. Faulkner, meanwhile, had been playing alongside his friend and work colleague Windsor at Newport Saracens and Cross Keys, and would be reunited in a year's time when the hooker made the journey to Pontypool Park, completing the most famous threesome in rugby history.

Anthony George Faulkner, known in rugby circles as Charlie, was an interesting character; a first dan black belt and former Welsh heavyweight champion in judo. A jovial man who, like Windsor, never has a chuckle far from his lips, he explains, 'Judo taught you balance and how to weigh up your opponent very early. It taught you to always be alert no matter how tired you are and it also meant that foot positions became natural to me. It definitely helped my rugby.'

He continues, 'I scored in a trial at Pontypool so they picked me against Bath but I had to cry off because I had blisters through training in a borrowed pair of boots. When I got back in the next game, I didn't miss a match throughout the season.'

Faulkner's age at the time of his arrival at Pontypool was anyone's guess. When he first played for Wales, he was reported as being 32, although in early 1975 *Rugby World* was describing him as 29. Eventually it would emerge that he had been born in February 1941, making him almost 34 when he made his debut and past 38 when he played his final game for Wales. 'They used to talk about my age all the time and I had a laugh about it. I would tell them any old bullshit. I said that as long as I do the business on the field the selectors will be happy.'

Even at his advanced age, Faulkner found it easy to improve under the guidance of Prosser. 'Charlie was a steady sort of prop,' says Price. 'But Pross could see what he had to offer and got to grips with him. He rode him, got him fitter and got him playing the way he wanted him to.' Faulkner recalls that Prosser had 'no time for bullshit', adding, 'He was straight to the point but very fair and a stickler for protocol and fitness. We used to train with Wales on a Thursday before an international but we still had to go to Pontypool on the Wednesday and he was harder on the internationals than on the rest of the side. He poured it on and said it would hold you in good stead.'

Price adds, 'I might come back from playing well for Wales, but I knew if I went back half a pace in one of the early scrums, he would say, "Don't you go bringing back those sloppy Wales habits to Pontypool."'

Faulkner continues, 'We all loved him. I had developed bad habits over the years and he taught me the fundamental principles of scrummaging, the basics of body position and helped me develop the right attitude. People can talk about the front row all they want but unless you have been there you can't coach it. You have to understand what is going on and you develop a feel for it. Ray wouldn't have you running around and neglecting the scrum. That was your first job and everything else went from there. He used to tell us, "You people up front carry water for other people to drink."'

Windsor also stresses that performance in the set scrum was the most important of the front row's duties. 'You have about 100 stones up your arse and 120 coming at you. You can be physically hurt; your neck, your ribs, your back. If you are not on top you feel like you have got divers' boots on, but if you are doing well you run round like a two year old.'

Signed in 1973–74, shortly before breaking into the Wales team, Windsor was the last of the trio to wear the Pontypool shirt. 'Alan Talbot, the Pontypool hooker was going to finish and he said, "Bob, go to Pontypool because Ray Prosser is getting some boys together and if you want to get on you have got to move."' Renowned for his strength in the rolling maul, Windsor is described as 'the strongest scrummaging hooker I ever knew' by Price, who adds, 'If he appeared flippant it merely disguised an innate and thorough knowledge which few players possessed.'

Windsor, meanwhile, acknowledges Prosser for 'telling us how you could do things in scrummages, rucks and mauls'. He continues, 'He taught us about three techniques for each and told us, "If you try them all you will find which one works for you." Then when you were in trouble you could always switch to something else. They call us donkeys in the front row but you had to be a clever donkey. In certain games I would like Graham to go as low as he could. If he went low I could lay across on him. On other occasions I would want him to take the prop on; other times grab the prop by the sleeve. When you see the elbow go up you know you are pulling him out to take the pressure off. When you played a side like France there was a hell of a lot of pressure. I could tell when Graham was having a bit of bother. He liked to take his opponent down as low as possible in the scrummage to nullify his ability to disrupt. A guy with eyes almost on the ground isn't able to do much in an attacking sense. Also in rucks and mauls, we got used to each other's play.'

Faulkner takes up the theme. 'You supported each other. Bobby and I worked together: we would go high, or he would come over with me and we would both go for the tight head's breastbone. We would go for a breastbone each and put tremendous pressure on him.'

Windsor explains that there was an acceptance among teammates that the trio would often have to tread a line bordering on illegality. 'The boys who are the gentlemen of today knew what we had to get up to in order to get them the ball. That is why they could run round to the posts, wave to the girls and put the ball down. I was once pulled up by one young debonair gentleman who played on the wing and he said, "Bob, I have seen what you did and there is no place for that." I replied, "Let me tell you what was happening. They were coming through and grabbing me round the face so I couldn't see the ball. If I had come off and said I was sorry but I couldn't get the ball in the scrum because this chap was cheating, what would you say?" He said, "Fair enough." I had to do what I had to do. It was my job. We knew that we just had to get our back line the ball and they would do the business. You also had to protect your halfbacks and if one of their forwards bumped them you made sure he got a bump back.'

According to Price, 'Each of us learned pretty quickly that to survive in big-time rugby we had to develop mental as well as physical hardness. Possibly the other two, being ex-steelworkers, had the edge on me. Charlie knew a little more than either Bobby or me about close-quarter combat. We were well prepared to handle most situations and when one of us was getting a bit of a going over the other two went to his assistance. You beat them or they beat you. A punch, a raking, a boot in the head – occasionally anything goes in the front row.'

The indestructible nature of the trio was even captured in song by Max Boyce, whose tribute characterised them as super heroes sorting out everything from football hooliganism to rogue Ugandan President Idi Amin. And as the Pontypool Front Row's reputation grew, so did the determination of opponents to bring them down, literally in some cases. Price continues, 'I remember playing at Gloucester and Charlie was up against Mike Burton. Before the first scrum Charlie knew Burton was going to go low and collapse the scrum. He said to our second-row, John Perkins, "If he decides to collapse the scrum, turn his head into a money box." Mind you, John would often get Charlie instead as he came through.

'In exhibition and charity matches it is usually an old pals' act. The ball goes with the head and you don't push in the scrum; you just run about the field and enjoy yourself. But whenever the Pontypool Front Row was picked it was never like that. The other front row would want to have a pop at us; people wanted to test themselves out. Because we had our reputation, we knew what to expect.'

Windsor recalls, 'Without a doubt people wanted to take us on. We had days when we got turned over and there were some who were intimidated by our reputation – and we did our best to make them believe it. We never had any easy games. We would have signals. If I wanted Charlie to hit someone in the chops, I would say, "Popeye." One time against France this bloke was biting me and when Charlie smacked him he had my ear in his mouth and I ended up with sixteen stitches.'

Each standing a little under or over 5ft 10in. and weighing above 15st., the Pontypool men's compatibility and camaraderie extended only so far beyond the field. 'We were close until it came to getting into the bar,' laughs Windsor. 'Pricey never liked the bar very much. Charlie and I were born and bred in Newport, have been friends for 40 or 50 years now and worked in the same steelworks. We looked after Graham because he was a young pup. I was the leader because I was the talker, whereas Graham is quieter, especially when it's his round. Charlie is more abrasive, so I had to get one of them up and keep the other one down.'

Price, who jokingly recalls Faulkner's hatred of baggy shorts – 'which seemed to emphasise his gawky, thin legs' – says that 'we didn't spend much time together after the game because we were from different backgrounds', while Faulkner recalls that his and Windsor's obsession with their craft dominated their time in each other's company. 'We trained together and shared hotel rooms and front-row play was all we talked about. People probably got fed up with us. We would go into details about opponents and were always finding answers. The backs didn't know what was going on. The one who really appreciated it was Gareth Edwards. He put the ball in the scrum and could see what was happening.'

A season after coming together for their club, the Pontypool men became the first club front row to represent Wales when they teamed up in the famous victory in Paris. Price had watched from the bench as Windsor and Faulkner played in the unofficial Test against New Zealand late in 1974 and Faulkner recalls how that match opened the door for his fellow prop, explaining, 'The scrum kept turning and turning. It was going back on Barry Llewellyn's side.' Installed alongside Windsor and fellow debutant Faulkner against France, Price recalled that 'we took them to the cleaners in every aspect of the match'. The 'Viet Gwent', as Boyce would christen them, had been born.

A former soldier from Caerphilly is one of Britain's first victims of the new craze of glue sniffing. The 19 year old, unable to find a job in four months since leaving the Royal Welsh Fusiliers, is found dead in his lodgings in Great Yarmouth after inhaling aerosol glue.

While the British Lions players had been otherwise engaged in the mud and rain of New Zealand, the nation's Jubilee summer of 1977 had gone on in their absence, marked by blazing sunshine, Virginia Wade's triumph at Wimbledon and the Sex Pistols storming the charts with 'God Save the Queen'. There had also been an Ashes victory for England's cricketers, but it was the dominant news story surrounding that series that provoked comment in the rugby world. An autumn free of international commitments allowed for much speculation on the possible impact on rugby of the cricket 'circus' being set up by Australian television magnate Kerry Packer. Having failed to win Australian TV rights for his own Channel Nine company he responded by corralling the best players in the world to play in his own World Series Cricket competition. The riches on offer were too good to be true.

As Packer embarked on what would be the first of two Australian summer schedules before he won his TV rights and called the whole thing off, rugby wondered whether it could be susceptible to a similar 'pirate' scheme. Its players, after all, received nothing for their endeavours and could be even more vulnerable to a Packer-type offer than their cricketing counterparts.

An organisation called World Professional Rugby Football Ltd quickly emerged, proposing a New Zealand versus British Lions series that would kick off in March 1978 and then head to South Africa. Former All Black captains Andy Leslie and Ian Kirkpatrick were said to have made themselves available. South African Board President Danie Craven said he 'viewed those threats seriously', while Barry John warned, 'Don't discount the chances of a professional circus skimming off the cream from the ranks of established stars.'

Veteran writer Vivian Jenkins was not about to give in to panic, however. 'It would sort out the sheep from the goats and skim off those who want to play for money as opposed to those who play for fun,' he huffed. 'Defections will do more good than harm to the amateur game.' In the end, it all came to nothing and the rugby world breathed again.

And so to the business of the Five Nations, where the Pontypool Front Row was back in harness as Wales travelled to Twickenham to open the season. With Ray Gravell fit once more in the centre, it meant another old friend was returning. On a bog of a Twickenham pitch in a high wind, it turned out to be the kind of game that tested even the renowned combative spirits of such players. The teams were quickly indistinguishable from each other, both kits a deep, dirty grey. 'Going out on freezing cold, rainy day? It was bloody murder trying to play rugby in that,' says Bobby Windsor. 'I liked to run with the ball, so playing in South Africa on hard grounds suited my game better. But I always loved playing against England because you knew all the players from club rugby.'

Gareth Edwards, winning his 50th Welsh cap, and captain Phil Bennett gave Wales the upper hand because their tactical kicking was superior to that of English counterparts Malcolm Young and John Horton. The rucks and mauls, meanwhile, were marginally in favour of England. In the end, the decisive balance was with Wales, Bennett kicking three of his four penalty attempts, while England full-back Alastair Hignell managed only two out of six, twice giving his side a lead they failed to hold. The three-quarters were mere spectators and even J.P.R. Williams was denied his traditional Twickenham try when held up on a scissors move. The kick that gave Wales their victory was an easy effort eight minutes from time, although Hignell missed an equalising opportunity with seconds running out.

It had been the kind of game that a Welsh team founded upon its fleet-footed backs might have lost a few years previously. This team, however, with the Pontypool trio in harness and Allan Martin and Geoff Wheel locking behind them, was a different proposition. Graham Price recalls the game falling during a golden period for his colleagues. 'Terry Cobner had been given overall control of the forwards on the Lions tour. We murdered the All Blacks forwards and it was down to the absolute basics of the game. It was so bloody obvious. For a few months we couldn't do a thing wrong. We kicked the shit out of the opposition, playing in the Lions way. It soon came back to being "you dirty Pontypool bastards" again, though.'

After the mud of Twickenham, Wales found snow piled round the perimeter of the National Stadium pitch when they took on Scotland. A good number of the day's sporting events were victims of the weather, while Wales's worst blizzards for fifteen years had isolated many remote areas and caused three deaths on the Snowdon mountain range. Players and spectators would be stuck in Cardiff because routes out of the capital were cut off.

Wales chose to give Scotland the advantage of the first-half wind and resolved to run at them at every occasion. That they had the opportunity to put the plan into practice owed much to their ability to win significant ball against the head and their excellence in the loose, where Derek Quinnell's efforts stood out. Trailing 3–0 to a Doug Morgan penalty, Gerald Davies made space where none existed and tiptoed to within striking distance of the line. Wales won a scrum five yards out and Edwards dummied to Gravell before breaking through tackles on the blindside and stretching out for his twentieth and final try for his country. Scotland regained the lead after Jim Renwick took a final pass from Bruce Hay to jink past a tackle to score. But Wales were in front before half-time after J.P.R. Williams and Davies attacked the left side of the defence and panicked them into being on the wrong side in the loose. Although the penalty was inside the 22, Wales opted to run and Gravell took a pass from Edwards to force his way over in unfussy fashion for his first international try.

Wales made the game safe with one of those second-half bursts in which they specialised – fourteen points in the first fifteen minutes, beginning with a Bennett dropped goal. A fierce push from their scrum produced more Welsh possession, the ball passing through several pairs of hands before Gravell found J.J. Williams as he was going down in a tackle. As the winger was halted, the ball went forward, yet Fenwick was quickest to fall on it in the in-goal area. Scottish protestors had apparently forgotten the new ruling that a ball going forward from a tackle was not considered a knock-on.

Bennett added a penalty after Scotland collapsed the scrum and then Quinnell was rewarded for his outstanding game. Edwards and J.J. Williams attacked the blindside and Quinnell, his right arm stuck out like a knight's lance, made the 20 yards to the line with defenders bouncing off him. Only an easing up by the home side allowed a Morgan penalty and a try by Alan Tomes to give the score a respectable look at 22–14.

19

WE CAN BE HEROES

'When the crowd burst into song I thought, "God Almighty, this is the time to go." It was emotional; you knew you had been part of something special'
– *Phil Bennett*

Bobby Windsor recalls games against Ireland with a certain amount of wryness. 'Playing the Irish was lovely,' he says. 'They would kick ahead – any head. That's what they used to say about them. But after the game you would have a good sing-song with them, win or lose.'

There was plenty of relationship repair work to be done in the bar after Wales's third match of the 1978 Five Nations campaign in Dublin. They came out on the winning end of a 20–16 scoreline, but this was a day that did more than any other single game to hasten Gareth Edwards, Gerald Davies and Phil Bennett out of international rugby. 'It was one of the dirtiest international matches that I've ever played in,' was Bennett's verdict in his autobiography, 'which I have no doubt accelerated my retirement decision.'

He'd feared the worst when he and referee George Domercq visited the Irish dressing-room for the coin toss, only to have the door slammed in their faces. The bad feeling that had been just under the surface for the previous decade and which exploded like an ugly boil a year earlier with the dismissals of Geoff Wheel and Willie Duggan was the dominant element of the game. Ireland played at a high level of intensity and the action was constantly interrupted by penalties, often caused by the violent force of their forward play. It was a day when the poise of veteran players like Edwards and J.P.R. Williams was a match-winning asset.

Bennett would state, 'It was quite frightening. In the end players on both sides were equally to blame.' Indeed, JPR managed to make himself a target of abuse from the crowd with a late tackle on local hero Mike Gibson, who was setting a world record with his 64th cap. Williams insisted it was an accidental 'reflex action' and apologised to his British Lions teammate.

After enduring early pressure, Wales went ahead with two Steve Fenwick penalties either side of the halfway line. Ireland fly-half Tony Ward, whose resemblance to new Hollywood heart-throb John Travolta extended beyond his dark good looks to his fancy footwork, narrowed the gap before Fenwick struck again. The first Welsh try followed Ray Gravell's surge and Graham Price's efforts in working the ball to Fenwick, who charged along the diagonal one pace ahead of his pursuers to score in the corner.

Still trailing 13–6 at half-time after a second Ward penalty, Ireland fought back to level the game as forwards Moss Keane, Fergus Slattery and Duggan rampaged. According to Edwards, 'Slats stopped at nothing to subdue us. His mania affected the other Irish forwards, who let fly with everything they possessed – boots, knuckles, fingernails, elbows.' Ward scored with a drop and then kicked high towards the posts. JPR sliced his clearance as he was hit by a green shirt, sending the ball behind him into the in-goal area, where Moloney touched down.

Welsh fans feared the worst and Gerald Davies recalled the additional effort now required. 'You can come out of the dressing-room feeling such inspiration but halfway through the second half it is very difficult to summon up the right emotions. At those moments you need to play with skill and with a cool head.' Fifteen minutes of fierce, evenly balanced play followed before Wales won a lineout on the right. Edwards directed play left towards Fenwick and the centre, again showing his knack for engineering an opening, lobbed a blind pass to J.J. Williams, who had the easy job of finishing the move. With four minutes remaining, Fenwick kicked Wales into a seven-point lead and Ward's penalty, which made the final score 20–16, was all Ireland could manage in response.

Wales had shown their ability to play on the back foot and been rewarded with a third consecutive Triple Crown. Yet there was a subdued air in the dressing-room under the Lansdowne Road stands. When some of the selectors entered 15 minutes after the game they found that the players had not yet summoned the energy to remove their jerseys. 'There was no jubilation after that victory, no immediate sense of celebration,' said Davies. 'The players were drained after the final few minutes' effort on the field.'

Edwards asked himself whether he could ever go through such an afternoon again, while Bennett said the game left 'a few of us wondering if all this, the recriminations, the sourness and the exhaustion, was worth the effort'. In fact, it underscored the decision Bennett had already made that the championship finale against France would be his last Wales appearance.

'I had always been a big boxing fan and I had seen so many of the great fighters go on one fight too long,' he explains. 'After being away from home almost every summer for ten years I thought it was about time I put something back into my family. I wanted to see my children grow up. I remember driving to Afan Lido one Sunday and within a couple of miles of leaving my village I had passed about four couples out with their kiddies. I thought, "Jesus, I won't get home until six and won't see my little boy all day."'

British Steel Corporation leaders are warned that the cost of closing its Ebbw Vale plant months ahead of schedule could be £6 million. Workers will demand 40 weeks' wages in addition to their standard redundancy payments to compensate for being out of work earlier than originally outlined.

France at home, with the Grand Slam for the taking. Wales had been here two years earlier. This time the French, reigning champions, arrived as favourites, their famous back row as good as ever and new scrum-half Jerome Gallion injecting energy and verve behind them. Wales knew they needed to contain this unit before taking the game to the visitors. Their attacking options had been reduced by Gerald Davies's injured hamstring, which saw Newport's Gareth Evans earn his first start in a Wales jersey, with J.J. Williams moving to the right wing.

Edwards admits that the Ireland game had induced a degree of self-doubt. He took the field in Cardiff uncertain whether this would be his final international and feared that a bad performance would have people questioning whether he had gone on too long. Meanwhile, although no one knew that Phil Bennett had already determined his future, it would unfold as a day of triumph for the Welsh captain, a fitting finale to a career he would close with a European record of 166 points in 29 Tests for his country.[11]

Yet he, too, had been fearful going into the game after what he felt was a below-par squad training session. Also, France had been given four weeks to prepare after winning on each of the championship's first three weekends and had enjoyed time off while Wales were taking a pounding in Dublin. Bennett's own participation in the game had been in doubt until two days before kick-off because of a toe injury on his right foot and he owed much to the generosity of Swansea City's new manager John Toshack, who put his club's medical facilities at his disposal.

After 24 minutes, it appeared that Bennett's concerns were well founded as France sat on a 7–0 lead. They had scored after a lineout when Paparemborde gathered in and, from the resulting drive, Skrela was credited with touching the ball down. Fly-half Bernard Viviès then landed a dropped goal from long range after a French free-kick.

Yet Wales were to take decisive steps towards the Grand Slam in what remained of the half. Allan Martin was increasingly dominant in the lineout and he allowed Edwards to hoist a cross-kick from the right touchline, instilling a defensive panic that led to a scrum five yards out. Wales turned the set-piece, Martin flipped the ball out to Bennett on the blindside and he cut inside a tackler to score a try that he converted himself.

---

11 Adding his Lions tally took him to a world-record 210, three ahead of New Zealand's Don Clarke.

Edwards sent over a steep dropped goal after Jeff Squire palmed down to Graham Price and, from the maul that followed the restart, he missiled a bouncing kick down the right to within five yards of the French line. Martin won the French throw, Gravell drove and kept the ball alive and Fenwick sent it back to the right to Edwards. His break saw him weaving past three defenders and passing to J.J. Williams, who flung the ball back infield for Bennett to plunge over, becoming the first Welsh fly-half to score two tries in a game for forty-seven years.

When Viviès missed his second penalty it preserved the 13–7 Welsh lead at half-time. As the pace of the game dropped, Aguirre hit the woodwork with a booming effort from inside his own half and the nervy Viviès failed to reach the posts with a simpler kick. Evans relieved the growing tension with an eye-catching break inside from the left, leading to J.J. Williams being ankle tackled just short of the line. More indicative of the mounting pressure felt by both teams were the outbreaks of fighting, with Quinnell holding his face after one exchange and exacting revenge by swinging fists at the next breakdown. Referee Alan Welsby administered warnings to captains Bennett and Bastiat.

With three minutes left, Wales gave themselves the breathing space of a nine-point lead. J.P.R. Williams gatecrashed the French defence as they attempted to deal with Bennett's kick and, from the resulting scrum, Edwards's untidy pass unintentionally missed Bennett but fell into the grasp of Fenwick, who calmly sent his drop between the posts. There was something appropriately poignant about the fact that, even with a misjudged pass, Edwards set up a score with his final contribution in international rugby. He and Bennett ran back to the halfway line locked happily in each other's arms.

Bennett recalls, 'Gallion was going to be the new star, but Gareth absolutely devoured him with a little break here, a chip there, a tackle here. He destroyed the young pretender. I wasn't a great try scorer, so to have got two was marvellous. With a minute to go I knew we were going to win the Grand Slam and I knew I had made the right decision to retire. We had been down on our knees and it was spirit that pulled us through. The crowd were singing us home for the final 20 minutes and it was inspirational. It made the hairs on your neck stand up. I was thinking, "Thanks, it has been brilliant. This is the time to go." I hoped I had done the Welsh nation proud because I know they did me proud.'

The last few seconds ticked away as songs of celebration tumbled down from the stands and the final whistle found the Welsh players battling back to the tunnel through a logjam of fans. Edwards was collared by Jean-Pierre Rives, who said, 'Gareth, wait until Paris next year!' Edwards knew in his heart he would not be there. Slumping on the bench in the changing-room, he said to no one in particular, 'That's it. I can't take any more.'

Bennett continues, 'When Gareth came in, I shook his hand and said, "Gar, it has been a privilege and a pleasure." He asked what I meant and I told him it was my last game. He said, "It is my last game too," and we burst out laughing. Neither of us had said anything because the press would have built it up.'

When composure had been regained, Bennett told reporters, 'We didn't play well but the tactic of hoisting high balls for Aguirre and allowing Ray Gravell and Steve Fenwick to hound him all afternoon did the trick.' But perhaps a bigger factor in the Grand Slam than getting tactics right in individual games had been continuity in the squad. Other than the arrival of Squire and Quinnell in the back row in place of Trevor Evans and Mervyn Davies, the third Slam of the decade had been won by the same first-choice unit as two years previously. For Quinnell, in particular, it felt good to have played a leading role instead of waiting in the wings, as he had in '71 and '76. 'I'd always been there or thereabouts, so to actually play all the games and be part of it was special. The Ireland game was probably the most difficult. It was good to be a part of sneaking that one.'

Even as Wales celebrated, some were looking beyond the boundaries of their triumph and wondering about the direction international rugby was taking. Acknowledging the Welsh public's often unfair expectation that their team should not only win but do it with style, Barry John still penned this somewhat ambivalent assessment of the season:

Welsh rugby of the past three years has been distinctly different from that of previous years. It may have settled into predictability and not be as pleasing to the eye as the French game or games of the early Seventies, but there is no doubting its effectiveness. It was a tragedy that so little was seen of Gerald Davies and J.J. Williams. To attack down the flanks and use their natural skills and talents would have added another exciting new dimension to the team and it was sad, particularly against Scotland, to see Davies holding his head in his hands with frustration.

Meanwhile, France's most recognisable figure, Rives, suggested that he was falling out of love with the game. 'In France we have made the move from just playing to winning rugby, but we have lost the excitement along the way. All the fun has gone out of our game. Even if we had beaten Wales at Cardiff it would still have been true. I do not like playing rugby any more. There is nothing but strong, hard play: pressure from the pack and nothing else.'

The Welsh management, however, had more parochial issues to worry about than upholding the beauty of the game and had little time to take in the scale of the team's achievement. While Prime Minister James Callaghan was inviting the squad to Downing Street, Edwards was not yet confirming his long-term intentions, announcing only that family and business commitments would absent him from his country's summer trip to Australia. Similarly, Bennett at this stage merely opted out of the first major Welsh Test tour for nine years. Clive Rowlands, named as manager, failed to change their minds and Terry Cobner was announced as captain for the nine-match trip.

The eleven uncapped players selected among the twenty-five tourists included four halfbacks, although scrum-half Brynmoor Williams, recently moved from Cardiff to Newport, had played for the Lions a year earlier and had worn a Wales jersey in 1974 against Tonga. Terry Holmes would compete with him for the number 9 shirt, while Cardiff clubmate Gareth Davies, who had helped Oxford to victory over Cambridge in the season's Varsity Match, was thought to be the steadier option than Swansea's David Richards at outside-half.

Australia were beginning to emerge as a stronger force than they had been earlier in the decade and stories were flying around that they were prepared to go to any lengths to achieve victory in the two-Test series. Having won four of their first five tour matches, Wales were given an uncomfortable taste of what was in store when local referee R.T. Burnett awarded twice as many penalties to the home team during a narrow win against Queensland. After the Australian RFU proposed him as referee for the first Test in Brisbane, Welsh objections came to nothing. When Wales players heard him announce during the course of the game, 'It's our ball,' they knew they were in for a long day.

Halfbacks Williams and Davies took their places in what was otherwise the full-strength Grand Slam team but found themselves 9–4 down at half-time after three Australian penalties and a try by Gerald Davies, who ran onto a diagonal kick from the new outside-half. With 15 minutes played in the second half, it was Williams's turn to make an impact, starting a move, supporting his back row and taking an inside pass from Gravell to score. Yet the Australian forwards were playing well and good ball from a ruck saw left-wing Phil Crowe cut through the defence. Paul McLean kicked the conversion and his fourth penalty produced a final score of 18–8.

The last provincial game of the tour was even more unsatisfactory, a 21–20 defeat against a weak Capital Territory side, even though Wales scored four tries to their opponents' one. The tourists made no attempt to hide their displeasure at the referee's penalty awards.

The second Test was little short of a farce, with the tone set by the absence of the entire Wales back row of Cobner, Squire and Quinnell through injury. Cardiff wing-forward Stuart Lane and Newbridge's Clive Davis, usually a lock, were joined in the back row by J.P.R. Williams, fulfilling an ambition by lining up for Wales at flanker. Meanwhile Swansea centre Alun Donovan filled the full-back position and Holmes took over at scrum-half. Brynmoor Williams, therefore, found himself back on the bench, from where he had been forced to watch so many of Gareth Edwards's performances. Steve Fenwick recalls, 'Brynmoor said to me once, "You know, Gareth

Edwards is a national hero. The only bloke who used to hope he would break both his legs on a Saturday was my old man!'"

A common knock on Williams's game was that his passing was erratic, although Gareth Davies said, 'Whenever I played outside Brynmoor that consistency was the equal of any other scrum-half I've played with.' Even Holmes acknowledged that his call-up was less about the perception that he was playing better than Williams than it was about the style of rugby Wales needed to employ. With a patched-up team, the requirement was to keep the game tight and Holmes accepted that his 6ft, 13st. build equipped him to give greater physical support to the makeshift back row.

It took only three minutes for the Wales line-up to suffer further when Aussie prop Steve Finnane landed a punch on Graham Price, who was led from the field with a bloodied face and broken jaw. Before half-time, Donovan injured his knee, bringing Gareth Evans into the action. His first touch of the ball saw him tackled high, resulting in a depressed fracture of the cheekbone. With the injury replacements already used, JPR had to leave the scrum to take over at full-back, with Evans and J.J. Williams, who had hurt his ankle in the meantime, attempting to share the left-wing duties.

Remarkably, Wales still made a game of it, Gareth Davies's penalty and dropped goal keeping them within reach at 9–6 at half-time. Early in the second half, they took the lead when Holmes barged over, but lost it when Australia number 8 Mark Loane scored from a lineout. The moment that compounded the Welsh opinion of Australian refereeing was the dropped goal attempt by McLean that was ruled as three points after appearing to clearly miss the target. Wales could still have saved the game after Gerald Davies celebrated his captaincy for the day by tying Edwards's Welsh record of twenty tries when he scored from ten yards. Yet Gareth Davies's failed conversion from wide condemned them to a 19–17 defeat.

Having seen his team score thirty-seven tries to their opponents' seven during the tour yet still lose four of their nine games, Rowlands was in no mood for diplomacy when he spoke at the post-match dinner. 'If we are rugby people and endorse thuggery, then I don't want any part of it,' he told his audience. 'What an effect it must have had on the thousands of schoolchildren present.'

Australian coach Darrell Haberlecht responded, after Wales had left the country, by saying that the tourists had been at fault for trampling in the rucks. Looking back on the tour, the *Rothmans Rugby Yearbook* would point out that Wales had not been blameless, while noting that even Rowlands had admitted that the discipline of his players may 'possibly' have been a problem.

The debate did, however, help convince the International Rugby Board that it was time to appoint neutral referees. Rowlands recalls, 'That was the last tour with home referees. I couldn't understand why they wouldn't even have a Queensland referee in New South Wales or the other way round. It was even more unfair because we really helped them money-wise on that tour and the gates were fantastic.'

J.P.R. Williams also believes that the team came home with the kind of resolve that the 1969 side had brought back from their beating in New Zealand. 'The best game was the second Test when they broke Graham Price's jaw and won the game with a dropped goal that was literally ten yards wide,' he says sardonically. 'Three reporters came in to show us a photograph of that. I wasn't captain that day so I don't know why I did this, but I sat everyone down and said, "There is no disgrace here. We have been cheated out of it and they have broken Pricey's jaw, so let's get ourselves back for next season. Also let's go out and drink them under the table."'

20

TURN IT ON AGAIN

'We did pretty well with a new side. We'd had a hard
time in Australia and that was the basis of the following
season' – *J.P.R. Williams*

If there was a lesson for Welsh rugby as the summer of 1978
faded into memory, maybe it could be found in the music charts,
where Genesis had shrugged off the departure of lead singer Peter
Gabriel to enjoy their biggest commercial success with the single
'Follow You, Follow Me'. If the Wales selectors could have dipped
into the future, their granddaughters could have assured them that even
Take That would find there was life after Robbie Williams. On the
other hand, the Sex Pistols had been floundering in a sea of imitations
and cheap gimmicks since Johnny Rotten walked out on them earlier
in the year. The question, then, as the 1978–79 international season
approached, was whether Wales, without Gareth Edwards, Phil Bennett
and Gerald Davies, would find their Phil Collins and retain their
number one position, or would their season be a mere pastiche of former
glories, like Sid Vicious croaking out old Eddie Cochran hits?

Edwards, still only 31, had confirmed his retirement during the
summer and was preparing for the release of his autobiography.
Davies, a relative veteran at 33, was quick to follow suit and, as
autumn arrived, Bennett announced that he would be stepping down
from international rugby at the age of 30. Ironically, just as in the year
of Barry John's abdication, a visit from the All Blacks beckoned, but

even that could not drag a few more weeks out of the trio. Edwards said he would not play in one game when he couldn't guarantee being able to give 100 per cent in the intervening matches.

Bennett, who would continue in club rugby for a few more years, says, 'I perhaps could have stayed on. I went back and played some of the finest rugby of my life for Llanelli but all of a sudden I wasn't spending the whole weekend training.' Even so, J.J. Williams struggled to understand his teammate's decision. 'Phil was getting over the hill slightly, but he still played for Llanelli and even for the Barbarians against New Zealand,' he says. 'I told him he was missing the best part, playing for Wales, but that was Phil. He was different. Gareth Davies came in and did quite well, but he was no Phil.'

The new halfback combination of Davies and Terry Holmes would be upgraded from stand-in to permanent status, remaining the pre-eminent men in their positions until Davies retired from rugby in 1985 and Holmes went to play for Bradford Northern later that same year. Both would captain their country. As well as making their international debuts on the same tour, they had previously played their first games for Cardiff within a few days of each other in 1975, Holmes having graduated through the Cardiff youth team and Davies switching from Llanelli after enrolling at the University of Wales Institute of Science and Technology.

Recovering from the setback of breaking his ankle in an unofficial game on Boxing Day morning in 1976, Holmes made big enough strides behind Gareth Edwards and Brynmoor Williams in the club's pecking order of scrum-halves that Williams moved to Newport. Steve Fenwick recalls the growing reputation of the young dark-haired man whose physical presence on the field belied a quiet, thoughtful personality. 'In many games Terry was as effective, if not more so, than Gareth Edwards. In a tight game where you needed someone to stand up and be an extra back-row forward he was fantastic. The first time I saw him he was about 18 and we were playing Cardiff in Bridgend. The tannoy announced that Gareth had withdrawn and we all thought, "Great, we have a better chance of winning." But then Terry took us apart on his own and we were standing around saying, "Fucking hell, where did they get him from?"'

If there was a concern over Holmes's play, it was that his delivery lacked a certain zip. But Davies, who became his closest friend as well as on-field colleague, said, 'Terry was criticised for the slowness of his pass by everyone except the man who had to take it. It was always just where I wanted it.'

Holmes, in turn, was fiercely loyal to Davies, a product of the famous Gwendraeth Grammar School that turned out other Wales fly-halves in Carwyn James, Barry John and Jonathan Davies. Gareth Davies was clearly more in the mould of John than his immediate predecessor Bennett, both in his languid, elegant style of play and the innate confidence he carried to the field. According to Holmes, 'Even when we were being well beaten, Gareth never believed we could lose.'

And Davies was not exactly suited to the physical side of the game either. 'Barry John used to describe himself as a fingertip tackler,' Holmes continued. 'Gareth didn't even bother with such niceties. He would only make a tackle if he had to or if he couldn't get out of the way.'

Overlooked in the retirement of the three big names was the decision of Terry Cobner to step aside because he felt he could no longer maintain the fitness required for international rugby. As well as leaving a hole to be filled in the back row, it meant that five players who had captained the team had bowed out within the space of two years.

J.P.R. Williams, the one certain selection remaining from coach John Dawes's own days as Wales skipper, was the man to whom the country turned, although he admits, 'I was not really expecting the captaincy and I never yearned it. I was more thrilled at being captain of Bridgend in their centenary season and I guess the captaincy of Wales came after that. You'd have to ask the players if I was a good captain, but I led from the front.'

As well as the new halfback pairing, Williams's first side featured London Welshman Clive Rees on the left wing, with J.J. Williams getting another rare chance on the right. Llanelli flanker Paul Ringer was chosen to replace the departed Cobner.

The New Zealand side they faced arrived in Cardiff a week after beating Ireland in the first international of their tour. The All Blacks had set out on something of a charm offensive, designed to erase the ugly memories of their last full British visit six years earlier. But defeat to Munster in the week preceding the Test match in Dublin had signalled a shifting of priorities. As *Rothmans Rugby Yearbook* would note, 'The All Blacks, who up to then had been moving the ball around in comparatively light-hearted fashion, revised their tactics and went in for a more purposeful, less spectacular game.' The Welsh, in particular, would once again be left with reason for umbrage by the time the All Blacks headed home.

New Zealand had at least reintroduced the *haka* to their pre-game routine, although little did Bill McLaren know the irony of pointing out to viewers that the words included the promise that 'anything unsportsmanlike we shall set aside'. A quarter of a century on from the last Welsh victory against New Zealand, it was clear that the home team had to meet the physical challenge of Graham Mourie's men head-on and scuffles broke out on a regular basis, causing the captains to be called together for peace talks by referee Roger Quittenton.

In the front row, the Pontypool trio enhanced their reputations even further by winning steady possession and Wales carried the game to the All Blacks, with Ringer to the fore. The Cardiff halfbacks looked assured and two penalties by Davies and a long one by Steve Fenwick – his torn number twelve shirt hanging down his back – had the home side ahead midway through the first half. The fear, however, was that Wales would pay for lacking the penetration to cross the New Zealand line, although the visitors looked no more likely to succeed in that area until they won the ball on the left after 25 minutes and moved it into the centre. Bill Osborne chipped towards the right corner and Stuart Wilson raced in to score.

Penalties by Davies and Brian McKechnie, an early substitute after full-back Clive Currie suffered a broken jaw, left Wales leading 12–7 as the teams changed ends. Davies missed an uncomplicated opportunity to add three more to the Welsh advantage and moments later McKechnie brought it back to two points with one of his long toe-pokes. The closest the home team came to pulling away was when Holmes could not quite finish a 30-yard break by getting the ball cleanly to J.J. Williams. With only seconds left, and the Arms

Park almost choking on the uncertainty of the outcome, the score remained 12–10 as Wales prepared for a lineout on their right wing, a short distance outside their own 22.

Black-jerseyed bodies tumbled to the floor as Windsor's throw hovered above them and Quittenton signalled for a New Zealand penalty, indicating his belief that Geoff Wheel had leant on Frank Oliver. The kick was bludgeoned through the posts by a delighted McKechnie and there was to be no end to 25 years of Welsh hurt against New Zealand.

What incensed the whole of Wales when the incident was shown on replay was that both Oliver and, even more blatantly, fellow lock Andy Haden had thrown themselves out of the line with a show of dramatics that could have been for no other purpose than deceiving the referee. Wheel was perhaps asking for trouble by attempting to win the ball with his outside arm, which critics suggested showed a certain naivety. Wouldn't it have been better, they asked, to have played safe by allowing New Zealand clean possession and forcing them to score a try or dropped goal?

Yet two points incensed Wales. First was the blatant gamesmanship of their opponents. Oliver appeared to have made up his mind to hit the deck regardless of Wheel's actions, while Haden's performance – possibly shielded from the referee's direct line of sight – was laughably obvious. Second was the fact that Quittenton had kept his whistle in his pocket for every other lineout, including several instances of players jumping with the outside arm. 'I was nonplussed by Roger's action,' said Holmes. 'He had refereed the lineout all afternoon with a casual disregard for all infringements. He didn't give one penalty at any lineout until that last one.'

New Zealand skipper Mourie has said in recent years that he remembered Haden telling him during the game that 'he was going to do it', while Haden would claim in his autobiography some years later, 'Our act, while premeditated, was born of desperation on the spur of the moment.'

J.P.R. Williams would comment, 'If their players can stoop that low to win a game, what was New Zealand rugby coming to?' Three decades on, though, he is prepared to take a diplomatic view.

'I see Andy Haden every year in Bermuda at a golf tournament,' he explains. 'There is a very big difference in practising cheating and doing something in the heat of the moment.'

Fenwick, however, has no such time for niceties. 'It was absolutely heartbreaking because we were the better side. I couldn't believe they had to resort to that; to win it on that sort of thing, diving out of the lineout. I have never seen it before or since. It was sickening. It won the game, but the fact they had to do it said a lot about the game. We were much better than them.'

Much of the post-game uproar was because New Zealand's antics struck at the heart of the notion of rugby being a 'man's game'. If anything illegal was going to happen, so the feeling went, it was better for it to be the Pontypool Front Row and their French counterparts giving each other an honest thumping in the scrum than the kind of gamesmanship more associated with Continental football teams. It was the cold-blooded intent that made this incident so damnable. When Haden and Oliver decided to take their dives, neither knew that Wheel would do just enough to allow them to get away with it. Mourie says of the incident, 'It has probably been mythologised a little bit. The Welsh see it as the reason they lost. In talking to the referee, he would say it wasn't.'

Either way, another controversial chapter in the history of Wales–All Blacks rugby had been written, and another Welsh defeat had been followed by acrimony and recrimination. There had been JPR's disallowed try against New Zealand in 1972; the 'Blind Irish Referee' at Twickenham in 1974; the phantom dropped goal in Australia a few months earlier; and now this. Was it a run of bad luck or did Wales, as their opponents sometimes suggested, not know how to take defeat without bleating? Certainly each of those defeats had given them genuine reason to feel hard done by, but hadn't they also got away with it when Brian Price thumped Noel Murphy back in 1969?

Ignored somewhat is the poignant fact that it was Wheel, who the previous year had been the first man sent off in a Wales shirt, who was the fall guy once again. 'I didn't do anything, honestly,' he pleaded after the game. Holmes is among those who believe it is unfair for Wheel's international career to be so quickly remembered for those two incidents. 'I have always thought his achievements received paltry acknowledgement both at the time and since.'

By the time the tourists were back to spend the final week of the tour in Wales, they had been victorious in fourteen of their fifteen games, winning all four internationals against the home nations, something none of their predecessors had achieved. Few fans were discussing that feat, however, after the events at Bridgend's Brewery Field in their final midweek match, a 17–6 victory in a game staged as part of the home team's centenary celebrations.

When J.P.R. Williams had found himself caught at the bottom of a ruck, he was brutally stamped on by prop forward John Ashworth. The action ripped a massive hole in his right cheek, causing the loss of two pints of blood and the insertion of thirty stitches. At first, Williams, who managed to play on after some initial patching up, had assumed it was accidental, but having seen the television replay – a clip that is still regularly viewed 30 years later on YouTube – he was left in no doubt about the intent that was involved. Speaking the next day through the pain of the jagged, crescent-shaped scar on his face, Williams said, 'I had some great tussles with the All Blacks but after yesterday's game I've got no wish to play against them again.'

He now says, 'To be honest, what annoyed me most about that incident was that Ashworth never apologised. When I saw the replay there was no doubt it was deliberate and when my father, who was giving a speech at the post-match dinner, drew attention to it, ten of the All Blacks got up and walked out.'

Further insult was added to injury three days later when Ashworth, by now the most unpopular man in Wales, was brought on as a substitute during the All Blacks' tour finale against the Barbarians at Cardiff, a game they won 18–16.

As the Labour government's 'Winter of Discontent' produces widespread work stoppages, it is the strike of lorry drivers that causes most distress in Wales, with rural areas unable to restock groceries, farmers fearful that adequate animal food stocks will not be delivered and pharmacies concerned about their supplies.

Neath winger Elgan Rees, who had been the traditional uncapped player in the Baa-baas side against the All Blacks, was the one change to the Wales team beaten by the tourists when the Five Nations season opened with a disastrous first half against Scotland. Rees took the place of namesake Clive, with J.J. Williams back in the number 11 jersey, but after taking a first-minute lead through Fenwick's penalty Wales trailed 13–6 at the turnaround. Andy Irvine kicked three penalties and also began and finished a twenty-fourth-minute move that involved a decisive break by fly-half John Rutherford.

Fenwick's third penalty early in the second half signalled Wales's intention to prove that their new team was as resilient as its predecessors and, with the strong wind in their favour, they proved too powerful for their opponents. Derek Quinnell and Jeff Squire were dominant behind an efficient front five and a period of pressure resulted in JPR chipping ahead for Rees to take the ball on the full and level the scores. Fenwick helped set up another score with a high kick that his forwards charged after, with Quinnell twice halted just short of the line. Wales drove hard and wheeled the resulting scrum, allowing Holmes to drop on the ball. Fenwick's conversion made the final score 19–13.

The build-up to the home game against Ireland was dominated by Britain's ongoing industrial strife. Cardiff Council pleaded unsuccessfully with cleansing department workers to break their strike to ensure that public toilets were operational and that mounting piles of refuse were cleared, especially with an additional seven tons of rubbish expected on game day. Instead, fans were urged to take their litter home and to cross their legs until they got to the National Stadium's working lavatories.

On the field, Wales built a 21–9 lead before fading in the final quarter and winning only 24–21, the most points they had ever allowed against Ireland. That they won at all was largely due to Fenwick outkicking Tony Ward. Otherwise, it was a performance lacking in precision, with Holmes grateful to Davies for his ability to make the most of inconsistent service. Wales were six points in arrears before Irish full-back Dick Spring fluffed Davies's high kick into the in-goal area and Allan Martin was quickest to react. Another error served up a further Wales try early in the second half, by which time the home side led 12–9. Scrum-half Colin Patterson, under pressure from Holmes, shovelled the ball into no-man's-land, where Ringer dropped down for his first international try.

A self-employed builder, Ringer's dark features and drooping moustache gave him a bandit look that matched his abrasive style of play. Llanelli clubmate Phil Bennett described him as 'one of a dying breed – flankers who flew off a scrum to take out the stand-off and crowd the midfield'. Hard-working and sharp to react to the ebb and flow of the action, he had caught the attention of selector Keith Rowlands while playing for Ebbw Vale at the start of the season and had put himself more squarely in the spotlight with a move to Llanelli. He had previously played for Leicester while attending Madeley College, Cobner's alma mater, although he had feared for his career when forced to miss half a season with a lung infection.

By the end of the Ireland game, Ringer was part of a reshuffled back row. Wheel's injury forced Quinnell to move to lock and brought Cardiff's Stuart Lane into the action. Ireland's breakaway trio proved a handful and left-wing Freddie McClennan and Patterson crossed for late tries either side of another Fenwick penalty.

As usual, France would provide the most meaningful test of the season, and Wales would come within a point of passing it. Barry Clegg won his first cap in place of injured clubmate Wheel, while Ray Gravell was sacrificed for the additional attacking options offered by another Swansea man, fly-half Dave Richards. It was hard to begrudge Richards his promotion after several years around the fringes of the team, but the timing was unexpected. A contest in Paris was always likely to have more call for Gravell's defensive ability than the creativity of his replacement.

Jean-Pierre Rives was intense and driven as he led his pack round the field, doubtless making Gareth Edwards even more relieved that he had declined that invitation to meet again in the Parc des Princes. Holmes emerged with honours for the way in which he kept Jerome Gallion in check and both he and Davies needed all the skills contained within their boots. After Fenwick's penalty opened the scoring, both scrum-halves touched down. Gallion cut inside J.P.R. Williams to score at speed before Holmes burrowed into the loose to emerge with the ball after a shortened lineout. Jean-Michel Aguirre and Fenwick landed two penalties each, but Wales were beaten when Gallion's quick release following a ruck gave Roland Bertranne the chance to put Jean-Francois Gourdon in at the corner. This time there was no saving tackle from J.P.R. Williams, and the Welsh captain admitted, 'Defeat would have been a terrible injustice to our opponents.'

Two weeks later ill-advised tactics and bad kicking sent the inconsistent French to defeat at Twickenham, meaning that Wales could win the championship outright, as well as a record fourth consecutive Triple Crown, if they beat England in the final Five Nations match of the decade at Cardiff. Whether Williams would be taking his place at the head of the team, however, was in doubt.

He had been working on his autobiography, a fact that emerged when his publisher, Collins, began a publicity campaign for its imminent release. The act of writing a book did not automatically compromise a player's amateur status, but receiving money from it did. The sport's rules even outlawed 'the promise of future payment or benefit'. John Reason argued in the *Daily Telegraph* that payment must have been made by the publisher and questioned its destination, while *The Sun* speculated that Williams had received a £10,000 advance. 'It was horrible,' Williams recalls. 'It was almost like they wanted to stop me playing for Wales against England. It was ridiculous. A friend of mine who was a lawyer said, "You should sue."'

Williams was called before the WRU and forced to explain to secretary Bill Clement that the money was going not into his own bank account, but to the Bridgend Sports Injury Clinic Foundation, which he was setting up in order to help fund a new treatment centre in his home town. Having been cleared to play against England, and in club games beyond his international retirement, Williams did sue the *Daily Telegraph* and *The Sun*. The latter settled without formal proceedings but the *Telegraph* case went to court three years later. Williams won £20,000 in costs and damages but the verdict was overturned on appeal, at which point he abandoned the campaign, despite thoughts of moving onto the European courts. 'We won the case, but the judge was too biased towards me and so we ended up in appeal. I couldn't afford to go on any more. It was an interesting experience.'

Meanwhile, Wales needed to reshape their pack for a season finale that also contained championship possibilities for England, whose only defeat of the season had been in Dublin. London Welsh stalwart Mike Roberts was brought back to cover for the absent Wheel, his first cap for four years, while injuries in the front row meant debuts for Cardiff hooker Alan Phillips and Aberavon prop John Richardson. The absence of Bobby Windsor was caused by lime burns he had received in a game on a council pitch.

With the season on the line, Wales gave their best performance by a long way, a perfect blend of forward power and flair in the back division, where Richards took the opportunity to demonstrate the skills that had earned his selection. Even the unusually wayward kicking of Fenwick, who missed five penalty attempts, had no bearing on the outcome of the game, other than to keep England in contention at 7–3 down after an hour.

Gareth Davies had opened the scoring with a dropped goal and the first try came from an unopposed run to the line by Richards after Jeff Squire's drive had set up Holmes to feed the backs. Richards could have had a second score but knocked on after a strong run by Holmes. England's best period coincided with JPR having a gashed calf stitched up, but after being held up just short of the line three times they never looked as threatening again. And in the final quarter, despite Clive Griffiths of Swansea having now replaced the wounded skipper, Wales made their superiority tell.

Roberts made his comeback even more remarkable by stealing possession at an England line and diving over to score – 'a sizzling burst from six inches', as he delighted in describing his only international try. Then J.J. Williams carried down the left and the ball was taken deep inside the English 22 by Fenwick, whose well-timed pass allowed Ringer an easy passage to the line. Richards used his pace to create a break from which Williams scored untouched after Wales had spread the ball right and left. The victory was completed after Davies launched an attack, Griffiths kicked ahead and Elgan Rees won the race to finish the move. Fenwick's conversion made the score 27–3 and equalled Phil Bennett's Five Nations record of 38 points in a season.

The party that had started long before the final whistle continued as J.P.R. Williams, after what was assumed to be his final international, was called to take a bow from the main stand while hordes of revelling fans gathered on the field. 'I have never been with a better bunch of lads,' he said. 'It has been a difficult season for us with injuries and illness but a tribute to Welsh strength.'

And with that image of the smiling features of someone who had grown during the decade from a nervous teenager on Edinburgh's Princes Street into a battle-scarred and decorated veteran, so an era came to an end.

Welsh voters come out four to one against allowing a national assembly in Cardiff to take over many of the governmental functions of Whitehall. Prime Minister James Callaghan is disappointed after calling for a 'yes' vote in the referendum on devolution, saying, 'The people of Wales are entitled to a bigger say in the decisions that affect their lives. Devolution will result in better government, not more government.'

It had been, without fear of contradiction, the greatest sustained period of success that Welsh rugby had known, bearing comparison with any period of dominance by any team in any sport. It began with an unforeseen Triple Crown in 1969 and ended ten years later with, appropriately, a similar achievement, this one a last hurrah eked out by many of those responsible for the triumphs of the previous decade.

In winning six outright championships, plus two shared, six Triple Crowns and three Grand Slams, Wales had won thirty-three of their forty-three games in the Five Nations Championship, posting an unbeaten home record along the way. The factors that contributed to those statistics have already been discussed in some detail, but few would begrudge the role of summariser for the purposes of this book being given to a man who, more than anyone, remains the personification of his team's achievements and with whom we prefaced the story of this golden period.

'We were lucky that there were a number of young, talented players who came together at the same time,' Gareth Edwards reflects. 'But you can put other ingredients in with that. A lot of our communities were based on working in heavy industry. I am not saying every coal miner and steel man could play for Wales but a lot played the game themselves and were hard, physical men. Then you can't be dismissive of the education system and the fact that many of our players were physical education students and therefore had a good grounding in important areas. When it came to the new era of weight training, coaching and preparation, we probably stole a march.

'It helped us to play a type of game we all revelled in. I don't want to suggest that we gathered together one day and said "this is how we are going to play" but Clive Rowlands saw the type of player he had at hand, like JPR coming in as a running full-back. What we had were guys who could play the game avoiding contact. When you grow up playing against physically bigger people, if you have any sense you avoid the contact. There was a Welsh style of play – with people like Cliff Morgan and Bleddyn Williams before us – that we tried to follow a great deal of the time.'

Having played in every Wales international over a period of 53 games, finishing with a then-record-equalling 20 tries, Edwards draws as much satisfaction from the manner of his country's accomplishments as the volume. That, after all, is why recollection of his team is such a joyful experience. 'I was at a function,' he concludes, 'and a soccer guy in London, a Chelsea fan, said to me, "You were the only team we used to watch. You were like the Brazil of rugby." A number of people from many countries have said that and it is a very kind compliment. It is much appreciated when people say it was a special era.'

He pauses briefly and adds with a chuckle, 'Mind you, we were not aware of it at the time. All we were doing was fighting for our lives.'

POSTSCRIPT

WALLS COME TUMBLING DOWN

'Shirley Williams closed the grammar schools, we closed
the mines – and that's why [Wales] were rubbish for 20
years' – *former Conservative MP Jeffrey Archer*

Much of this book was written with Wales once again at
the pinnacle of European rugby. A Grand Slam in the Six
Nations Championship of 2008 was followed later in the year by
the achievement of beating Australia in Cardiff, the only victory by
a home nation over one of the three southern hemisphere powers in
the autumn internationals. Three years earlier, the first Welsh Grand
Slam for twenty-seven years had preceded one victory in each of the
next two seasons and a humiliating World Cup exit in the group stage
at the hands of Fiji. This time, with New Zealander Warren Gatland
at the helm and in spite of the failure to repeat their championship
triumph in 2009 and 2010, there is hope that Wales's occupancy of
an elevated position in the rugby hierarchy will be sustained.

It has been a tortuous journey back towards the sport's summit,
one that few saw stretching out ahead when Wales entered the '80s
under John Lloyd, who had followed John Dawes as national coach
– just as he had succeeded him as captain eight years earlier. Only
twice in the next twenty years would Wales win more than two
games in a single Five Nations season. The fact that, in 1980, they
suffered their first defeat against England for 17 years – a game that
saw Paul Ringer sent off for a late tackle on John Horton – was a

warning sign. So was the home defeat to Scotland in 1982, their first championship loss in Cardiff in 14 years.

It had been defeat against the Scots at Murrayfield a year earlier that caused the permanent discarding of stalwarts Steve Fenwick and J.P.R. Williams, back in the team after rescinding his international retirement. Allan Martin went voluntarily at the end of the season, leaving Graham Price as the only major figure among the '70s Grand Slam winners still in the picture. By 1983, he too was stepping down, giving a damning indictment of the Welsh set-up in his autobiography, *Price of Wales*:

> The chief reason I quit was that I was thoroughly fed up with the way the Welsh team was being run. I dislike incompetence of any kind. What was happening in the Welsh team appalled me and with no channels open to express my opinion of the decline in the standard of selection, squad sessions and coaching, I resolved the best thing was to inform the selectors that I was no longer available.
>
> I considered myself more enthusiastic than most. Rugby meant a lot to me. I made the sacrifices willingly. But even my interest was dulled to the extent that by the end of the international season I would have been quite happy to throw my boots into the broom cupboard and forget about everything until the start of the new season.

By that time, former fly-half John Bevan was in charge of the team, assisted by Terry Cobner, whose involvement with the WRU would continue into the new century in his role as director of rugby. Bevan was given a rough ride by the critics, although Terry Holmes commented, 'Wales didn't produce the goods but that wasn't necessarily John's fault. There was a shortage of talent in some areas.' Bevan stepped down in 1985 due to ill health and, the following June, lost his battle against cancer, dying at the age of 38.

Holmes was soon heading to Bradford Northern, while halfback partner Gareth Davies retired to begin a successful business career that took in appointments as head of sport for BBC Wales, chief executive of Cardiff RFC, chairman of the Sports Council for Wales and chief executive of the Royal Mail in Wales.

Among the men whose era Holmes and Davies had followed, J.P.R. Williams was on his way to becoming orthopaedic consultant at the Prince of Wales Hospital in Bridgend and would continue to play club rugby into his fifties. John Dawes accepted the post of national coaching organiser, a role he confesses he did not enjoy or excel at. Gareth Edwards and Barry John continued to pursue successful media careers and remain among the most sought-after personalities in Wales, while Gerald Davies sits on the WRU committee and was appointed to manage the British Lions on their 2009 tour of South Africa. Phil Bennett has worked as a sports development officer for Carmarthenshire County Council; his predecessor as captain, Mervyn Davies, is a regular after-dinner speaker, like many of his peers.

Fenwick and Tom David were partners for a decade in an industrial chemicals supply company, while Brian Price gave up working for the BBC after 30 years because 'I was becoming bored of the repetitive nature of the game.' Graham Price is a media figure in Wales, as well as an after-dinner and motivational speaker, while J.J. Williams established a successful industrial painting company. Others followed their playing days by continuing careers as sales reps, teachers and electricity board employees. Many combined their day jobs with coaching, such as Charlie Faulkner at Newport and Allan Martin at Aberavon.

Derek Quinnell was named to assist Wales team coach Tony Gray in New Zealand and Australia at the inaugural World Cup in 1987, for which Clive Rowlands was given the role of team manager. After topping their group and beating England in the quarter-finals, a lesson in reality was administered in the form of a 49–6 thrashing by New Zealand in the semi-final in Brisbane. A last-gasp 22–21 win over Australia in the third-place play-off was thought by many to have covered up some of the problems, especially when Wales proceeded to win their first Triple Crown in nine years the following spring. And they were brutally brought back to earth with two wallopings in New Zealand, who racked up more than fifty points in each game.

Quinnell, who now runs a chemical supply company in Llanelli, recalls, 'We got a group of players together who I thought could become similar to what we were in the '70s; players like Robert Jones, Jonathan Davies, Adrian Hadley and Bleddyn Bowen. We were third in the world in 1987 and then we won at Twickenham in 1988. Tony Gray had done a good job as coach but all of a sudden we got beat in a few Tests and never got invited back again. We were a couple of positions short but in the main I was happy that for the next five or six years we would be in there. Then Davies, Hadley, John Devereux and Paul Moriarty all went north. If we could have kept that group together and added a couple of players we could have done well.'

Instead, aside from a championship victory in 1994 under skipper Ieuan Evans – beating England on points differential – the 1990s were even more dismal than the previous decade, with a revolving door of coaches unable to shut out the chill of disappointment. That championship success came in the midst of a run of five wooden spoons in seven seasons, while Wales failed to get past the group stages in the 1991 and 1995 World Cups. They at least reached the quarter-finals in the next two, although 2003 had earlier seen them suffer their first five-game whitewash since Italy joined an expanded Six Nations tournament. By the time coach Mike Ruddock led them to a triumphant 2005, there were plenty of regular visitors to Welsh international matches for whom such achievement existed only in the memories of older relatives.

It would take a book fully devoted to the subject to properly explore the reasons why the uplifting years of the 1970s were followed by almost three decades of Welsh subsidence. A cross-section of views is offered here as an illustration of the diverse factors that are considered to have contributed.

In *The Essential History of Rugby Union: Wales*, authors Steve Lewis and John Griffiths suggest, 'The administrators of the other leading rugby playing nations in the 21st century had been looking forward 20 years, while their Welsh counterparts were very much guilty of looking back.'

It is a view held by J.J. Williams, who agrees that success created complacency, an unfounded belief that things would somehow turn out right. 'In those days they all thought we had a divine right to win. It didn't happen when the exceptional players had gone and when the WRU were left to their own devices they came up short. The leaders must take the responsibility because they had no answers. They thought they were the cause of the '70s success, but they weren't. It was great individuals and great schooling. Since those days the schooling system has changed but the WRU should have adjusted.'

Ieuan Evans, who won the first of his 72 Welsh caps in 1987, adds, 'Going into the late '80s and '90s, we became too blasé about winning and were caught short. The game moved on and we didn't. I wouldn't blame it on the success of the '70s, but on the people who thought it was a right of ours to be successful rather than develop and evolve the game.'

Lack of continuity in and around the Wales team is cited by many. Clive Rowlands, who followed his management of Wales in the 1987 World Cup by guiding the British Lions in Australia two years later, says, 'During the 1970s we had only two coaches and the players knew each other inside out. That was a big help for us. I am still the guy who has coached the longest, six years, and John Dawes is next with five. In the '80s and '90s we had more coaches than people have hot dinners.'

Rowlands also believes that the loss of key players to rugby league eventually left too big a gap in the ranks of Welsh players, although former captain Arthur Lewis, who went on to coach Ebbw Vale and Cross Keys, blames the selectors for not looking hard enough to identify the available talent. 'You have to look at selection policies,' he says. 'I took the B team to Italy with Leighton Davies and they just ignored the report we gave back. The selectors believed in the players they saw in their small circle. When I mentioned Ebbw Vale's hooker Ian Watkins they had never heard of him.'

The arrival of professional rugby in 1995 presented fresh challenges to everyone involved in the game. Kevin Bowring, the first Wales coach of the new era, recalls, 'The game changed suddenly. I was appointed in September 1995 and the game had just gone open.

One week guys were amateurs and suddenly they were being paid. It required an immediate change in attitude. Players like Rob Howley were able to do it instantly but for others it was a battle. If you stand still in sport you get overtaken and we had some years when the structure didn't allow us to move forward.'

J.P.R. Williams believes that the advent of professionalism might actually have turned away good players unwilling to gamble everything on the sport offering them a comfortable living. 'We don't have the numbers coming through because since we went professional a lot of the good young players are choosing to go to university instead,' he suggests. 'I think they are wise.'

J.J. Williams argues that, for too long, the development of young players left much to be desired. 'I tried to help coach the Welsh Under–20s but they didn't want any of us there. In the '80s, the young Welsh teams were the most unfit teams ever. We always felt that when England got organised they would be awesome and they did just that. Wales didn't frighten them any more; all we did was argue among ourselves. It has come around now because people are getting to grips with professionalism.'

Stuart Gallacher, chief executive at Llanelli and then the regional Scarlets, agrees that it took too long for Welsh rugby to embrace the new age. 'Everyone was expecting to get paid all of a sudden but it took us ten years to get broadcasting contracts and decent value in place.'

Even the structure of the sport in Wales continues to cause frequent debate, with the professional game now centred on four regional teams: (Cardiff) Blues, (Llanelli) Scarlets, (Newport Gwent) Dragons and (Neath-Swansea) Ospreys. Steve Fenwick, a former coach at Bridgend and Newport, says, 'The worst thing to happen is taking away regional rugby from the mid-district of Bridgend and Pontypridd, which is where much of the talent comes from.'

In early 2009, it was rugby league that endeavoured to fill that void with the arrival of the Celtic Warriors in the Super League. On the eve of the new season, Allan Bateman, a Welsh international in both codes of the sport, argued, 'They made a massive mistake taking a region out of that area and rugby league is taking full advantage.

It's an untapped mine of talent. Youngsters are going to become battle-hardened rugby league players.'

Fenwick continues, 'Cardiff and Newport are only ten miles apart and then it is fifty-six miles before the next club. It will affect the national team eventually because promising players from that area used to watch Neil Jenkins and Gareth Thomas. Kids have got to have heroes.'

These days those champions of children's dreams no longer perform in the National Stadium at the Arms Park, but in the Millennium Stadium, built on the same site and incorporating a small part of the old building. Meanwhile, the demographics of the Welsh working population are much changed from the days of coal and steel domination, and today's technologically advanced fans consume the game via a range of media that Bill McLaren, Cliff Morgan and good old J.B.G Thomas could never have imagined.

Yet there is still one thing guaranteed to make the valleys, and all their clubs, pubs, schools and workplaces, come alive: victory for Wales. In that respect nothing has changed.

The Sunday morning smiles that John Dawes recalls seeing on the streets as he returned home from another triumph are worn just as broadly. As Stuart Gallacher notes, 'The goodwill and feeling of well-being you get from Wales winning should never be underestimated. It totally wraps everybody up. Thankfully rugby is still our national sport. We all feel part of it and feel we have played our part when the team is successful.'

Max Boyce, that most famous of Welsh fans, concurs. 'I don't think a lot has changed. Supporters are younger and more colourful and the game is less affordable for people in villages like mine, but the game is just as important. We are a small country and it is still one of the few sports where we walk the world stage. We take great pride in that and it is hugely important to people, rightly or wrongly, for Welsh rugby to be successful. On a Monday morning after beating England, people will go to work with a smile on their face. It definitely lifts the spirit and remains part of the fabric of life.'

Yet it is not just the re-emergence of Wales as a winning force in world rugby that is resonant of the 1970s. Welsh retailers reported a 'frightening fall' in sales as the world's financial crisis took hold. As budgets for the new economic era are projected, the valleys' industries, like their counterparts around the globe, have resorted to shrinking the workforce in order to reduce costs. How many new winters of discontent now lie in store? In these times of turmoil, it will be down to the rugby community of Wales to ease its people's burden once again with an extended age of on-field prosperity.

If that doesn't work out, well, there will always be the 1970s, an era whose light will never go out and whose stars live on through DVDs and retro sports channels. When fortunes on Welsh rugby fields are bad, that decade's passing is mourned and its personalities most acutely missed. When the good times return, comparison with the teams of Dawes and Mervyn Davies is used to evaluate and validate new achievements.

And should younger fans grow weary of hearing Shane Williams mentioned in the same breath as Gerald Davies – or wish for the shadow of Gareth Edwards and Barry John to be removed from above Mike Phillips and Stephen Jones – there will always be someone quick to remind them how those bygone names breathed life into a nation; into a whole sport for those of us lucky enough to have been watching.

No one would begrudge those men the gift of eternal life. Not even an All Blacks captain.

APPENDIX

WALES FULL INTERNATIONALS, 1969–79

Played: 53. Won: 36. Drawn: 4. Lost: 13
Grand Slams: 1971, 1976, 1978
Triple Crowns: 1969, 1971, 1976, 1977, 1978, 1979
Five Nations Championships: 1969, 1970 (shared), 1971,
1973 (five-way tie), 1975, 1976, 1978, 1979. (Note: unbeaten
in incomplete 1972 season.)

1969
1 February 1969: Scotland 3, Wales 17 (Murrayfield)
Wales: J.P.R. Williams, S.J. Watkins, K.S. Jarrett, T.G.R.
Davies, M.C.R. Richards, B. John, G.O. Edwards; D.
Williams, J. Young, D.J. Lloyd, B. Price (captain), B. Thomas,
W.D. Morris, T.M. Davies, J. Taylor.
Tries: John, Edwards, Richards. Con: Jarrett. Pen: Jarrett 2.

8 March 1969: Wales 24, Ireland 11 (Cardiff)
Wales: J.P.R. Williams, S.J. Watkins, K.S. Jarrett, T.G.R.
Davies, M.C.R. Richards, B. John, G.O. Edwards; D.
Williams, J. Young, D.J. Lloyd, B. Price (captain), B. Thomas,
W.D. Morris, T.M. Davies, J. Taylor.
Tries: Watkins, Morris, Taylor, D. Williams. Con: Jarrett 3.
Pen: Jarrett. DG: John.

22 March 1969: France 8, Wales 8 (Paris)
Wales: J.P.R. Williams, S.J. Watkins, K.S. Jarrett, T.G.R.
Davies (Rep: P. Bennett), M.C.R. Richards, B. John, G.O.
Edwards; D. Williams, J. Young, D.J. Lloyd, B. Price
(captain), B. Thomas, W.D. Morris, T.M. Davies, J. Taylor.
Tries: Edwards, Richards. Con: Jarrett.

12 April 1969: Wales 30, England 9 (Cardiff)
Wales: J.P.R. Williams, S.J. Watkins, K.S. Jarrett, T.G.R.
Davies, M.C.R. Richards, B. John, G.O. Edwards (captain);
D. Williams, J. Young, D.J. Lloyd, W.D. Thomas, B. Thomas,
W.D. Morris, T.M. Davies, J. Taylor.
Tries: Richards 4, John. Con: Jarrett 3. Pen: Jarrett 2. DG:
John.

31 May 1969: New Zealand 19, Wales 0 (Christchurch)
Wales: J.P.R. Williams, S.J. Watkins, K.S. Jarrett, T.G.R.
Davies, M.C.R. Richards, B. John, G.O. Edwards; D.
Williams, J. Young (Rep: N.R. Gale), D.J. Lloyd, B. Price
(captain), B. Thomas, W.D. Morris, T.M. Davies, J. Taylor.

14 June 1969: New Zealand 33, Wales 12 (Auckland)
Wales: J.P.R. Williams, T.G.R. Davies, K.S. Jarrett, S.J.
Dawes, M.C.R. Richards, B. John, G.O. Edwards; D.
Williams, N.R. Gale, B. Thomas, B. Price (captain), W.D.
Thomas, W.D. Morris, T.M. Davies, D. Hughes.
Tries: Jarrett, Richards. Pen: Jarrett 2.

21 June 1969: Australia 16, Wales 19 (Sydney)
Wales: J.P.R. Williams, T.G.R. Davies, K.S. Jarrett, S.J.
Dawes, M.C.R. Richards, B. John, G.O. Edwards; D.
Williams, N.R. Gale, D.J. Lloyd, B. Price (captain), W.D.
Thomas, W.D. Morris, T.M. Davies, J. Taylor.
Tries: Morris, T.G.R. Davies, Taylor. Con: Jarrett 2. Pen:
Jarrett 2.

APPENDIX

1970

24 January 1970: Wales 6, South Africa 6 (Cardiff)
Wales: J.P.R. Williams, P. Bennett, S.J. Dawes, W.H.
Raybould, I. Hall, B. John, G.O. Edwards (captain); D.
Williams, V.C. Perrins, D.B. Llewellyn, W.D. Thomas, T.G.
Evans, W.D. Morris, T.M. Davies, D. Hughes.
Tries: Edwards. Pen: Edwards.

7 February 1970: Wales 18, Scotland 9 (Cardiff)
Wales: J.P.R. Williams, L.T.D. Daniels, S.J. Dawes, P.
Bennett, I. Hall, B. John, G.O. Edwards (captain); D.
Williams, V.C. Perrins, D.B. Llewellyn, W.D. Thomas, T.G.
Evans, W.D. Morris, T.M. Davies, D. Hughes.
Tries: Daniel, Llewellyn, Dawes, Morris. Con: Edwards 2,
Daniel.

28 February 1970: England 13, Wales 17 (Twickenham)
Wales: J.P.R. Williams, S.J. Watkins, S.J. Dawes, W.H.
Raybould, I. Hall, B. John, G.O. Edwards (captain Rep:
R. Hopkins); D. Williams, J. Young, D.B. Llewellyn, W.D.
Thomas, T.G. Evans, W.D. Morris, T.M. Davies, D. Hughes.
Tries: T.M. Davies, John, J.P.R. Williams, Hopkins. Con:
J.P.R. Williams. DG: John.

14 March 1970: Ireland 14, Wales 0 (Dublin)
Wales: J.P.R. Williams, S.J. Watkins, S.J. Dawes, W.H.
Raybould, I. Hall, B. John, G.O. Edwards (captain); D.
Williams, J. Young, D.B. Llewellyn, W.D. Thomas, T.G.
Evans, W.D. Morris, T.M. Davies, D. Hughes.

4 April 1970: Wales 11, France 6 (Cardiff)
Wales: J.P.R. Williams, J.L. Shanklin, S.J. Dawes (captain),
A.J. Lewis, R. Mathias, B. John, G.O. Edwards; D.J. Lloyd,
J. Young, D.B. Llewellyn, W.D. Thomas, I.S. Gallacher, W.D.
Morris, T.M. Davies, J. Taylor.
Tries: Morris. Con: J.P.R. Williams. Pen: J.P.R. Williams 2.

1971

16 January 1971: Wales 22, England 6 (Cardiff)
Wales: J.P.R. Williams, T.G.R. Davies, S.J. Dawes (captain),
A.J. Lewis, J.C. Bevan, B. John, G.O. Edwards; D. Williams,
J. Young, D.B. Llewellyn, W.D. Thomas, M.G. Roberts,
W.D. Morris, T.M. Davies, J. Taylor.
Tries: T.G.R. Davies 2, Bevan. Con: Taylor 2. Pen: J.P.R.
Williams. DG: John 2.

6 February 1971: Scotland 18, Wales 19 (Murrayfield)
Wales: J.P.R. Williams, T.G.R. Davies, S.J. Dawes (captain),
I. Hall, J.C. Bevan, B. John, G.O. Edwards; D. Williams, J.
Young, D.B. Llewellyn, W.D. Thomas, M.G. Roberts, W.D.
Morris, T.M. Davies, J. Taylor.
Tries: Taylor, Edwards, John, T.G.R. Davies. Con: John,
Taylor. Pen: John.

13 March 1971: Wales 23, Ireland 9 (Cardiff)
Wales: J.P.R. Williams, T.G.R. Davies, S.J. Dawes (captain),
A.J. Lewis, J.C. Bevan, B. John, G.O. Edwards; D. Williams,
J. Young, D.B. Llewellyn, W.D. Thomas, M.G. Roberts,
W.D. Morris, T.M. Davies, J. Taylor.
Tries: T.G.R. Davies 2, Edwards 2. Con: John. Pen: John 2.
DG: John.

27 March 1971: France 5, Wales 9 (Paris)
Wales: J.P.R. Williams, T.G.R. Davies, S.J. Dawes (captain),
A.J. Lewis, J.C. Bevan, B. John, G.O. Edwards; D. Williams,
J. Young, D.B. Llewellyn, W.D. Thomas, M.G. Roberts,
W.D. Morris, T.M. Davies, J. Taylor.
Tries: Edwards, John. Pen: John.

1972

15 January 1972: England 3, Wales 12 (Twickenham)
Wales: J.P.R. Williams, T.G.R. Davies, R.T.E. Bergiers,
A.J. Lewis, J.C. Bevan, B. John, G.O. Edwards; D.J. Lloyd

(captain), J. Young, D.B. Llewellyn, W.D. Thomas, T.G. Evans, W.D. Morris, T.M. Davies, J. Taylor.
Tries: J.P.R. Williams. Con: John. Pen: John 2.

5 February 1972: Wales 35, Scotland 12 (Cardiff)
Wales: J.P.R. Williams, T.G.R. Davies, R.T.E. Bergiers, A.J. Lewis, J.C. Bevan, B. John, G.O. Edwards; D.J. Lloyd (captain), J. Young, D.B. Llewellyn, W.D. Thomas, T.G. Evans, W.D. Morris, T.M. Davies, J. Taylor.
Tries: Edwards 2, T.G.R. Davies, Bergiers, Taylor. Con: John 3. Pen: John 3.

25 March 1972: Wales 20, France 6 (Cardiff)
Wales: J.P.R. Williams, T.G.R. Davies, R.T.E. Bergiers, A.J. Lewis, J.C. Bevan, B. John, G.O. Edwards; D.J. Lloyd (captain), J. Young, D.B. Llewellyn, W.D. Thomas, T.G. Evans, W.D. Morris, T.M. Davies (Rep: D.L. Quinnell), J. Taylor.
Tries: T.G.R. Davies, Bevan. Pen: John 4.

2 December 1972: Wales 16, New Zealand 19 (Cardiff)
Wales: J.P.R. Williams, T.G.R. Davies, R.T.E. Bergiers, J.L. Shanklin, J.C. Bevan, P. Bennett, G.O. Edwards; G. Shaw, J. Young, D.B. Llewellyn, W.D. Thomas (captain), D.L. Quinnell, W.D. Morris, T.M. Davies, J. Taylor.
Tries: Bevan. Pen: Bennett 4.

1973
20 January 1973: Wales 25, England 9 (Cardiff)
Wales: J.P.R. Williams, T.G.R. Davies, R.T.E. Bergiers, A.J. Lewis (captain), J.C. Bevan, P. Bennett, G.O. Edwards; D.J. Lloyd, J. Young, G. Shaw, W.D. Thomas, D.L. Quinnell, W.D. Morris, T.M. Davies, J. Taylor.
Tries: Bevan 2, T.G.R. Davies, Edwards, Lewis. Con: Bennett. Pen: Taylor.

3 February 1973: Scotland 10, Wales 9 (Murrayfield)
Wales: J.P.R. Williams, T.G.R. Davies, R.T.E. Bergiers, A.J.
Lewis (captain), J.C. Bevan, P. Bennett, G.O. Edwards; D.J.
Lloyd, J. Young, G. Shaw, W.D. Thomas, D.L. Quinnell,
W.D. Morris, T.M. Davies, J. Taylor.
Pen: Bennett 2, Taylor.

10 March 1973: Wales 16, Ireland 12 (Cardiff)
Wales: J.P.R. Williams, T.G.R. Davies, R.T.E. Bergiers, A.J.
Lewis (captain), J.L. Shanklin, P. Bennett, G.O. Edwards;
P. D. Llewellyn, J. Young, G. Shaw, W.D. Thomas, D.L.
Quinnell, W.D. Morris, T.M. Davies, J. Taylor.
Tries: Shanklin, Edwards. Con: Bennett. Pen: Bennett 2.

24 March 1973: France 12, Wales 3 (Paris)
Wales: J.P.R. Williams, T.G.R. Davies, R.T.E. Bergiers, A.J.
Lewis (captain. Rep: J.J. Williams), J.L. Shanklin, P. Bennett,
G.O. Edwards; P. D. Llewellyn, J. Young, G. Shaw, W.D.
Thomas, M.G. Roberts, T. David, T.M. Davies, J. Taylor.
Pen: Bennett.

10 November 1973: Wales 24, Australia 0 (Cardiff)
Wales: J.P.R. Williams, T.G.R. Davies, R.T.E. Bergiers, K.
Hughes, J.J. Williams, P. Bennett, G.O. Edwards (captain);
G. Shaw, R.W. Windsor, P.D. Llewellyn, A.J. Martin, D.L.
Quinnell, W.D. Morris, T.M. Davies, T. David.
Tries: Morris, Windsor, T.G.R. Davies. Pen: Bennett 4.

1974
19 January 1974: Wales 6, Scotland 0 (Cardiff)
Wales: J.P.R. Williams, T.G.R. Davies, I. Hall, K. Hughes,
J.J. Williams, P. Bennett, G.O. Edwards (captain); G. Shaw,
R.W. Windsor, P.D. Llewellyn, A.J. Martin, D.L. Quinnell,
W.D. Morris, T.M. Davies, T. Cobner.
Tries: Cobner. Con: Bennett.

2 February 1974: Ireland 9, Wales 9 (Dublin)
Wales: J.P.R. Williams, C.F.W. Rees, I. Hall, A.A.J.
Finlayson, J.J. Williams, P. Bennett, G.O. Edwards (captain);
G. Shaw, R.W. Windsor, W.P.J. Williams, A.J. Martin,
G.A.D. Wheel, W.D. Morris, T.M. Davies, T. Cobner.
Tries: J.J. Williams. Con: Bennett. Pen: Bennett.

16 February 1974: Wales 16, France 16 (Cardiff)
Wales: J.P.R. Williams, T.G.R. Davies, I. Hall, A.A.J.
Finlayson, J.J. Williams, P. Bennett, G.O. Edwards (captain);
G. Shaw, R.W. Windsor, W.P.J. Williams, I.R. Robinson,
D.L. Quinnell, W.D. Morris, T.M. Davies, T. Cobner.
Tries: J.J. Williams. Con: Bennett 3. DG: Edwards.

16 March 1974: England 16, Wales 12 (Twickenham)
Wales: W.R. Blyth, T.G.R. Davies, R.T.E. Bergiers, A.A.J.
Finlayson, J.J. Williams, P. Bennett, G.O. Edwards (captain);
P.D. Llewellyn, R.W. Windsor, G. Shaw, W.D. Thomas, I.R.
Robinson (Rep: G.A.D. Wheel), W.D. Morris, T.M. Davies,
T.J. Cobner.
Tries: T.M. Davies. Con: Bennett. Pen: Bennett 2.

1975
18 January 1975: France 10, Wales 25 (Paris)
Wales: J.P.R. Williams, T.G.R. Davies, R.W.R. Gravell, S.P.
Fenwick, J.J. Williams, J.D. Bevan, G.O. Edwards; A.G.
Faulkner, R.W. Windsor, G. Price, A.J. Martin, G.A.D.
Wheel, T.P. Evans, T.M. Davies (captain), T.J. Cobner.
Tries: Fenwick, Cobner, T.G.R. Davies, Edwards, Price. Con:
Fenwick. Pen: Fenwick.

15 February 1975: Wales 20, England 4 (Cardiff)
Wales: J.P.R. Williams, T.G.R. Davies, R.W.R. Gravell, S.P.
Fenwick, J.J. Williams, J.D. Bevan, G.O. Edwards; A.G.
Faulkner, R.W. Windsor, G. Price, A.J. Martin, G.A.D.
Wheel, T.P. Evans, T.M. Davies (captain), T.J. Cobner.

Tries: T.G.R. Davies, J.J. Williams, Fenwick. Con: Martin.
Pen: Martin 2.

1 March 1975: Scotland 12, Wales 10 (Murrayfield)
Wales: J.P.R. Williams, T.G.R. Davies, R.W.R. Gravell, S.P.
Fenwick (Rep: W.R. Blyth), J.J. Williams, J.D. Bevan (Rep:
P. Bennett), G.O. Edwards; A.G. Faulkner, R.W. Windsor,
G. Price, A.J. Martin, M.G. Roberts, T.P. Evans, T.M.
Davies (captain), T.J. Cobner.
Tries: Evans. Pen: Fenwick 2.

15 March 1975: Wales 32, Ireland 4 (Cardiff)
Wales: J.P.R. Williams, T.G.R. Davies, R.W.R. Gravell,
R.T.E. Bergiers, P. Bennett, G.O. Edwards; A.G. Faulkner,
R.W. Windsor, G. Price, A.J. Martin, G.A.D. Wheel, T.P.
Evans, T.M. Davies (captain), T.J. Cobner.
Tries: Edwards, T.G.R. Davies, Faulkner, J.J. Williams,
Bergiers. Con: Bennett 3. Pen: Bennett 2.

20 December 1975: Wales 28, Australia 3 (Cardiff)
Wales: J.P.R. Williams, J.J. Williams, R.W.R. Gravell, S.P.
Fenwick, C.F.W. Rees, J.D. Bevan, G.O. Edwards; A.G.
Faulkner, R.W. Windsor, G. Price, A.J. Martin, G.A.D.
Wheel, T.P. Evans, T.M. Davies (captain), T.J. Cobner.
Tries: J.J. Williams 3, Edwards. Con: Fenwick 2, Martin.
Pen: Fenwick. DG: Bevan.

1976
17 January 1976: England 9, Wales 21 (Twickenham)
Wales: J.P.R. Williams, T.G.R. Davies, R.W.R. Gravell, S.P.
Fenwick, J.J. Williams, P. Bennett, G.O. Edwards; A.G.
Faulkner, R.W. Windsor, G. Price, A.J. Martin, G.A.D.
Wheel, T.P. Evans, T.M. Davies (captain), T.J. Cobner.
Tries: J.P.R. Williams 2, Edwards. Con: Fenwick 3. Pen:
Martin.

APPENDIX

7 February 1976: Wales 28, Scotland 6 (Cardiff)
Wales: J.P.R. Williams, T.G.R. Davies, R.W.R. Gravell, S.P.
Fenwick, J.J. Williams, P. Bennett, G.O. Edwards; A.G.
Faulkner, R.W. Windsor, G. Price, A.J. Martin, G.A.D.
Wheel, T.P. Evans, T.M. Davies (captain), T.J. Cobner.
Tries: J.J. Williams, Edwards, Evans. Con: Bennett 2. Pen:
Bennett 3. DG: Fenwick.

21 February 1976: Ireland 9, Wales 34 (Dublin)
Wales: J.P.R. Williams, T.G.R. Davies, R.W.R. Gravell, S.P.
Fenwick, J.J. Williams, P. Bennett, G.O. Edwards; A.G.
Faulkner, R.W. Windsor, G. Price, A.J. Martin, G.A.D.
Wheel, T.P. Evans, T.M. Davies (captain), T. David.
Tries: T.G.R. Davies 2, Edwards, Bennett. Con: Bennett 3.
Pen: Bennett 3, Martin.

6 March 1976: Wales 19, France 13 (Cardiff)
Wales: J.P.R. Williams, T.G.R. Davies, R.W.R. Gravell, S.P.
Fenwick, J.J. Williams, P. Bennett, G.O. Edwards; A.G.
Faulkner, R.W. Windsor, G. Price, A.J. Martin, G.A.D.
Wheel, T.P. Evans, T.M. Davies (captain), T. David.
Tries: J.J. Williams. Pen: Bennett 2, Fenwick 2, Martin.

1977

8 January 1977: Wales 25, Ireland 9 (Cardiff)
Wales: J.P.R. Williams, T.G.R. Davies, D.H. Burcher, S.P.
Fenwick, J.J. Williams, P. Bennett (captain), G.O. Edwards;
G. Shaw, R.W. Windsor, G. Price, A.J. Martin, G.A.D.
Wheel, T.P. Evans, J. Squire, R.C. Burgess.
Tries: T.G.R. Davies, J.P.R. Williams, Burgess. Con: Bennett
2. Pen: Bennett 2. DG: Fenwick.

5 February 1977: France 16, Wales 9 (Paris)
Wales: J.P.R. Williams, T.G.R. Davies, D.H. Burcher, S.P.
Fenwick, J.J. Williams, P. Bennett (captain), G.O. Edwards;
G. Shaw, R.W. Windsor, G. Price, A.J. Martin, D.L.

Quinnell, R.C. Burgess, J. Squire, T.J. Cobner.
Pen: Fenwick 3.

5 March 1977: Wales 14, England 9 (Cardiff)
Wales: J.P.R. Williams, T.G.R. Davies, D.H. Burcher, S.P.
Fenwick, J.J. Williams, P. Bennett (captain), G.O. Edwards;
C. Williams, R.W. Windsor, G. Price, A.J. Martin, G.A.D.
Wheel, R.C. Burgess, D.L. Quinnell, T.J. Cobner.
Tries: Edwards, J.P.R. Williams. Pen: Fenwick 2.

19 March 1977: Scotland 9, Wales 18 (Murrayfield)
Wales: J.P.R. Williams, T.G.R. Davies, D.H. Burcher, S.P.
Fenwick, J.J. Williams, P. Bennett (captain), G.O. Edwards;
C. Williams, R.W. Windsor, G. Price, A.J. Martin, G.A.D.
Wheel, R.C. Burgess, D.L. Quinnell, T.J. Cobner.
Tries: J.J. Williams, Bennett. Con: Bennett 2. Pen: Bennett 2.

1978
4 February 1978: England 6, Wales 9 (Twickenham)
Wales: J.P.R. Williams, T.G.R. Davies, R.W.R. Gravell, S.P.
Fenwick, J.J. Williams, P. Bennett (captain), G.O. Edwards;
A.G. Faulkner, R.W. Windsor, G. Price, A.J. Martin,
G.A.D. Wheel, J. Squire, D.L. Quinnell, T.J. Cobner.
Pen: Bennett 3.

18 February 1978: Wales 22, Scotland 14 (Cardiff)
Wales: J.P.R. Williams, T.G.R. Davies, R.W.R. Gravell, S.P.
Fenwick, J.J. Williams, P. Bennett (captain), G.O. Edwards;
A.G. Faulkner, R.W. Windsor, G. Price, A.J. Martin,
G.A.D. Wheel, J. Squire, D.L. Quinnell, T.J. Cobner.
Tries: Edwards, Gravell, Fenwick, Quinnell. Pen: Bennett.
DG: Bennett.

4 March 1978: Ireland 16, Wales 20 (Dublin)
Wales: J.P.R. Williams, T.G.R. Davies, R.W.R. Gravell, S.P.
Fenwick, J.J. Williams, P. Bennett (captain), G.O. Edwards;

A.G. Faulkner, R.W. Windsor, G. Price, A.J. Martin,
G.A.D. Wheel, J. Squire, D.L. Quinnell, T.J. Cobner.
Tries: Fenwick, J.J. Williams. Pen: Fenwick 4.

18 March 1978: Wales 16, France 7 (Cardiff)
Wales: J.P.R. Williams, J.J. Williams, R.W.R. Gravell, S.P.
Fenwick, G.L. Evans, P. Bennett (captain), G.O. Edwards;
A.G. Faulkner, R.W. Windsor, G. Price, A.J. Martin,
G.A.D. Wheel, J. Squire, D.L. Quinnell, T.J. Cobner.
Tries: Bennett 2. Con: Bennett. DG: Edwards, Fenwick.

11 June 1978: Australia 18, Wales 8 (Brisbane)
Wales: J.P.R. Williams, T.G.R. Davies, R.W.R. Gravell, S.P.
Fenwick, J.J. Williams, W.G. Davies, D.B. Williams; A.G.
Faulkner, R.W. Windsor, G. Price, A.J. Martin, G.A.D.
Wheel, J. Squire (Rep: S.M. Lane), D.L. Quinnell, T.J.
Cobner (captain).
Tries: T.G.R. Davies, D.B. Williams.

17 June 1978: Australia 19, Wales 17 (Sydney)
Wales: A.J. Donovan (Rep: G.L. Evans), T.G.R. Davies
(captain), R.W.R. Gravell, S.P. Fenwick, J.J. Williams, W.G.
Davies, T.D. Holmes; A.G. Faulkner, R.W. Windsor, G.
Price (Rep: S.J. Richardson), A.J. Martin, G.A.D. Wheel,
J.P.R. Williams, C.E. Davis, S.M. Lane.
Tries: T.G.R. Davies, Holmes. Pen: W.G. Davies 2. DG:
W.G. Davies.

11 November 1978: Wales 12, New Zealand 13 (Cardiff)
Wales: J.P.R. Williams (captain), J.J. Williams, R.W.R.
Gravell, S.P. Fenwick, C.F.W. Rees, W.G. Davies, T.D.
Holmes; A.G. Faulkner, R.W. Windsor, G. Price, A.J.
Martin, G.A.D. Wheel, P. Ringer, D.L. Quinnell, J. Squire.
Pen: W.G. Davies 3, Fenwick.

1979

20 January 1979: Scotland 13, Wales 19 (Murrayfield)
Wales: J.P.R. Williams (captain), H.E. Rees, R.W.R. Gravell,
S.P. Fenwick, J.J. Williams, W.G. Davies, T.D. Holmes; A.G.
Faulkner, R.W. Windsor, G. Price, A.J. Martin, G.A.D.
Wheel, P. Ringer, D.L. Quinnell, J. Squire.
Tries: Holmes, Rees. Con: Fenwick. Pen: Fenwick 3.

3 February 1979: Wales 24, Ireland 21 (Cardiff)
Wales: J.P.R. Williams (captain), H.E. Rees, R.W.R. Gravell,
S.P. Fenwick, J.J. Williams, W.G. Davies, T.D. Holmes; A.G.
Faulkner, R.W. Windsor, G. Price, A.J. Martin, G.A.D.
Wheel (Rep: S.M. Lane), P. Ringer, D.L. Quinnell, J. Squire.
Tries: Martin, Ringer. Con: Fenwick 2. Pen: Fenwick 4.

17 February 1979: France 14, Wales 13 (Paris)
Wales: J.P.R. Williams (captain), H.E. Rees, D.S. Richards,
S.P. Fenwick, J.J. Williams, W.G. Davies, T.D. Holmes; A.G.
Faulkner, R.W. Windsor, G. Price, A.J. Martin, B.J. Clegg, P.
Ringer, D.L. Quinnell, J. Squire.
Tries: Holmes. Pen: Fenwick 3.

17 March 1979: Wales 27, England 3 (Cardiff)
Wales: J.P.R. Williams (captain), H.E. Rees, D.S. Richards,
S.P. Fenwick, J.J. Williams, W.G. Davies, T.D. Holmes;
S.J. Richardson, A.J. Phillips, G. Price, A.J. Martin, M.G.
Roberts, P. Ringer, D.L. Quinnell, J. Squire.
Tries: Richards, Ringer, Roberts, Rees, J.J. Williams. Con:
Martin, Fenwick. DG: Davies.

APPENDIX

WELSH CHARITABLES RUGBY UNION FOOTBALL

The Welsh Charitables RFC raises funds for a number of charities through the medium of rugby. The charities supported by the club include Ty Hafan, the Children's Hospice in Wales; St Anne's Hospice; St David's Foundation Hospice Care; the Welsh Rugby International Players' Benevolent Association; and the Welsh Rugby Charitable Trust, which support players seriously injured while playing the sport.

The club, which has launched its 'We Want A Million Appeal', stages events including sportsmen's dinners, golf days, tribute dinners and charity games, all of which are supported by former Wales players. Further information about the club can be found at www.welshcharitablesrfc.com.

WELSH RUGBY INTERNATIONAL PLAYERS' BENEVOLENT ASSOCIATION

The Welsh Rugby International Players' Benevolent Association (registered charity 1102 484) is the charitable arm of the Welsh International Former Players' Association and was set up to aid the relief of poverty and hardship of former Welsh internationals and their families and dependents. Help is given to those requiring medical treatment for illness or injury relating to their playing days, or those whose earning capacity has been adversely impacted by rugby-related injury or illness.

The organisation is administered by a group of trustees, whose J.J. Williams explains, 'While charities exist to help those seriously injured on the field, we wanted to provide support to those who have given so much for their country on the field of play but whose problems are very varied.' Further information can be found at www.wrex.co.uk.

BIBLIOGRAPHY

Bennett, Phil and Martyn Williams, *Everywhere for Wales: An Autobiography* (Stanley Paul, 1981)

David, Tom, *Tommy David* (Thomson Media Services, 1983)

Davies, Gareth with Terry Godwin *Standing Off: My Life in Rugby* (Macdonald Queen Anne Press, 1986)

Davies, Gerald, *Gerald Davies: An Autobiography* (George Allen & Unwin, 1979)

Davies, Mervyn with David Parry-Jones, *No. 8* (Pelham Books, 1977)

Dawes, John (editor), *Thinking Rugby* (George Allen & Unwin, 1979)

Edwards, Gareth, *Gareth: An Autobiography* (Stanley Paul, 1978)

Edwards, Gareth, *The Golden Years of Welsh Rugby* (Harrap, 1982)

Edwards, Gareth with Peter Bills, *Tackling Rugby: The Changing World of Professional Rugby* (Headline, 2003)

Holmes, Terry *My Life in Rugby* (MacMillan, 1988)

John, Barry with Paul Abbandonato, *Barry John: The King* (Mainstream, 2000)

Lewis, Steve and John Griffiths, *The Essential History of Rugby Union: Wales* (Headline, 2003)

Morgan, Kenneth O., *Wales 1880–1980: Rebirth of a Nation* (University of Wales Press, 1981)

Parry-Jones, David, *The Dawes Decades: John Dawes and the Third Golden Era of Welsh Rugby* (Seren, 2005)

Price, Graham with Terry Godwin, *Price of Wales* (Collins Willow, 1984)

BIBLIOGRAPHY

Reason, John (editor), *How We Beat the All Blacks: 1971 Lions Speak* (Aurum, 2005)

Richards, Alun, *Carwyn: A Personal Memoir* (Michael Joseph, 1984)

Richards, Huw, *Dragons and All Blacks: Wales v. New Zealand – 1953 and a Century of Rivalry* (Mainstream, 2004)

Richards, Huw, Peter Stead and Gareth Williams (editors), *Heart and Soul: The Character of Welsh Rugby* (University of Wales Press, 1998)

Rowlands, Clive and John Evans, *Clive Rowlands: Top Cat* (Mainstream, 2002)

Rowlands, Clive and David Farmer (editors), *Giants of Post-War Welsh Rugby* (Malcolm Press, 1990)

Reyburn, Wallace, *The Winter Men: The Seventh All Blacks Tour* (Stanley Paul, 1973)

Samuel, Bill, *Rugby: Body and Soul* (Mainstream, 1998)

Taylor, John, *Decade of the Dragon* (Hodder and Stoughton, 1980)

Thomas, Clem and Geoffrey Nicholson, *Welsh Rugby: The Crowning Years 1968–1980* (Collins, 1980)

Thomas, J.B.G., *The Roaring Lions* (Pelham Books, 1971)

Thomas, J.B.G., *The Greatest Lions* (Pelham Books, 1974)

Turner, Alwyn W., *Crisis? What Crisis? Britain in the 1970s* (Aurum, 2008)

Watkins, David, *David Watkins: An Autobiography* (Cassell, 1980)

Williams, J.P.R., *JPR: An Autobiography* (Collins, 1979)

Williams, J.P.R., *Given The Breaks: My Life in Rugby* (Hodder and Stoughton, 2006)

Wilson, Jonathan, *Inverting the Pyramid: The History of Football Tactics* (Orion, 2008)

The following annuals, publications and periodicals were also of valuable assistance:

Rothmans Rugby Yearbook (Macdonald and Jane's/Queen Anne Press, various years), *Rugby Annual for Wales* (Welsh Brewers, various years), *World of Rugby* (W.H. Allen and Christopher Davies, various years), *Rugby World, Welsh Rugby, Western Mail, South Wales Argus* and various national newspapers.